Using the Brain to Spell

Effective Strategies for All Levels

Sally E. Burkhardt

ROWMAN & LITTLEFIELD EDUCATION

A division of
ROWMAN & LITTLEFIELD PUBLISHERS, INC.
Lanham • New York • Toronto • Plymouth, UK

KH

Published by Rowman & Littlefield Education
A division of Rowman & Littlefield Publishers, Inc.
A wholly owned subsidary of The Rowman & Littlefield Publishing Group, Inc.
4501 Forbes Boulevard, Suite 200, Lanham, Maryland 20706
http://www.rowmaneducation.com

Estover Road, Plymouth PL6 7PY, United Kingdom

British Library Cataloguing in Publication Information Available

Library of Congress Cataloging-in-Publication Data
Burkhardt, Sally E.
  Using the brain to spell : effective strategies for all levels / Sally E. Burkhardt.
     p. cm.
  Includes bibliographical references and index.
  ISBN 978-1-60709-698-6 (cloth : alk. paper) — ISBN 978-1-60709-699-3
(pbk. : alk. paper) — ISBN 978-1-60709-700-6 (ebook)
  1. English language—Orthography and spelling—Study and teaching. I. Title.
  LB1574.B87 2011
  372.63'2--dc22
                                    2010047155

∞™ The paper used in this publication meets the minimum requirements of
American National Standard for Information Sciences—Permanence of
Paper for Printed Library Materials, ANSI/NISO Z39.48-1992.

Printed in the United States of America

3/19/12

To Bill for his advice,

"Make research your own!"

Contents

List of Figures

List of Tables

Foreword

More than twenty years ago, Sally Burkhardt, a graduate student in English education at Virginia Commonwealth University, submitted a fascinating paper to me, a fledgling study on teaching spelling to seventh graders. A respected middle-school teacher in the Chesterfield County School District in Virginia, she felt frustration in following the spelling program her system mandated. Inspired to research this language component, she championed spelling and developed methods of teaching it in brief segments that occupy fifteen to forty-five minutes of class time weekly. The result is a fun-filled, theoretically grounded approach to integrating spelling into a whole-language-based curriculum for language arts.

In the intervening two decades, she retired from full-time teaching and became a sought-after substitute teacher to her colleagues and the "Spelling Lady" to hundreds of middle-school students. In *Using the Brain to Spell*, Sally Burkhardt offers readers the hard-earned wisdom of a career-long teacher-researcher and passionate whole language teacher.

Using the Brain to Spell is an engaging, sensible, and accessible work grounded in theory and practice. Burkhardt embraces whole language with a vengeance and makes language learning fun for both students and teachers. In her discussion of "guessing games," she inductively foregrounds logical rules for hands-on exercises that let students teach themselves with teacher guidance. But she does not offer readers panaceas; instead, she offers us practical advice, tempered with student-centered wisdom. She encourages us to become guides and reminds readers frequently, "Only one teacher can teach spelling. In all cases, the person is the same because that person is the learner! Humans teach themselves to spell! A person learns to spell by becoming his or her own spelling teacher."

Using the Brain to Spell echoes Chekhov's definition of grace—when a writer "spends the least possible number of movements over some definite action, that is grace" (Letter to Gorky 1899). Sally Burkhardt gracefully synthesizes years of thinking, researching, and practicing ways of introducing and guiding students to the logic of spelling. Through creative, interactive exercises, she demonstrates visual, auditory, and kinesthetic ways of showing students how words work. Both beginning and seasoned teachers will find her methods useful.

Always returning to her opening chapters and the powerful concept of moving from the known to the unknown, from the familiar to the unfamiliar, she explains how teachers can guide students to tap into tacit memory rather than waste time doing well-intended but pedagogically pointless exercises. She wisely cautions teachers not to expect instant growth; instead, she often reminds the reader that progress in spelling develops slowly over time. Her book gives teachers glimpses into the ways they may engage students in play, from rhymes to basketball, from tongue twisters to bingo, from classrooms to grocery stores. The extensive word lists she provides and advice on how to use them are generous gifts to readers. As I read *Using the Brain to Spell,* I kept thinking, "Yes, I'm in the hands of a master teacher-researcher, whose enthusiasm is unflagging and whose suggestions are perfect for me and my students."

Her narrative unfolds so clearly that it is in itself a metaphor for successful scaffolding. The self-discoveries she makes as a teacher-researcher show us her own learning style as she focuses and refocuses her energies, a journey that is more recursive and less linear than she first assumed. In chapter 5, "Eye Openers," my favorite chapter, she invites us along on her arduous journey from intended success to sudden realization that she must rework all her summer efforts to pay homage to copyright laws.

Using the Brain to Spell is a smart, well-told story that shows the trials and the successes of a tenacious teacher-researcher. The student commentary sprinkled throughout the text lets us hear the candor of those who liked and disliked her approaches to spelling. Most of all, we hear a committed teacher constantly rethinking her practice, even when it seems to work extraordinarily well.

The piéce de resistance of *Using the Brain to Spell* occurs unexpectedly in chapter 5. In response to a letter she had written him about rhymed, comic verse, Roald Dahl, only months from death, wrote to her attesting to the effects of wordplay on his imagination in childhood. This letter from Roald Dahl is the perfect dramatic endorsement of the significance of wordplay and Burkhardt's creative approach to spelling.

Using the Brain to Spell has been a long time coming, but for me, it is well worth the wait.

William E. Smith

William E. Smith is professor of English and coordinator of professional and technical writing at Western Washington University, in Bellingham, Washington

Acknowledgments

Many than years have passed since I first started researching the teaching of spelling that started when I took Dr. William E. Smith's "Teaching of Composition" class in the fall of 1988, a course required for my master of arts in English/English education program at Virginia Commonwealth University in Richmond, Virginia. Always directing his students to call him "Bill," he is a supportive, knowledgeable professor whose enthusiasm for teaching captivates his students. At the same time, he is a demanding teacher who requires constant readings as well as frequent and challenging writing assignments.

As I wrote this book, I could hear in my brain Bill's voice advising me. How pleased I was that when, years later, in the spring of 2006, I sent him a copy of my first draft, Bill took time out of his busy schedule at Western Washington University to read "over . . . three days . . . every word" in my book. He then wrote me a lengthy, complimentary review I will always treasure.

In addition, he has spent a great deal of his time to write the foreword. Bill is one of those rare professors who care more about serving their students than themselves.

Three other well-known professors have agreed to read my work and give input: Leila Christenberry, PhD, of Virginia Commonwealth University; Patricia McAlexander, PhD, retired professor of University of Georgia; and Sandra Wilde, PhD, of Hunter College in New York. Some of their opinions have guided me in revising a few parts to improve my book. I so appreciate their willingness to read or look over my book and share their expertise.

I am especially thankful for the time Dr. McAlexander spent reading my book and then writing a complimentary review, of which a condensed form appears on the back cover. In addition to her approving comments, she made several suggestions and corrections that I used to improve my work.

Beth Boone Bradford started me on the way to writing this book by accepting me to be a fellow in the 1985 Capital Writing Project at Virginia Commonwealth University when I did not have a teaching position but only hopes of gaining one. Her teaching expertise helped me hone my writing and presentational skills, and three of my CWP writings were published soon after. In addition, I gave my CWP presentation at two state-level conferences.

When I recently contacted her about some points she and Ada Hill make about Maslow's teaching philosophy, she quickly replied with pertinent information. Beth is another of those caring teachers who are always willing to help present and past students in any way they can.

I so appreciate Nancy Austin, PhD in psycholinguistics, for teaching the course I took in her subject area when pursuing my master's degree at VCU. Her ability to explain complex language psychology in simplified ways made these complicated concepts easier to understand. I think that knowledge of psycholinguistics is very important and that a course in this subject should be a requirement for all potential educators of language arts.

I will always appreciate Francis Evans, my high school Latin teacher at West High School in Columbus, Ohio, for being a strict authoritarian who zealously drilled her students to memorize all English grammar counterparts to Latin syntax. Her instruction gave me a thorough knowledge of traditional English grammar, which helped me understand quickly in my undergraduate studies at Ohio State University that little correlation exists between Latin and English language rules. Readers will discover this book reveals that spelling ability correlates to a tacit knowledge of English grammar.

Another constant supporter has been my good friend and golfing buddy, Raney Jones. She has endured listening to me talk about my spelling research right from my beginning efforts. Her constant encouragement throughout the years motivated me to stop talking and start writing my book as well as to continue working on its completion. When I called to tell her I had a contract to publish it, she gave a loud war whoop. What a dear friend she is!

In attempting to gain endorsements, I emphasized to each person who requested copies that I wanted both negative and positive reactions: The few suggestions I received put me back to work to revise pertinent parts of my book.

The copies I sent were mostly to educators, but I have also given two copies to parents homeschooling their children who I knew would find my book of value.

The eight educators listed below read my entire work and sent me responses, time I appreciate very much. One teacher responded, "I have been COMPLETELY overwhelmed with work this year!" in regret for her inability to find time to review the book and provide input: Teaching is a difficult profession for those committed to instructing their students the best way they possibly can. Caring parents and grandparents also have busy lives to handle.

I am thankful to the following educators of The Villages Charter Schools for reading my book and writing me responses: Shannon Cree and Kimberly Wittenberger of The Villages Charter Elementary School; Lori Hogan and Nancy Jones of The Villages Charter Middle School; and William C. Zwick, PhD, principal; Keith Baumann; and Kristan Liner of The Villages Charter High School. *Note:* The Villages Charter Schools, located in The Villages, Florida, are known for excellence.

I especially value Alison Lewis's positive comments since she gained certification in reading when completing her master's program at Cleveland State University. She understands that spelling ability correlates to reading only if the reader takes time to focus on deviant letter patterns that can appear in numerous English words. In addition, her comments are especially relevant because she recently retired after thirty-six years of successfully teaching elementary level students.

The David Higham Associates in London, who are handling the estate of Roald Dahl, have been very generous in allowing me to include in my book a copy of the letter Roald Dahl wrote me granting permission to use his poetry in my English classes. I thank them for this gesture.

Tom Koerner, PhD, vice president and editorial director at Rowman & Littlefield Education, has always responded quickly to any questions and e-mails I have sent. In turn, he has suggested changes that enhanced my work. I am especially thankful to him for offering me a contract. He made a good decision!

Preface

Dear Readers,

I deliberated at length when composing my subtitle, *Effective Strategies for ALL Levels*. I started researching spelling back in the fall of 1988, with the intention to use my findings for teaching my seventh-grade students, especially those who had serious problems in spelling. Over the many years that have passed since then, my conclusions have resulted in discovering various areas of spelling that can apply to all ages, from newborns to even centenarians. Instead of individual booklets on specific areas that each would interest only a few readers, my book discusses all these possibilities. While I would be delighted with any reader who reads the entire book, I would like to direct interested readers to applicable sections.

All should give chapter 1, "In the Beginning," a careful reading because it covers important educational philosophies, especially those that psycholinguistic professors express. I hope readers will have no trouble comprehending the numerous educational principles I have tried to hone to simple explanations. The main reason readers need to absorb this information is that most of the chapters refer at times to one or several of these principles.

Probably the vast majority of readers will be teachers of language arts, but many will find that not all chapters apply to their teaching levels. Teachers in preschool and lower grades in elementary school will benefit most by reading chapter 4, "Focusing on Letter Patterns," to understand the reasoning in the following chapter, "Eye Openers," which stresses the importance of reading poetry to young children as well as engaging them in word play.

Teachers of second graders and higher should read and apply the strategies given in chapters 2 through 5. Those who teach highly gifted learners and instruct higher elementary grades will find many items of value in chapters 6 through 8.

Most middle-school teachers and high-school teachers of students on grade level will want to read chapter 2, "Priming the Spelling Pump." They will then probably want to skip to chapter 6, "Rules Rule," and finish the rest of the book.

All secondary level teachers will want to give special attention to chapter 8, "Fine Tuning," which describes numerous concepts any English teacher of advanced levels should stress.

Teachers of extremely weak spellers in all grade levels will probably want to concentrate on chapters 2 through 4.

Parents and grandparents, even of newly born infants, should also find my book of interest, because a child starts developing spelling ability with his or her first word. They will also realize that they can guide their youngsters to notice words, especially during numerous activities, even a trip to a store. Of course they will also want to read to their little ones books containing poetry and wordplay, which they can find easily in many libraries. As their children become older, parents and grandparents might try applying the strategies I provide for teachers of various age levels. Homeschooling parents will find this book especially valuable for the many activities and strategies I supply for various levels of learners.

Over the years, I have frequently talked about my spelling research to many different friends, some of whom have commented that they have always had difficulty spelling many words correctly. Most are extremely bright, and my book clearly explains the reason for their difficulties, especially in the section titled "No Correlation to Intelligence and/or Reading Ability" in chapter 1. Such adults will also benefit from understanding and applying concepts discussed in chapter 4, "Focusing on Letter Patterns," which explains that identifying deviant patterns in words they see every day will help them make great strides in spelling ability. Most will also improve in spelling, as I did, from learning and applying the spelling rules provided in chapter 6, "Rules Rule."

Several times I have talked with friends who claim their spelling ability is so weak that they usually can't even look up a word in the dictionary. Such adults will greatly benefit from the strategies I discuss in chapter 3, "Using Logic to Spell." When they learn and start applying these strategies, they will improve in spelling ability.

One pattern of errors I frequently find in adults' writings is misspelling common homonyms. They will benefit from reading chapter 7, "Which One?," to understand how to compose a memory trick to learn the correct spelling of any homonym. They might want to keep this book for the extensive source list in appendix N.

All adults should find chapter 8, "Fine Tuning," of interest, especially the sections that describe developing vocabulary, a process they should continue for the rest of their lives.

Readers will probably think my book has "acute appendicitis"—pun intended—because it has twenty-two appendixes. Throughout the many years I experimented with teaching spelling, I probably spent more time developing word banks and exercises than I did planning lessons on spelling that would hold the attention of my seventh-grade students. Listing them separately makes my book more interesting for readers who are not educators.

Above all, readers must understand that the most important consideration when selecting any strategy or activity is to make it fun, because humans love to play!

Sincerely,
Sally E. Burkhardt

1

In the Beginning

THE BIRTH OF SPELLING

My nine-month-old son sat patiently before me in his feeding table while I warmed his breakfast. He babbled contentedly, fingering dexterously the tabletop beads, so unlike his aimless batterings of just a few months before.

I smiled to myself when he murmured "dada," which my husband would always insist was "Daddy." I never disagreed even though I knew this is one of the first sounds most babies make.

Suddenly, from outside the kitchen window burst the morning song of a bird welcoming the new day. I'll never forget my baby's reaction. His eyes widened with surprise and pleasure. Pointing, he said, "bur."

"Bird," I pronounced distinctly, articulating naturally the final "d." I beamed at him with elation. Our child had just said his first word!

Today, I would add that he was beginning to spell!

When I first conducted my spelling research in the late 1980s, most teachers at that time would have had little interest in comprehending this statement because the majority viewed spelling as a boring subject, a separate entity from teaching language skills, one that consisted only of dictating and grading weekly spelling tests. Teaching spelling in most language arts classes was little more. Then, only a few considered this issue the way my assistant principal did during my interview for the middle-school English teaching position I was lucky to obtain.

My inability to answer continued to haunt me, especially when I tried to implement zealously the school system's spelling program in my sixth- and seventh-grade English classes. The spelling book adopted by the system was typical of most spelling programs. Each weekly lesson listed twenty-odd words that in most cases had little connection to one another. Following this list were various senseless exercises for student practice. At the end of the week, I dictated a test on these words. Grading these tests was always disappointing because I would note little if any improvement. The best spellers scored well; the poor usually failed.

In the late 1980s, probably no other area cried out more for improved strategies than the teaching of spelling. Most secondary-level English teachers would find approaching this subject one of their greatest nemeses because weak spellers—even those who struggle valiantly—usually make very little improvement. Others seem to spell even the most difficult words effortlessly, "catching spelling as easily as they catch singing" (Peters 1985, 24).

RESEARCHING THE TEACHING OF SPELLING

A number of my courses in graduate school emphasized making connections between communication skills—reading, writing, speaking, and listening. Understanding the importance of making these connections in a language arts classroom started my thinking about how spelling should fit into a whole-language curriculum. The term "whole" implies that language instruction should not be separated into parts but should be presented together as an entirety. In other words, language proficiency improves when connecting reading, writing, listening, and speaking skills, a philosophy that I continually tried to implement in my language arts classroom when I returned to teaching in 1985.

My attempts to teach spelling, however, continued with perfunctory weekly tests and exercises until I decided to research this area—first in a cursory project in a graduate-level course and then in an independent study.

I tackled this task with enthusiasm, fully intending to read every book and article I could find. When I developed a bibliography that listed hundreds of entries, I realized what an overwhelming project I had undertaken. I had selected a subject that was probably better researched than any other area. Unfortunately, pedagogical language often obscured meaning in many writings. Most works frequently required reading numerous times for complete comprehension. Many of the studies were so difficult and seemingly irrelevant that there is little wonder few were translated into practical applications.

As one who enjoys scholarly research, I might still be contentedly researching if my professor, Dr. William Smith, hadn't thrown his hands up in disgust, remonstrating, "Stop reading and start writing. You've read enough. Start making this your own." Although what I had studied represented only a small percentage of the published material on the teaching of spelling, I had avidly consumed everything I could for several months. The bulky stack of relevant material I had collected was certainly enough to "make my own."

The resulting study, finished in the spring of 1989, was more than forty pages long. It was an adequate account of spelling research along with numerous creative innovations of my own. In addition, I collected numerous selections of mostly teacher-produced activities that would help spelling instruction become more "interesting." My project also included an extensive compilation of appealing poetry that teachers could use to foster spelling improvement. Both of these collections resulted in two separate bound books.

My major concern was to discover how to implement these research findings in my classroom. Even though I had an armory of completed research, I still could not see clearly how spelling connects in a whole language curriculum. At best, I had a collection of sundry ideas with little notion where to start in attempting classroom applications.

My idealistic energy quickly gained control over my quandaries, especially when my school system gave me the green light to abandon the deadly spelling texts to conduct spelling research in my classroom. My students were receptive, but anything would have been an improvement over the usual spelling lessons. In the eleven years that followed before I retired in June 2000, I actively pursued the teaching of spelling as a classroom teacher-researcher. In addition, I have applied my resulting methods to several long-term substitute-teaching assignments.

What I have discovered has clearly guided me to conclude that spelling abilities and language skills develop interdependently, a process that stems from a child's first word. Understanding this connection brings a realization that spelling acquisition does not result from boring drills and tests. In fact, many students improve in spelling skills naturally as their proficiency in language grows (Peters 1985, 7). At the same time, teachers should not dismiss spelling-deficient students as "dumb" or "too lazy to learn."

WHERE ARE WE GOING?

Unlike most books on the teaching of spelling, the focus of this book is not on philosophies, theories, or conducted research, which usually discuss only what should be involved in spelling instruction and why. Instead, it focuses on how I have implemented my research in my classroom. Discussions of resulting strategies provide specific details. I can say with confidence that applying these numerous, often enjoyable methods will help poor spellers improve. Most are so deceptively simple that the reader might assume they emerged quickly. Quite the reverse is true; many first attempts proved disastrous. Only through perseverance and constant evaluation of failures have I evolved successful techniques.

At times discussions—particularly in this chapter—involve explanation of relevant educational philosophies and theories. Most are succinct summaries of major studies to explain the rationales behind resulting methods. Though many answers will be clear, readers need to beware that these possibilities are not a panacea for eliminating spelling problems.

The most exciting result of my spelling research is detailed in chapter 3, "Using Logic to Spell." This chapter describes how to teach basic concepts about common spelling patterns, information especially helpful to extremely poor spellers. First they need to learn and apply some fundamentals I term "logical spelling" techniques. Once they have learned and applied this information, many can become "functional" spellers, who can correct most of their misspellings with a computer. Data are also included in chapter 3 to support these results.

What I have discovered is only a smattering of helpful strategies. I probably still have more questions today than solutions; many more roads lie ahead.

WHAT A DIFFERENCE TODAY!

"In the last twenty years, few areas of elementary school curriculum have changed more than spelling" (Laminack and Wood 1996, ix).

When I thought this book was in an acceptable state to submit to publishers, reading online submission guidelines of various publishers made me realize otherwise. I was unable to explain how my book would "stand out among its competition" because most citations in my book were from research I had conducted in 1989.

As a result, I spent numerous hours in the beginning months of 2007 reading recently published books and articles on spelling to understand current thinking on the teaching of spelling. After developing an extensive bibliography, I was able to find and review fifty-seven sources. I purchased two of the books: Laminack and Wood's *Spelling in Use* (1996) and McAlexander, Dobie, and Gregg's *Beyond the "Sp" Label* (1992).

My findings reveal that most English educators have abandoned traditional spelling texts and instead teach spelling as an integral part of a whole-language curriculum that constantly connects reading, writing, speaking, and listening, a philosophy my book also expounds. As a result, I completely revised my book to incorporate many pertinent points from these sources.

Many of these works focus on teaching reading in the primary grades, with a heavy emphasis on phonics, with spelling taught through directing students to complete word sorts, word walls, pattern sorts, wordplay, rhymes and jingles, and many games: Bear 2004; Bolton and Snowball 1993; Brand 2004; Chandler and Mapleton Teacher Research Group 1999, 2000; Cramer 1998; Fountas and Pinnell 1999; Fresch and Wheaton 2002; Gentry 1993, 2004; Henry 2003; Hiskes 2005; Laminack and Wood 1996; Marland 2002; Marten 2003; O'Sullivan 2007; Phenix 2001, 2003; Pinnell 1998; Podhaizer 1998; Rosencrans 1998; Rycick 2007; Simon 2004; Snowball and Bolton 1999; Templeton 1998, 2004; Westwood 2005; and Wilde 1992, 1996, 1997, 2004.

Examining Houghton Mifflin spelling texts for grades 1 through 8 was especially refreshing. These books are a far cry from the traditional texts my school system required. Publishers are finally producing spelling textbooks based on current spelling research, which will definitely help students improve their spelling abilities (Templeton 1998).

My findings from conducting this recent research support the unique approaches briefly described below, which my book promotes:

- Gentry's list of 500 high-frequency words, reorganized by logical and deviant letter patterns—see chapter 2, "Priming the Spelling Pump."
- Specific strategies to teach poor spellers how to make educated guesses to spell unknown words, including word lists that are valuable for practice—see chapter 3, "Using Logic to Spell."
- Organizing word lists only by letter pattern and not by sound/letter correspondences, since students note deviant patterns in words visually, not phonetically—see chapter 4, "Focusing on Letter Patterns."
- Resourceful ways to help students note deviant patterns in words to help them develop memory banks of words containing unusual letter patterns, memory banks necessary for learning the spelling of new words—see chapter 5, "Eye Openers."
- Innovative ways to help students learn spelling rules, including extensive word banks—see chapter 6, "Rules Rule."
- Teaching students how to write memory tricks for remembering spellings of homonyms and words commonly confused, including a comprehensive source list of homonyms with accompanying words with the same letter patterns—see chapter 7, "Which One?"
- Creative ways to teach advanced spellers how to learn spelling demons, broaden vocabulary, understand the difference between denotation and connotation of words, and develop the suffix sense necessary for using the correct grammatical forms of any newly learned vocabulary word—see chapter 8, "Fine Tuning."
- Innumerable, fun-filled activities and games teachers will find invaluable for teaching spelling rather than dwelling on a pedagogic analysis of student spelling errors.

SPELLING IS DEVELOPMENTAL

In 1975, Charles Read opened a new frontier in spelling research when he published *Children's Categorization of Speech Sounds in English*. In examining children's spelling errors, he was able to identify and describe distinct developmental spelling stages (Fisher and Studier 1977; Henderson and Beers 1980; Hodges 1981; Manning and Manning 1981):

- Initial Stage: During the beginning stage, children use a letter name strategy to spell. For example, a preschooler might write "Wot u pla wf me" (Fisher and Studier 1977, 1).
- Intermediate Stage: Children progress to the next level once they start realizing that various letter combinations can spell the same sound. During this middle stage, children discover such concepts as that all vowels can spell a schwa sound and that different letter combinations can represent the same vowel sound. For example, "ai" can spell a long "a" sound as in "rain," "ea" as in "pear," "eigh" as in "eight," and "ay" as in "tray." They also discover that unusual consonant combinations can represent common consonant sounds. Realizing that "ph" and "gh" are "f" sounds as in "phone" and "laugh," that "ps" and "z" can stand for an "s" sound as in "psalm" and "maltz," and that "kn" and "gn" as in "knot" and "gnat" are "n" sounds might be just a few of their observations.
- Highest Level: At the highest level, competent spellers acquire more sophisticated information about spelling other than sound–letter correspondences. They observe that a word's position in a sentence influences not only spelling but also meaning. For example, the word "beautiful" becomes "beauty," "beautify," "beautification," and "beautiful" when placed in other sentences. They become aware of homonyms and other words often confused that are pronounced the same but have different meanings and spellings, such as the words "gnu" and "new." In addition, they draw complex conclusions about other spelling intricacies, a process that intertwines with language development.

A number of researchers, under the direction of Edmund Henderson at University of Virginia, continued studies of children's spelling errors and concluded, "The ability to spell is a complex intellectual and developmental achievement" (Hodges 1981, 10).

As is also true in the writing process, growth in spelling ability is recursive, with no set sequential levels. In other words "when one new stage begins, previous ones" will not necessarily be completed (Laminack and Wood 1996, 11). Educators therefore "cannot assume that spelling develops in a lock-step progression from one stage to the next" (Laminack and Wood 1996, 8).

As an Oak

Alfred Lord Tennyson once wrote in his poem "Flower in a Crannied Wall," published in 1869, that if he could understand a flower "root and all, all in all, [he] . . . should know what God and man is" (Wikipedia 2010, 6). While our purpose is not so ethereal, making a similar comparison between the growth of an oak tree and the spelling process might better illuminate the developmental nature of spelling ability.

Both acorn and infant contain everything needed to develop to their fullest potential if nurtured. When dropped on fertile ground, the acorn sprouts its first root, in the same way that a baby utters a first word in a world surrounded by love and language. Like an acorn rising to the world above, a baby learns additional words from numerous ones repeated daily. The plant sprouts additional roots and leaves; a baby starts speaking in short sentences.

The preschooler becomes an oak sapling in speaking fluency, expertly manipulating language complexities with ease. In fact, long before young children are officially taught to read and write, they have developed a highly sophisticated knowledge of their native language.

Sometime during this sapling period children discover there are written symbols for the words they love to say. This revelation motivates most to learn how to read and write. They memorize the alphabet, pointing to the letters in words they notice in the world around them. Usually starting as pretend readers and scribble writers, they quickly progress to recognizing simple words and writing according to the "initial stage" described above.

Perhaps "initial" is a misnomer, since it implies the beginning of a process. The oak tree analogy shows that spelling ability is at best the ending branches and leaves in language development, ending points that sprout from a complex interconnection among speaking, listening, reading, and writing skills. A sapling would never sprout additional branches if invading insects severely damaged its trunk or root systems. Likewise, the more language deficient a child is, the greater the problem he or she will have developing spelling abilities.

The "initial" stage of spelling, therefore, builds on a child's fluency in language. A child's language tree must have a healthy trunk, roots, and branches to support orthographic leaves and branches. As an oak sapling grows into a larger tree, so a child's expertise in speaking, listening, reading, and writing skills keeps increasing. A tree is a complex entity of numerous systems supporting one another. Language development is an intricate interaction among these four communication skills. Growth in any one of these areas will produce greater facility in others.

Most children improve in spelling abilities as their knowledge of language expands, especially with growth in writing expertise. Learned spelling concepts bud from language capabilities that grow in complexity as the language oak enlarges.

Annually, children competing in the National Spelling Bee demonstrate this facility for language. To correctly spell the difficult words given in this contest, a contestant must tap into an extensive vocabulary that builds on knowledge of complex grammatical concepts. "Afflatus," "cinnabar," and "esquamulose"—all words on which National Spelling Bee championships have been won or lost (Shefter 1976, 252)—are so rare that many college professors would probably stumble spelling them. National Spelling Bee winners and final contenders should be revered in the same way Olympic stars are, because they demonstrate exceptional language mastery, much as winning Olympians exhibit physical prowess.

Few develop such spelling proficiency, but most grow in spelling ability. In all cases, each spelling concept acquired interconnects with communication counterparts, connections that represent not just three stages, but hundreds, thousands, millions—probably even more—of different parts. Each link stems to the utterance of a child's first word, the taproot of language development.

PSYCHOWHAT?

Psycholinguistics is the psychological study of language that examines how humans acquire, produce, and comprehend language. Most textbooks on this subject contain an immersion of complicated terms and concepts to describe the complex interacting processes involved in the acquisition of language knowledge. Absorbing this material will require diligent efforts even for proficient readers. Language arts teachers, however, will find such effort worthwhile, because numerous practical applications for improving language arts programs hide in psycholinguistic jargon. Several of these concepts are highly relevant to understanding the additional processes involved in language and spelling improvement.

Tacit versus Explicit

Fluent speakers have a tacit knowledge of their language (Carroll, 1986, 6). In other words, they produce meaning with little or no comprehension of the explicit or technical processes that a linguist or other language expert would delight in describing with professional magniloquence. For example, fluent preschoolers have complex knowledge of grammatical structures, which they manipulate automatically in the sentences they speak. They use such words as "see," "bring," "give," and "buy" correctly with no ability to apply such labels as "transitive" and "intransitive" verbs.

Most authorities today agree with Noam Chomsky's theory that a child's ability to use words appropriately according to rules of language is innate (Carroll, 1986, 18–19). Chomsky believes a child is born with language knowledge. In other words, if a number of babies could be raised in a loving environment but without any exposure to language, the group would most likely develop a new language with grammatical rules similar to any other language in the world.

Avoiding explicit language analysis with young children, therefore, is an important application. Comprehending technical principles requires abstract thinking powers and correlates little with language improvement. The noted educational psychologist Jean Piaget discovered years ago that young children start developing abstract thinking skills around age eleven, which fully develop around the age of fifteen (Brainerd 1976, 38).

Even so, complex terminology and abstract analysis dominate many elementary and middle-school curriculums. For example, one of my friends recently bemoaned the fact that her third-grade child has great difficulty understanding "medial vowels," a term that aptly describes the vowel sound in such words as dog, cat, sit, bet, etc. No doubt that same child would have no difficulty repeating the medial vowel sounds in one-syllable words after being given a few examples. A child speaks such words daily, articulating naturally all sounds in each word. Even a preschooler could pronounce "the sound in the middle" with ease.

Curriculums, programs, lesson plans, and books should focus on information that connects immediately to a child's vocabulary and understanding. Teaching terminology used only on professional levels is of little value when guiding children's growth in language. To teach a child, translate knowledge into the language of a child. In other words, hone material to its simplest terms that will connect easily to a child's viewpoint.

In presenting the concept of "medial vowels," therefore, the term "medial" would definitely fall by the wayside. The label "vowel" and its counterpart "consonant" are terms worth keeping because they will occur frequently in future language discussions. Perhaps a game titled "Name That Sound" could be played for vowel and consonant sounds, a game that could be complicated later with their syllable positions. Many other possibilities exist. Creative, innovative teachers easily develop effective, enjoyable strategies that build on children's natural, tacit knowledge of language. Children do not need to learn abstract, explicit terms to describe what they already know. Teaching to tacit knowledge will make learning fun; explaining explicitly will make it drudgery.

Tapping into Memory

Short-term memory requires attention to learning for only a brief period. Unless this information continues to receive attention, it escapes as a forgotten thought until once again retrieved for attention. For example, most people will forget a telephone number they have just looked up as soon as they have finished dialing. Our lives are filled with memorizing and releasing such tidbits of information.

Information must receive repeated attention to be transferred into permanent memory. Carol Scearce, the former director of staff development in Chesterfield County Schools in Virginia (the system I taught in for fourteen years), stated that a concept must receive attention as many as twenty times before it emerges into the permanent knowledge base. She emphasized this point during her presentation "Enlightening," a fascinating lecture on how the human brain functions. She continues to give presentations to various school systems around the United States, ones that

I guarantee will be valuable. Readers can contact her at the Corwin Press Web Site (corwinpressspeakers.com).

Driving a Point!

Learning to drive a car with a manual transmission clearly illustrates this process. The driver must attend to a number of tasks in the first lessons. The left hand holds the steering column while the right hand shifts gears, an operation that must be perfectly synchronized with the left foot pumping the clutch and the right foot operating the accelerator pedal. In addition, the driver must still attend to driving the vehicle, which is no minor feat, as anyone learning to drive a car with an automatic transmission can attest. Jerky starts and stops interspersed with a shrill grinding noise characterize beginning attempts. Operating a car with a stick shift smoothly requires intensive attention and practice.

Gradually the driver improves, until the car runs as smoothly as one with an automatic transmission. Even so, the beginning driver must pay careful attention to coordinating all operations. Only after a great deal of practice is attention no longer needed, because suddenly all the interrelated tasks can be performed automatically, signifying the transference of the operational knowledge into "permanent memory."

Learning a new word follows the same process. Before my son pronounced his first word, he had made a number of visual observations that were often accompanied by his parents, along with other relatives and friends, saying "bird." His utterance of "bur" was immediately preceded by listening to a bird's song. We soon discovered, however, that he used "bur" not as an ornithological description but as a synonym for any animal; he also called cows, horses, and monkeys in the zoo "bur." Only after numerous experiences involving multiple sensory perceptions did the meaning and pronunciation of "bird" become clear.

As his comprehension of this word grew, he was of course also learning numerous other words, a continuing process that often led him to discovering how meanings interrelated. Eventually he could automatically retrieve any of these words, speaking them clearly and correctly as does any fluent speaker, obvious signals that this information was embedded into his permanent memory base.

Spreading Activation Models

Most psycholinguists agree that *spreading activation models* best describe how the human brain stores words. These models resemble spider webs that store concepts as interconnected parts that interweave according to structural and functional characteristics. A model of semantic knowledge will reveal how a person's brain might make connections between words. For example, the word "red" might conjure in a person's brain images of roses, cherries, fire, other colors, and even a fire engine. Thinking of a fire engine might bring thoughts of other vehicles—ambulance, car, truck, bus, etc. (Carroll 1986, 157).

Words used most often are the easiest to access. Recall of infrequently used expressions follows a "spreading activation" process. Retrieval begins at a single node and spreads from one closely related concept to the next, rippling through interconnected parts, similar to "the effect of dropping a rock into a pool of still water" (Carroll 1986, 158).

A spreading activation model resembles the clustering or brainstorming charts that writing process teachers encourage students to create. In fact, the reason these activities are such effective prewriting strategies is that they lead students to accessing ideas stored in their brains.

Jerome Bruner's scaffolding image also describes the same process. As the brain assimilates new information into the old, the scaffolding system expands, symbolizing cognitive growth (1996, 21). Additional scaffolds clearly connect to supporting bases, which must be strong enough to hold each addition. A weak support might cause the whole system to fail in the same way that a diseased root system would cause a tree to die.

Other metaphors could also aptly describe how complex and interconnecting the brain's storage of knowledge is. Scientific classification systems of the universe are equally complex and interrelated. The technical nomenclature for the world's plants and animals, for example, reveals a comparable ordering plan. Modern technology also reveals resemblances: Televisions, computers, engines, electrical systems, and telephone circuit boards all contain thousands of interconnecting parts that work together in a similar scheme. Even the organizational chart for a large corporation would show how each employee is an essential, mutually supporting member. The viability of any of these systems in all cases depends on the components maintaining interdependent connections.

In other words, a human's brain normally processes new knowledge by making connections to known material. A learner easily absorbs such information if it taps into knowledge already known. The more connections a learner can make, the easier the assimilation of the new material will be. Novel material that connects clearly to what is already known will be easily assimilated. If a learner's brain contains no information to make any connection with, he or she must first work on learning the basics from which future connections will stem,

For example, studying psycholinguistics is difficult for most beginning students because it comprises complex terminology and concepts. To make sense of the this subject, most students new to this subject must spend endless hours trying to comprehend psycholinguistic information. Many passages in the textbook must be re-read several times, with complete understanding often not developing until numerous questions are discussed with the attending professor.

The acquisition process, however, becomes easier as the knowledge base grows, as long as new concepts connect to primary information. Acquiring knowledge of any complicated subject follows the same process. Most schools across our nation today recognize the importance of developing curriculums that help students make connections in any knowledge acquisition process.

Developing spelling ability is also dependent on learning fundamentals that interconnect with increasing complexities in similar patterns found in a spreading activation chart. Tacit spellers discover these spelling building blocks naturally. Progression is "not made word by word, but spelling principle by spelling principle" (Henderson 1985, 87). Each learned spelling concept dictates the spellings and misspellings of succeeding words, an ordering strategy that helps the learner grow in spelling competence while also reducing the load on memory. "Non-achieving spellers, in contrast, are those who lack these principles of order. Notoriously, they spell by sound and tattered remnants of what they tried to remember but partially forgot" (Henderson 1985, 88).

Patience Is a Virtue

Understanding how information processes into permanent memory is particularly of value to language arts teachers. How often have I heard

English teachers complain that their students continue to make the same careless mistakes in spite of extensive instruction. For example, a teacher might have devoted a whole week to teaching spelling rules, yet only a few students seem to apply them to their writing. Teachers need to realize that little transfer is to be expected during initial instructional stages, and they should therefore be tolerant of their students' learning mistakes. Analysis of students' mistakes can serve as a guide to designing future lessons that will promote growth. Acquisition of language skills is a time-consuming process because so many attention exposures are necessary before the information transfers into permanent memory. No wonder the development of a language oak is so gradual!

Understanding the developmental nature of spelling acquisition, as well as the memory processes of the brain, leads one to realizing that spelling acquisition will be slow and often almost imperceptible. Daily growth changes are hardly noticeable in most developing organisms; likewise, children will not demonstrate spelling and language improvement over short periods.

Only comparisons of writing samples produced between widely separated periods can reveal progress. In the same way that a visiting relative remarks on the physical changes in a child not seen for several years, writing samples will reveal a child's growth in language and spelling ability. Often as much as a year will pass before noting significant changes in samples.

The speed of spelling improvement will, of course, depend on the amount of language mastery a student possesses: The greater the ability, the faster will be the improvement when a student starts applying the strategies suggested in this book. Once familiarized with the process that good spellers use, even the worst spellers can improve when learning how to observe the world of words they see each day.

NO CORRELATION BETWEEN SPELLING ABILITY AND INTELLIGENCE AND/OR READING ABILITY

Many people might consider poor spelling a sign of low intelligence. In the beginning of the novel *Flowers for Algernon* by Daniel Keyes, Charlie Gordon is a severely retarded adult whose IQ is only 68. His spelling skills are weak, as one of his written sentences reveals: "I hope I dont have to rite to much of these progris riports because it takes along time and I get to sleep very late and Im tired at werk in the morning" (1988, 4). After Charlie has his brain operation and some skilled tutoring, his spelling skills are superior: "So, I still don't know what I.Q. is, and everybody says it's something different. Mine is about a hundred now, and it's going to be over a hundred and fifty soon" (1988, 35). When Keyes reveals these differences in Charlie's spelling abilities, he gives readers a subliminal message that poor spelling skills indicate low intelligence.

Many weak spellers, however, are extremely intelligent. I will always remember one brilliant boy who was in my ninth-grade class of highly gifted students. Students needed a minimum IQ of 130 for placement in this group. His IQ was the highest in the entire class, close to 190, a number that classified him in the "genius" category.

My student's writings, however, were filled with many misspellings far worse than Charlie's. In addition, he wrote in print instead of cursive, writing that was almost illegible. I wish I knew then what I know now; maybe I could have helped him improve his poor spelling. I also would have encouraged him to practice cursive handwriting, which correlates with improving spelling ability (see "Promote Cursive Handwriting" in chapter 2).

Spelling ability also does not correlate with reading ability. Both excellent and weak readers can be poor spellers. At the same time, many poor readers develop excellent spelling skills.

The psycholinguistic terms "top-down" and "bottom-up" processing can help explain why. Most of the time, good readers use a top-down processing method, in which they quickly read chunks of words at a time. Such processing results in little attention to individual words and letter-pattern parts. On the other hand, poor readers use a bottom-up processing technique, in which they analyze one word or word part at a time (Carroll 1986, 129–130).

Bottom-up processing requires the close observation of words necessary for developing spelling skills, explaining how a poor reader can have excellent spelling skills. In all cases, students who have inferior spelling skills need to learn to start looking closely at words and word parts to improve their spelling.

MODELING MASLOW

Although many currently noted authorities express the importance of creating a secure classroom environment, Abraham Maslow is probably best known for emphasizing that educators should first focus on fulfilling the psychological needs of their students. All humans have these needs—for safety, belonging and love, self-esteem, aesthetic surroundings, and most of all mental understanding and self-actualization. Those who have these needs met attain the highest levels of achievement (1970, 80–106).

Maslow's hierarchy, depicted in a triangle, reveals that humans don't have higher level needs until their basic needs are met, progressing, as on a ladder, from one to the next. For example, if humans don't have food and shelter, they don't care much about belonging (1970, 80–106).

According to Hill and Boone-Bradford, Maslow's hierarchy of needs applies to the classroom: If kids don't have paper and pencil, basic writing needs, they can't write. If they were at the belonging level, they would work well in groups. Other parallels also apply (1982, 3–77).

ALL teachers, therefore, should concentrate on fulfilling their students' psychological needs to guide their students to their highest learning capabilities. The language arts teacher who adheres to Maslow's philosophies will help his or her students attain far greater growth in writing competency than an English teacher following "grim grader" approaches. Unfortunately, numerous language arts teachers—perhaps the majority of English teachers—delight in marking every error on a paper, even on a basic writer's composition. Some think they are being helpful in noting minute mistakes, even ones the majority of college-educated adults would probably make.

I'll never forget the reactions of my students when I was a beginning teacher over forty years ago, when I passed back their graded compositions. At that time I was teaching high school seniors who placed in the lower third of their class and one class of heterogeneously grouped juniors.

Once, one boy laughed when he saw his paper and questioned me in front of the entire class, gesturing dramatically, "Miss Miller, how do you grade these papers? I bet you take a red pen and shake it as hard as possible to sprinkle red spots throughout!" Of course, we all laughed at his seemingly intended joke. His remark, however, confused me. I literally spent countless hours working on marking all errors and writing a short commentary at the end of each paper. Often during those six years that I taught high school students, I would wonder why many of my students also seemed so unappreciative of my grading attempts.

Not until participating in the 1985 Capital Writing Project at Virginia Commonwealth University under Beth Boone-Bradford did I realize the ineffectiveness of "grim-grader" marking. Beth expounded against such methods. As director of the Capital Writing Project, she emphasized that marking every error is highly threatening, especially to basic writers. "Grim-grader" marks blast, not build, every psychological need Maslow describes. Teachers who are still using these outdated grading strategies need to become familiar with current research to realize that their zealous approach is probably harming their students more than helping them!

Teachers should not mark every spelling error, especially on the paper of a spelling-deficient student, for exactly the same reason. Be as accepting of your students' writing attempts, however wrong, as is a new mother when her baby utters his or her first word. When my baby blurted "bur," I didn't frown and correct him severely. Instead, I reacted with elation, articulating "bird" correctly so he would want to imitate its pronunciation exactly. If teachers who believe in a stern, severe classroom atmosphere would suddenly change to simulating the actions of a new mother responding to her infant, they would probably accomplish ten times more than they usually do. If all teachers modeled Maslow, what a better world we would be building.

Beware! These statements might mislead some teachers and make them think they will no longer have to grade student writings. Teachers will discover the opposite is true when reading this book's discussion of grading strategies in the following chapters. In fact, instead of throwing away their red pens, teachers will probably end up needing many more, including some of a different color. Teachers will also be surprised, perhaps pleased and relieved, to learn that there will be times when they need to zealously "grim grade" certain writing efforts!

THE WORLD OF YOUNG CHILDREN

Young children, even newborn infants, delight in responding to the world around them. Feeling, smelling, sucking, viewing, listening to, dropping, and even throwing objects are fascinating activities. Their surroundings are a source of constant entertainment and provide interminable delights.

Eventually all children reach the stage when they need "formal schooling." School for the majority means a change to daily drills and practice, a place where skill packs abound and teachers direct activities. Although most children adapt easily to a school with such structured learning, some flounder.

A number of teachers would probably purse their lips in disgust and label these "reluctant" learners with such demeaning descriptors as "lazy," "dumb," or "careless." After all, the unmotivated represent only a small minority.

Many students in this minority are intellectually talented but "handicapped because their abilities that fall outside the normal range are viewed often as weaknesses" (Coleman and Cross 2001, 22). Many gifted thinkers fail to achieve success because of boredom and lack of motivation when placed in traditional classrooms.

Over the years, I have had a number of highly gifted students in my regular and even low-level language arts classes in middle school. Their weak English skills and study habits were the reasons for these placements. Since I taught highly gifted learners for a number of years when a high school teacher, I could easily recognize the superior intellectual abilities of such reluctant learners. While I tried my best to meet their needs in my English class, often successfully, most failed to succeed in other classes.

If education is ever to effect cures for its many ills, it must first promote schools in which ALL students can experience success. Rationalizing student failure is a deadly disease that must be eradicated before success-oriented schools can be not just idealized platitudes but realities.

A few perceptive educators might observe that the real reason behind many students' lack of interest is that school is often a dreadfully boring place to be. Perhaps the most astute would realize that answers may lie in the lives of people in our everyday world, particularly in the environment of a normal preschool child. Studying children outside a traditional school points to universal truths about how humans learn, truths that are especially relevant to understanding the spelling process.

Joy in Learning

The most obvious principle that emerges in studying the behavior of young children is remarkable: Learning is not boring but fun! Actions of normal preschoolers reveal that gaining knowledge is so enjoyable that its pursuit absorbs most of their time. Curious about everything they encounter, little ones continuously ask questions about their surrounding world, questions that adults are often unable to answer.

Discovering answers usually brings additional questions about their surrounding world, a cycle that repeats with each new experience. Toddlers delight in knowing answers and performing skills to the delight of their parents, who no doubt brag to anyone willing to listen about the antics of their omniscient offspring. Unlike the numbers of "reluctant" students in many formal classrooms, normal preschoolers love learning. Any little one who acts as bored as many children act in school would quickly be labeled "abnormal." A scientist analyzing the activities of typical preschoolers would probably conclude that a thirst for knowledge is innate to human beings.

That same scientist would probably reach a similar conclusion when examining the adult world. Grown-ups, almost as much as children, love to play games, especially those requiring specific knowledge. The board game "Trivial Pursuit" is only one of many adult board games known for brain tickling. The card game bridge requires so much intellectual skill that learners eagerly attend classes and avidly read the many books and newspaper columns published by those who have earned the required points necessary to attain the revered title "Bridge Master."

How ironic it is that the numerous reluctant learners in our nation's schools form a counterargument. The same scientist might study this group and label them deviants displaying abnormal attitudes: They hate, not love, to learn, so much that they can't wait until they can quit school. No one would disagree that the major purpose of schools should be to promote learning, but far too many students end up dropping out of school.

Closely scrutinizing the behavior of "school haters," however, would probably reveal that these students, unbeknown to them, also love learning as much as any other human. The way a low-level student performs during a typical class spelling bee serves as an example. The class's worst speller who accidentally spells a word correctly will have an amazed expression, utter a sigh of relief, and give a broad smile to anyone who nods congratulations. The same student, however, when misspelling the next word given, will usually shrug his or her shoulders with an "I don't care" attitude that aptly expresses frustration.

The fact is clear: To know is fun; the reverse is not. Humans especially love possessing trivial tidbits of information. Spelling a difficult word brings pleasure to the speller: If it is the winning word in a National Spelling Bee, the speller gains world acclaim.

Can anyone imagine the opposite? Students so proud of misspellings they brag about their mistakes? Can anyone recall anyone who boasts seriously of his or her ignorance? Never! Humans are proud of what they know, and most revere the knowledge others possess. If we can accept the maxim that a love for learning is innate, then why are there so many unmotivated students in our nation's schools?

The answer would probably be obvious to our scientist: Schools need to simulate real world environments that foster learning. Schools should be places where all students thrive, not suffer, and where learning is fun. The immediate answer to "what" and "why" is simplistic; the solutions to "how" are not. Many school systems, probably a majority, still cling to traditional methods that make school a boring trap for large numbers of students.

The essence of a successful spelling program is that it be enjoyable and motivating. Children develop a love for language through a "rich experience with words which is a necessary condition for advancing phonological knowledge" (Henderson 1981, 51). "Word exploration activities and games can be used to enhance the young child's growing awareness of words and how they are spelled while at the same time providing enjoyable encounters with written language" (Hodges 1981, 15). In other words, any spelling program should above all be fun for students. Shouldn't such a philosophy pervade any educational method? Making spelling enjoyable has always been an important consideration when conducting my classroom spelling research.

JOY IN THE CLASSROOM

Teachers will usually obtain dramatic results when incorporating enjoyable approaches. For example, when I first started my spelling research, I devised a simple game for my X-level students to play in preparation for their weekly spelling test from the text mandated by the school system. "X-level" was the awful term my school system, Chesterfield County

Schools in Virginia, applied to the lowest level of a five-track system. Most students in this group had recently been mainstreamed from special education programs for learning disabled and educable mentally retarded students. The list of words contained a typical myriad of letter-string patterns that any group of weak spellers would find difficult.

A student would try to spell correctly in front of the class three words given by other students, to win a piece of candy as well as the right to choose the next contender. If a word was missed, the student asking the word could be the next player if he or she spelled the word correctly.

The test results were extraordinary. Every one of the students passed the test, instead of the usual number failing or barely passing, revealing that even low-level learners can achieve if highly motivated. Playing a game based on the words was far more effective than directing students to complete the meaningless drills in their spelling text.

My major mission as an English teacher has always been to present the required curriculum in enjoyable ways that motivate students to learn. While my first goal in any activity is to help students acquire required knowledge, I try to think of pleasurable ways for my students to absorb this information. Of course not all activities can be fun, but most can at least keep the majority of students attentive to learning.

At various points in this book, I describe activities that help to accomplish these purposes. Most of the time they are risk-free activities that encourage, not discourage, learning. The games I recommend will motivate learning. Likewise, the wordplay activities I suggest will foster interest and improvement in spelling. At times, I discuss drama activities that can reinforce learning. Although a casual observer might think many of these activities are frivolous time-fillers, all definitely connect to specific curriculum goals.

Many teachers offer candy prizes to increase attention, an incentive that makes most middle-schoolers more attentive to a lesson. Constantly doling out candy can be quite expensive. A better method is to give chance tickets for various desired behaviors during a class period. Giving a chance ticket to each student who has done the assigned homework is a typical reward.

My favorite way to dole out homework chance tickets was to divide students into groups to work on another activity while I checked to see if each student in a group had done the homework. If everyone in the group had completed the homework, I gave another chance ticket to each member. Students were quick to admonish any student who had failed to do his or her homework and had thus prevented them from earning additional chance tickets. I always smiled to myself as students scolded, knowing the offender would listen more to his or her peers than to me.

Throughout the period, I collected the tickets, and at the end I drew from a "chance box" three tickets to award three candy prizes. I then kept all the chance tickets collected each day for each class in separate envelopes, which I brought back periodically for a "Spinner Prize Day." My husband and I made a spinner from a bicycle wheel attached to the metal top of a fifty-gallon drum, complete with a clicker and forty-four numbers, just like lotto. A spinner can be used for many games, but I used it mostly for awarding prizes that I purchased from the catalog of the Oriental Trading Company—goofy ones like "third eyes," noise-makers, miniature stuffed animals, etc.

Students whose names were drawn from the saved chance tickets spun the wheel for prizes, with certain numbers selected for winners. All spinning contenders earned at minimum a "consolation prize," in most cases a pencil. I usually had spinner awards once every four weeks, for about fifteen minutes at the end of a period. Most school years, I would spend around $100 a year on candy and prizes, money I felt was well spent because these incentives created excitement and motivation in my classroom.

Creatures from Planet Spellingmess

One way I have made spelling memorable and enjoyable is by dressing up each year around Halloween as a creature from Planet Spellingmess. Each character described this imaginary planet as wonderful because it is a place where all syllable parts in words are spelled with "oddball" spellings. I discuss at length "oddball" syllable parts in chapter 4, "Focusing on Letter Patterns."

Each being insisted that she was a substitute teacher and gave out cards for the complicated spellings of her name. For example, Highness Homonym's card spelled her name as Whaikneast Whaumboapnaigm.

After the phonetic spelling, Hī' nəs Hom' ō nim, a spelling explanation followed:

h as in **wh**ole	s as in ca**s**tle	n as in **pn**eumonia
i as in **ai**sle	o as in h**au**nt	i as in ag**ai**n
n as in **kn**ife	m as in la**m**b	m as in phleg**m**
e as in inst**ea**d	o as in b**oa**t	

The focus of the day's lesson was explaining this card and discussing how English words have such few "oddball parts" in comparison to the complex spellings of Planet Spellingmess words. Each creature then discussed the concept she represented. After distributing some Planet Spellingmess food (candy), the being directed students to listen to some Planet Spellingmess music—a record of the many sounds of Halloween.

After reviewing prewriting strategies students could use, the creature instructed students to write down ideas for a story as they listened to the record. After a time, students started writing their story, until told to stop. Then, only if they wanted to, they could share with other students what they had written. Many were delighted with their beginning attempts and developed their story starts at a later date. I'll never forget one of my usually reluctant writers yelling out, "I'm on a roll"; he produced more writing than he had done on any other writing assignment.

Over the years, I have appeared as ten creatures and have pictures of all but one. Unfortunately, I have just a card for Lady Logica, who represents the logical spelling strategies I discuss in chapter 3, "Using Logic to Spell." Interested readers may view pictures and cards of all the creatures on my Web site (braintospell.com), as well as basic information about this book.

As each school year progressed, discussions of the appearing character were a springboard for various spelling concepts.

WHOLE BRAIN THINKING

My first character was Ms. Righta Left, who promoted "whole brain thinking," a concept American psychobiologist Roger W. Sperry developed in the 1960s. His research revealed that the human brain has two different ways of thinking. The right brain is the creative side, which processes the whole picture first and then the details. The left brain "processes information in an analytical and sequential way, looking first at pieces then putting them together to get the whole" (Boddy-Evans 2010, 1).

Readers will enjoy analyzing whether their brains are oriented more to the right side or to the left, but as Marion Boddy-Evans explains, "subsequent research has [shown both sides] aren't quite as polarized as once thought nor as simple" (2010, 1).

Ms. Righta Left had a small box on her forehead, which she used as a "brain shifter." When she moved the lever to the right, she would go "wild and crazy," and when she moved it to the left she would become "serious and somber."

When I was little I was a totally right brain thinker: In the elementary grades I put down any number in my math book, so that I could then spend my time reading or drawing. I drove my mother nuts as a small child! Our next door neighbor, Mrs. Hollis, called her frequently about my escapades, which also led my sixteen-month-older brother into mischief. Two examples follow:

"Do you know your children are crawling around on the roof?"

"Do you know your children are racing across the road trying to beat oncoming cars?"

My dad dubbed me "The Instigator"; my mother tried to cope. In later years she said I was getting "payback time" when raising my two sons, Doug and Brad.

However, when I entered high school I became interested in being a superior student. Francis Evans, my Latin teacher, was especially instrumental in this change, with her zealous instructional methods that helped me develop left-brain thinking skills. Studying geometry was a maze for me for most of the school year, but when I solved the Pythagorean theorem in late spring, geometric concepts became understandable. By the time I finished high school, I had developed "whole brain" thinking skills.

Those who acquire "whole brain" thinking skills will most likely make the greatest contributions to our world. Teachers need to guide students to gain both intellectual and creative skills: The serious ones need to learn that acting silly can be fun; the silly ones need to work on developing academic abilities to excel in educational pursuits.

SPELLING DOES COUNT!

Many students have become complacent about spelling because process writing assignments often end short of publication, especially on state writing assessments. Students were getting the message that "spelling doesn't count" (Thibodeau 2002, 20).

I could not disagree more with such a philosophy. All students in higher grades, even those with the weakest spelling abilities, need to be held accountable when producing revised, finished works, in various ways— checking in a dictionary for spellings, using spell checker on a computer, or conferencing with a competent speller.

When starting a peer conferencing session, I always cautioned proficient writers that they could only record correction symbols for errors they found in another student's work. If the writer continued to be unable to make a correction from the symbol, the student helper could dictate the answer for the writer to make on his or her own paper, allowing for some learning transfer.

At the same time, I caution parents to follow this same process in reading their child's writing. Correcting their child's mistakes will not be helpful; guiding him or her to making his or her her own corrections will promote writing growth.

NO TEACHERS BE

Kelly Chandler expresses what most excellent spellers usually remark about their spelling abilities: "spelling had always come easily, almost magically to me" (Chandler Teacher Research Group 2000, 88). Superior spellers usually fail to realize that their abilities have not come "magically," but rather through their fascination with letters in words when they were little and continued close observation of words they see daily.

Only one teacher can teach spelling. In all cases, that person is the learner! Humans teach themselves to spell. A person learns to spell by becoming his or her own spelling teacher. Poor spellers can improve by learning and applying strategies that good spellers develop tacitly. Once they understand the spelling process that good spellers follow, students should soon realize that no book, word list, or set of worksheets can teach spelling ability—although many will foster improvement. Learners can grow in spelling knowledge even while performing mundane tasks. An ordinary errand to the grocery store, the mall, or practically any other place humans go daily can become a spelling lesson.

Oglan's "Grocery Lists, Shopping, and a Child's Writing and Spelling Development" illustrates how a father turned trips to the grocery into writing and spelling exercises for his daughter, whose teacher labeled her "probably dyslexic" (2001, 2). The resulting lists reveal his daughter's growth in spelling and writing, improvement that will result when a child has a purpose for using words. A learner will improve in spelling ability only if he or she is willing to make a concentrated effort to observe closely the many words he or she sees daily.

2

Priming the Spelling Pump

A painter first applies primer to a wall to prepare the surface for painting. A lawyer usually primes a witness to prepare him or her before giving testimony in court. Likewise, a number of procedures will prime students' learning, especially in the teaching of spelling.

SELF-CORRECTION

In her research in 1981, Barbara Pflug found that the "single most important factor in learning to spell is the student correcting his or her own spelling test under the teacher's direction" (21). Such findings are not surprising when one considers that self-correction puts the student, not the teacher, in charge of his or her own learning.

In my former English classes before graduate school, I had a complex system for students grading papers. I would collect papers and then pass them out in a way that the student doing the grading would be at least two rows away from the student whose paper was to be graded. Many would be more concerned about their own scores than correcting another student's paper.

Students love a self-correction system because they are involved in checking their own work, not another student's. Many teachers think that students will cheat and change their answers. Cheating in my class is difficult because I require students to have a good supply of red pens and/

or red pencils for self-checking. When it is time to grade, students may have only their paper and the red pen or pencil on top of their desks: They place all other books, pens, pencils, notebooks, etc., on the floor. Before starting, I make sure each student has the required red writing tool; if not, the student loses the right to grade his or her paper, which I then collect to grade myself later. Once students realize that they will not be able to check their work, most—usually all—come well supplied on future days.

Of course I go over the papers checking for mistakes, marking off twice as much for any errors not marked. Instead of using red, I use either green or purple, so the student and his or her parents or guardians can differentiate my marks.

Many teachers feel grading should be their responsibility and refuse to try the self-correction methods I expound. They fail to realize that students' grading their own papers creates an additional learning activity rather than just a culminating test. After many years of directing students to do self-correction on various activities, I strongly believe that students performing self-correction is one of the most effective learning tools, which all teachers should use.

ACCURATE COPYING

Poor spellers have many reasons for misspelling a word. Miscopying a given word should not be one of them. Closely observing a word and its parts to copy its spelling accurately seems a simple task, especially to teachers and good spellers. The lowest level spellers, however, will find accurate copying of spellings a daunting task. I still remember one of my low-level students whose eyes would bug out when I pointed out spelling errors he had missed correcting. He would respond in surprise, "How do you do that?" as if I had some magical ability. Such a student needs lots of practice to help him or her develop the ability to look carefully at a word and copy all of its parts accurately.

One way that I give my students daily practice in accurate copying is with an "anticipatory set" activity that I term "The Ant." In her model of an ideal lesson, Madeline Hunter recommends such an activity to help students prepare for class (1990, 28).

A cartoon picture of an ant accompanies the transparency directing this activity. On my classroom wall is also a caricature of an ant with the saying "Start class with the Ant!," which leads students to the misconception at the beginning of the year that "The Ant" must be some game or other fun-filled but frivolous activity. Instead, it is usually a sentence-writing activity that students are required to start working on as soon as they enter the classroom, even before the bell has rung. Usually the activity culminates in students accurately copying a sentence from the literature text.

Since I have taught all grades at my middle school—sixth, seventh, and eighth—I have developed "Ant" sentence-writing activities from each of the corresponding *Literature and Language* texts published by McDougal, Littell in 1994, the texts Chesterfield County adopted for all English classes in the middle schools in the county. The sentences I select model syntactical structures that middle-school students need to use in their writing. They usually contain a mix of gerund, participial, and prepositional phrases as well as relative and adverb clauses without correlative conjunctions, which result in what would be labeled "simple" sentences in traditional grammar. A reader who understands the previous statement has explicit knowledge of English grammar; middle-school students, however, have no need to understand such terms.

I turn each sentence that I select into one of the following activities: sentence combining, sentence murdering, or sentence expanding. While I could write extensively on each of these sentence-writing activities, I will describe them only briefly here.

Sentence combining requires breaking down the selected sentence into basic sentences—teachers who have studied transformational grammar would use the term "kernel sentences." Directions guide students to try to combine these short sentences into fewer ones and into one sentence if possible. The major goal for students in composing resulting sentences is to avoid writing run-ons or comma splices. After several students share their attempts, a citation directs them to a specific sentence in the text for accurate copying.

At the beginning of each school year, I give students easier sentences to combine. The first story we study is "Charles" by Shirley Jackson (1994, 7–11). Following is the first sentence-combining activity I show on a transparency for students to complete:

Directions: Try to combine the following sentences into one correct sentence:
The teacher spanked him.
She made him stand in a corner.

After a few students share their attempts, I uncover an abbreviated code of the sentence citation:

P7, ¶ 11, S4 (Copy: page 7, paragraph 11, sentence 4.)

Students then open their texts and copy the selected sentence:

(The teacher spanked him and made him stand in the corner.)

I always require students to bring their textbooks to class daily. For any who have forgotten, I do not allow borrowing of another student's book. Instead, I remind them that they have to copy the sentence later for additional homework. I encourage parents to check their child's copying efforts. If they note any errors, they can then tell their child to try to find them. If their child still fails to find the mistake, they can then point it out to correct. Such checking for accuracy is an especially effective strategy for helping special education students' growth in language skills.

If any student has created the exact same sentence that is in the text, he or she writes instead, "I did it." As the school year progresses, many are able to make this claim. Occasionally I have found a student looking for the sentence in the text to save using his or her brain to compose a result. Fortunately, this rarely happens.

As the year progresses, so does the complexity of sentence exercises, until students can attempt more complicated ones, such as the following excerpt from the book *Exploring the Titanic* (1994, 94–105):

Both men had been at work for hours.
They were in the room.
The room was for the ship's radio.
The name of the ship was *Titanic*.
They tried to get caught up in sending out messages.

There were a large number of messages.
The messages were personal.

P98, ¶2, S4 (Copy page 98, paragraph 2, sentence 4.)
(Both men had been at work for hours in the *Titanic*'s radio room trying
to get caught up in sending out a large number of personal messages.)

Sentence-murdering and sentence-expanding activities are similar; both also culminate in students accurately copying a sentence in the textbook. In the sentence-murdering activity, I butcher a selected sentence, usually turning it into series of run-ons and comma splices, common errors beginning writers often make. In sentence expanding, I give students a phrase from the selected sentence for them to expand into as long a sentence as possible without using correlative conjunctions or committing any syntactical errors. Copying well-written sentences daily gives students a tacit knowledge of how to write complex sentences without learning any technical grammatical descriptions. By the end of the year a large number of my students are able to duplicate the selected sentence as well as compose highly complicated but grammatically correct sentences, revealing that they have acquired the highest level of syntactical skills.

In turn, students have to copy all parts accurately, including spelling and punctuation. I have always graded resulting papers harshly, lowering an otherwise perfect paper to an average grade—C under an A to F system—for ONE mistake in spelling or punctuation, or ONE miscopied part. On such a paper I also write "Look," making cartoon eyes out of the two "O's." I never grade a paper lower than a "C" unless the writer failed to complete other parts. Of course, for students with learning disabilities or limited language skills, I lower my expectations accordingly. The "Ant" activity is just one of many graded assignments throughout the grading period and has little impact on the resulting period grade for a student who otherwise usually earns honor roll ratings.

Some students are dyslexic and will reverse letters when copying a word. An understanding teacher will mark such errors for the student to correct until he or she can catch and correct these mistakes.

Sandra Stotsky, an educational consultant who specializes in teaching reading and writing, recommends accurate copying of sentences to help students internalize the structure of correctly written sentences. Stotsky cites various sources that expound on the value of copying text to improve writing. She states that Malcolm X taught himself command of English by reading and copying the dictionary (1984, 338). Meredith Hunter, a very talented English teacher in my school system, stated in an in-service presentation that she has helped basic writers make dramatic improvements by directing them to accurately copy selected literature passages.

Granted, I have had some students complain that my grading of "The Ant" is too severe. One mother scheduled a conference when her daughter expressed her anger, but the mother quickly gave me her support when she found out that my high expectations were teaching her daughter to edit accurately. Developing proofreading skills is an essential writing skill for beginning writers. The eighth-grade teachers at my school frequently commented that they could tell which of their students had been in my English 7 class because they always checked their writings very carefully. Editing accurately requires the ability to observe words carefully.

Another way I insist on accurate copying of spelling is to count any test answer wrong for misspelling a word given in a word bank, taking off as many points as for a wrong answer. Likewise, I penalize writings that misspell words given in directions, but certainly not as heavily as those on the "Ant." I also expect students to copy spellings accurately for words given on a transparency or the blackboard, but take off only partial points.

Another "accurate copying" activity is to give dictation exercises, a whole language activity that connects speaking, listening, writing, and reading. In other words, a teacher picks a passage from the students' text to dictate for writing. When they are finished, students open their books to the selected part and correct mistakes they find in their work. The teacher then grades the resulting papers on whether or not students made all the corrections. I frequently gave my X-level students dictation exercises.

Dr. Smith, in his graduate-level class, "The Teaching of Composition," often spoke of the number of dictation tapes he developed to help basic writers he taught at VCU improve in various writing skills. Each tape or set of tapes was devoted to helping a student correct a pattern of error, an excellent venue for individualizing instruction. Educational publishers should consider developing such tapes. Otherwise, leading an entire class in a dictation activity consumes a great deal of time, with not all students benefiting.

A Way to Teach Punctuation Tacitly

My daily anticipatory activity was also a way to teach students how to punctuate correctly the sentences they composed. On the front wall of my classroom, I had mini-posters of all punctuation marks with their correct names, for student reference. One of my mini-lessons in the beginning of each school year was to invite four students to come forward for some acting lessons, always a favorite activity. Then I stated that most students have a problem punctuating written sentences correctly because they never say the names of these marks in any conversation. We would therefore start making punctuation marks memorable by acting out various punctuation marks along with emphatically stating each mark's name. Modeling dramatically, I directed the group to say the name of a particular mark, with an appropriate gesture. Semicolon is a good one! The results brought laughter as well as building confidence in students to perform in front of the class.

For about a week thereafter, I required each student who shared his or her composed sentence, as well as the reading of the selected sentence in the text, to say each punctuation mark clearly along with making the appropriate gesture. I agreed with my students that this was a silly activity, but it was an excellent way to make punctuation marks memorable when writing. For the rest of the school year, any student who shared his or her writing or read aloud the sentence I had selected had to also say the name of each punctuation mark.

When grading the "Ant" sheets students produced weekly, I usually noted that the majority of my students carefully and distinctly made any punctuation marks in their written sentences, as well as in those they copied from the text.

An excellent closure activity is to have two students come up in front of the class and have a conversation, saying and acting out each appropriate punctuation mark. Acting out punctuation marks is an activity most of my students would probably remember performing; one year four students posed for a picture in the school yearbook of them punctuating in the air!

By the end of the year, the vast majority of students learned tacitly how to punctuate correctly the complicated but correctly constructed sentences they composed.

Teaching accurate observing and correct copying stresses one of the most important skills a weak speller needs to learn: to use his or her eyes in observing word parts. In addition, accurate copying of carefully selected sentences helps students develop a tacit understanding of many writing elements: correct syntactical construction, capitalization, punctuation, and spelling. Such activities immerse students in language development, of which spelling is just one important component.

All teachers should require their students to spell given words accurately. Unfortunately, many ignore spelling mistakes or impose only minor penalties, instilling in students the idea that spelling has little importance. Teachers should realize that reversing these practices will help students improve in spelling.

LISTENING TO CLASSICAL MUSIC INCREASES MEMORY AND LEARNING

One of the fellows in the 1985 Capital Writing Project was a music teacher, whose name I have forgotten. I have not forgotten her presentation, in which she stressed that students' listening to classical music increases their attention and promotes learning.

As a result, almost every day, when students first entered my classroom, I played part of a tape of a classical piece by a famous musical artist. At the beginning of each school year, I started with Peter Tchaikovsky's *Piano Concerto No. 1 in B Flat Minor*, a piece I could play on the piano when in my teens but only after constant practice for many weeks. I told my new students that I could once play it, but not presently. I could probably not even play one note because I stopped playing the piano when I started my undergraduate college studies.

I then directed my students to copy in capital letters on their daily "Ant Sheets" the name of the selected classical artist whose music I had played (e.g., TCHAIKOVSKY). I always directed them to start working before the bell rang. I also emphasized any unusual spelling in the artist's last name, and the name Tchaikovsky is an excellent example. Frequently, I gave a bonus question on a test or quiz, and sometimes I asked students to give the correct spelling of the week's classical artist.

Of course, some enjoyed the music while others hated having to listen to it before class even began. At a minimum, the music kept mischievous students from chasing each other around the room before the bell, typical behavior for seventh graders. Once a student visited me when he was in high school and commented that what he had enjoyed most about my English class was the classical music I played.

Laurence O'Donnell emphasizes how listening to classical music can positively influence learning:

> One simple way students can improve test scores is by listening to certain types of music such as Mozart's *Sonata for Two Pianos in D Major* before taking a test. This type of music releases neurons in the brain which help the body to relax. (2010, 3)

O'Donnell also explains how scientific testing reveals that listening to classical music positively influences students' learning (2010, 4).

Teachers incorporating classical music, even in small amounts, into their lesson plans will probably increase their students' learning in the subject area. Many readers, especially when stressed, will discover that listening to classical music is soothing.

PROMOTE CURSIVE HANDWRITING

When I taught high school for six years long ago, I always told my students they could write in print or cursive as long as their writing was legible. I gave my middle-school students the same directions, until I took Dr. Smith's "Teaching of Composition" class, a required course in my graduate program.

Dr. Smith expounded at length on the value of having students write in cursive. Once adept in cursive handwriting, students can write faster and thus more fluently. He stressed that a writing teacher's first concern should be to help students develop writing fluency or speed. A writer who struggles to put words on paper will lose thoughts in the process, but one who can write quickly will be much more likely to access relevant brain connections.

Research reveals that cursive handwriting also is also connected to spelling ability. The speed of writing seems to be a contributory subskill of spelling ability: "Carefulness in writing is significantly correlated with speed of handwriting, and both these factors correlate significantly with good spelling" (Peters 1985, 22). Forming letter shapes with certainty in an automatic, continuous flow will help a writer "concentrate on letter pattern and word structure rather than letter formation" (Peters 1985, 55). Establishing fluid writing patterns helps students remember spelling, because "children with swift motor control write groups of letters, for example, 'ing' 'ean' 'est,' in a connected form and this is the basis of knowledge about which letters stick together. This is the crux of spelling ability, for handwriting and spelling go hand in hand" (Peters 1985, 55). Having students copy in cursive will help them associate the letter patterns in words they copy (Kavanaugh and Venezky 1980, 218).

Ever since taking that course, I have insisted that my middle-school students write in cursive, over their many objections. I always explain that besides writing fluency and spelling connections, writing in cursive creates a greater impression of intelligence, since students learn cursive writing after printing. Providing students with writing models has been helpful to those who had forgotten certain letter formations. Writing legibility improved tremendously for many, especially those whose printing resembled awkward and usually illegible scratchings.

In her recent book, *Spelling, Handwriting, and Dyslexia: Overcoming Barriers to Learning*, Diane Montgomery discusses at length the importance of teaching cursive handwriting. "Handwriting is a motor activity which needs to be taught that will not develop like walking. The motor memory controls the direction and shape of each letter, and, therefore a continuous joined handwriting style established as early as possible, can help to gain automaticity" (2007, 35).

Automatically writing in cursive frees the brain to concentrate on other writing skills such as spelling, grammar, syntax, style, and content. "Any students who has not been able to develop a fast and legible script is at a disadvantage and likely to underachieve in school" (Montgomery 2007, 35). Using cursive writing promotes fluency and legibility at a "reasonable speed" (2007, 47). In cursive handwriting, each word or syllable is one continuous line that gives the writer a kinesthetic feedback.

"Handwriting, therefore, supports spelling and this contributes to literacy development" (2007, 53). A student's writing speed is a "crucial factor of academic success at the secondary level" (2007, 53).

Montgomery (2007, 54) also cites research showing that cursive writing

- aids left-to-right movement through words across the page;
- stops reversals and inversions of letters;
- induces greater fluency in writing, which enables greater speed to be developed without loss of legibility;
- enables more to be written in the time allowed;
- can make a difference of a grade at GCSE, a level or in degree programmes through increased speed and fluency;
- can improve spelling accuracy, as the motor programmes for spelling words, particularly their bases and affixes, are stored together by the brain (Kuczaj 1979);
- results in orderly and automatic space between letters and between words;
- enables a more efficient, fluent, and personal style to be developed;
- reduces the pain and difficulty experienced by pupils with handwriting coordination difficulties;
- improves legibility of writing;
- reinforces multisensory learning linking spelling, writing, and speaking;

In addition, if cursive writing is taught from the outset,

- it eliminates the need to relearn a whole new set of motor programmes after the infant stage;
- there is a more efficient use of movement because of cursive's flow.

STUDY HIGH-FREQUENCY WORD LISTS

Directing students to study and memorize the spellings in high-frequency lists is a logical approach that numerous current authors recommend (Gentry 1993, 2004; Marland 2002; Pinnell 1998; Sipe 2003; Smith 2001; Snowball and Bolton 1999; and Wilde 1992, 1996, 1997, 2004). Marland's book, *High Frequency Words: Strategies That Build Skills in Spelling, Vocabulary, and Word Play* (2002) focuses on many effective strategies for helping students to spell these words.

Carl Smith (2001, 39) notes that the twenty highest-frequency words appear in 25–28 percent of student and adult writing:

a	to	we	that	in
the	was	he	is	have
and	my	for	are	my
I	your	it	not	be

Elementary teachers should emphasize spelling these twenty wordsones correctly.

Many authors just list high-frequency words, with no particular organization. Gentry's "Five Hundred Words Most Frequently Used in Children's Writing" (1993; see appendix C) is a commonly cited list. To provide a more plausible approach for using this extensive list to teach spelling, I have reorganized these words according to logical and illogical spelling patterns (see appendix A). Chapters 3 and 4 provide detailed explanations of these groupings. Once teachers implement the strategies I recommend in these two chapters, they can present these words to their students according to their groups: The logically spelled words students will easily master; the illogical or "oddball" ones will be more difficult.

GUIDE STUDENTS TO BECOMING SPELLING DETECTIVES

Mina Shaughnessy is well known for *Errors and Expectations* (1977). When teaching basic writers at City University of New York, Shaungnessy discovered that students' writing errors fall into predictable patterns that often result from their misconceptions about formal written language. Her book explains explicitly how correcting one pattern of error usually significantly reduces the total number of errors students produce in future papers.

Students' spelling errors also fall into foreseeable patterns. Most teachers are thoroughly discouraged when trying to instruct a group of disphonetic spellers. Reading the following passage, which one of my students wrote, would make most teachers throw their hands up in frustration:

Whene I went to the hocky game fridy at the colocein it was croded on the
stans you could harly move around there were long lins in the place were

you get food. dering the game there where alot of fight's and players got kickt out of the gome for flghighting one person hit the gole and broak it and it came off and hit the gate and broak it and it came off and hit the glass and they sead that rechem is getting a hocky team to.

Such weak spellers need to learn and apply the logical spelling principles presented in chapter 3. Once students become skilled in using these simple concepts, they will make notable gains. Teachers' frustration should turn to excitement once they realize they can have the greatest impact on their lowest level spellers by teaching them how to spell words logically.

Several authors of current research recommend that teachers make periodic assessments of each student's spelling skills. Laminack and Wood promote a complicated "index of control" system and admit it is a "time-consuming process" but provides "invaluable" data (1996, 48). Fresch and Wheaton also have devised a complex assessment method they title the "Spelling Knowledge Inventory," which requires a teacher to record types of spelling errors for each student (2002, 61–82). Bear promotes a "Stage Assessment" model for students to show how to spell words and features analysis for Elementary Inventory, with a focus on analyzing spelling stages for each student (2004, 39). O'Sullivan recommends the CLPE Spelling Assessment framework (2007, 102–105, Appendix 1).

I can't imagine an elementary teacher keeping such data. Skimming writing to note patterns of errors is a more workable method. Focusing on assessing the types of spelling errors students make is a better approach. McAlexander, Dobie, and Gregg expound on "the major types of errors" caused by visual and auditory errors (1992, 19–30). They recommend a "Shaughnessy" type of error assessment rather than a complicated system that requires teachers to keep technical data on each student.

Other spelling researchers recommend that students, not teachers, be responsible for assessing spelling problems in their writing. "Teachers can help students become more independent in their editing by showing them how to scan their texts for one particular kind of error at a time" (Chandler and Mapleton Teacher Research Group 1999, 93). Each student needs to be accountable for learning: A teacher is only a guide. Students, not teachers, should keep track of spelling errors (McAlexander, Dobie, and Gregg

1992, 42). Sipe promotes students keeping spelling logs of problem words (2002, 28) and charts (2003, 17–19).

TEACH BASIC PHONETICS

One memorable class I took in undergraduate school at Ohio State University in the early 1960s was "History of English Language," memorable because I almost failed a major portion, English phonetics. The professor required memorizing all of the diacritical marks and corresponding sounds usually provided in a collegiate dictionary. The "Guide to Pronunciation" in *Webster's Ninth New Collegiate Dictionary* is eight pages long and in miniscule type. Before the listing "English Spelling and Sound Correspondences" is a warning that the given list is "representative . . . [and by] no means exhaustive" (1983, 37). At best, learning and understanding phonetics is a difficult process.

Memorizing diacritical marks was not my problem; listening to the vowel sounds in a word and transposing them correctly was my nemesis. I didn't seem to hear a vowel sound the same way my professor did. Psycholinguistics labels such difficulty as a *"problem of invariance"* (Carroll 1986, 117).

Teaching students how to pronounce unknown words from corresponding phonetic spellings is supplying them with invaluable knowledge they will use in future educational years. However, they do not need to comprehend all complex phonetic principles. Instead, they need to understand and apply three basic phonetic concepts:

- stressed syllables
- long vowels
- sound of schwa

Once students understand and can apply these basics, most will usually develop adequate proficiency to be able to pronounce, or closely pronounce, most unknown words from their phonetic spellings in a dictionary. In addition, students need to understand these simple principles in applying the spelling strategies discussed in following chapters. Helping students understand phonetics by focusing on these three fundamentals is highly enjoyable for most teachers and students.

Stressed Syllables

Explaining the meaning of a diacritical stress mark on a syllable—a diagonal slash over a syllable—involves a discussion of how to pronounce that word part. A few students might be able to state that such a mark indicates the syllable needs more emphasis when pronounced than the other syllables in that word. Such an explanation will not be enough for students to understand this concept.

Using first names of students in the class is an excellent way to help them understand a stressed syllable. I usually begin by giving my first name of "Sally" to discuss which syllable—"Sal" or "ly"—has greater emphasis. Most students will be able to reply that the "Sal" part gets greater stress than the "ly" part. I then ask students to pronounce my name but change the stress to the second syllable; this changes the sound of my name dramatically, giving it more of a French-sounding pronunciation. I then ask students to analyze several other names in the class and likewise change the stress in each pronunciation. Two-syllable names will be the easiest to discern until most students seem to understand. Then select a multisyllable name like "Angela" for more of a challenge. The resulting pronunciation of "Angela," stressing "gel" rather than "An," will bring smiles.

Most classes contain many students whose first names can lead to similar discussions and pronunciation changes to aid in understanding the concept of a stressed syllable. Using names of actual students in the class gains the interest of practically all of them. While some teachers might be concerned that the change in pronunciation will result in teasing of the selected student, I have never experienced such a problem. Usually those whose names have not been selected develop an interest in examining their own names. A number of parents have reported to me over the years how much they enjoyed hearing their children explain this name activity.

Long Vowels: Key to Pronouncing Vowel Sounds

Almost all middle-school students thoroughly understand the differences between vowels and consonants. Many might not know the meaning of a long mark over a vowel. Discuss with the class the fact that such a mark indicates the vowel has the same pronunciation as it has in the alphabet. Pronouncing each major vowel—a, e, i, o, and u—should make this concept clear. I supply my students with a handout titled "Key to Pronouncing Vowel Sounds." This guide provides a list of major sounds vowels make, each with several example words:

a: at, fat, lap	i: it, is, hit	oi: oil, boy
ā: age, ape, date	ī: bite, mile, tiger	ou: out, doubt
ä: father, car	o: hot, lot, top	ū: you, music, use
e: end, ten, let	ō: go, tone	ü: truly
ē: me, even, meet	ô: saw, all, caught	u: full, rule, wool
ë: term	oo: tool, troop	

This list is very fundamental, eliminating many other diacritical markings most dictionaries give. Understanding that vowels have long sounds as well as variations for short sounds is the most important concept for students to gain at this point. Students' understanding all of the diacritical marks and sounds for the short vowels is not important.

They do need to know why example words appear after each given vowel. Going over the list and having various students say the sound each short vowel represents will help them realize that the corresponding letter(s) in each example word illustrates how to speak each vowel sound. Have students then examine an extensive list in a dictionary to show them that short vowels have many different pronunciations.

Again, students' understanding the key on the given list will lead them to understanding how to use a dictionary key in the future when trying to decipher the pronunciation of an unknown word. Such dictionary activities will be valuable in the future but not at this point of instruction, since the purpose is to lead students to understanding just these three phonetic principles.

THE SCHWA SYMBOL

Include a discussion of the schwa symbol, an upside down "e" that represents an "uh" sound, the most common vowel sound in the English language. Instruction on the schwa sound will most likely be new to most students.

I delight in explaining to students my theory about why schwa is the most frequently occurring vowel sound. My guess is that prehistoric man probably communicated with many "ughs." As a result, an "uh" sound remained in many words as they evolved into English. A few moments of the whole class yelling "ugh" and gesturing like cave men—including myself modeling—will reinforce this concept. Students need to remember the schwa is an "uh" sound. The sound of schwa is an essential concept for students to understand and apply the logical spelling strategies discussed in chapter 3, "Using Logic to Spell," and chapter 4, "Focusing on Letter Patterns."

Schwa is a source of many spelling problems because it has so many different spellings. At the end of the "Key to Pronouncing Vowel Sounds" handout, I provide the following list to show that schwa can represent all five major vowels:

- For **a** as in **ago**
- For **e** as in **taken** or **agent**
- For **i** as in **pencil** and **sanity**
- For **o** as in **lemon** and **comply**
- For **u** as in **circus** and **focus**

One year I used Princess Schwa from Planet Spellingmess to demonstrate the variable ways to spell this sound. She wore a necklace of cards, each of which listed a pattern for spelling a schwa sound. (Appendix B lists the word examples I placed on each card.) Each card can be pulled to show word examples. The explanations and examples Princess Schwa gave made very clear to students why the schwa sound is so difficult to spell.

Reading and Writing in Phonetics

Once most students understand stressed syllables and basic vowel sounds including the schwa sound, I give them a letter from me written in phonetics (see figure 2.1).

Most will find translating this letter easy, but not the next assignment. For homework, I direct students to write an equally long letter to me, spelling all words phonetically. This assignment does not teach students how to write in phonetics, which is certainly not my goal; instead, it helps them become familiar with the phonetic fundamentals I have stressed so

Dēr Stü'dənts,
    Lern'ing fō·net'ik spel·ing
Kan bē fun bē·köz' it iz
līk ū'zing ə sē'krət cōd.
        I wənt yü tü lern hou
Tü rēd and prə'nounz wërdz
speld fō·net'ək·lē sō yü wil
bē ā'bül Tü prə·nounz' wërdz—
e'vun lăng, dif'ə·kült wërdz
yü dōn't nō.
        Ri'ting in fōnet'ikz iz
thə best wā Tü lern thə
fō·net'ik sim'bülz.
        I hōp yü in'joi fō·net'ikz!
            Sin·ser'lē,
            Mi'sus Berk'hart

Figure 2.1. Phonetic Letter to Students

far. I tell students to do their best in recording short vowel sounds, picking the closest one on the pronunciation key. I also have them note that a dot is placed after an unstressed syllable to separate it from a following syllable. Above all, they should strive to accurately record stressed syllables, long vowels, and schwa sounds.

The following day students usually report to me on how challenging this assignment was to complete, that it took a great deal of time. Though most students will do this assignment because it is one they enjoy, a few will fail to complete it. I separate these students and direct them to write as much of their phonetic letter as they can in class, giving partial credit for completed ones.

Students with completed letters trade with one another. Each then translates the phonetic spellings in the other student's writing. They then write a note—in regular English, not phonetics—to the student whose phonetic letter they have just translated, commenting on his or her writing and the assignment. Since a typical behavior of many students, elementary through high school, is to pass a note secretly in class, most students will enjoy being permitted to write to another class member.

Practice Pronouncing Phonetically Spelled Words

Completion of the phonetic letter activity prepares students for the next, a list of multisyllable words with their phonetic spellings (see figure 2.2).

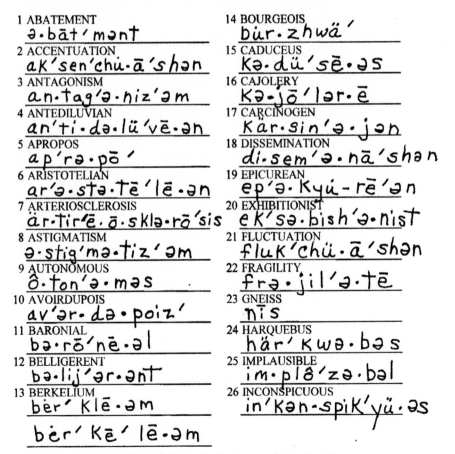

1 ABATEMENT	14 BOURGEOIS
2 ACCENTUATION	15 CADUCEUS
3 ANTAGONISM	16 CAJOLERY
4 ANTEDILUVIAN	17 CARCINOGEN
5 APROPOS	18 DISSEMINATION
6 ARISTOTELIAN	19 EPICUREAN
7 ARTERIOSCLEROSIS	20 EXHIBITIONIST
8 ASTIGMATISM	21 FLUCTUATION
9 AUTONOMOUS	22 FRAGILITY
10 AVOIRDUPOIS	23 GNEISS
11 BARONIAL	24 HARQUEBUS
12 BELLIGERENT	25 IMPLAUSIBLE
13 BERKELIUM	26 INCONSPICUOUS

Figure 2.2. Phonetically Spelled Words for Pronunciation Practice

As an additional reinforcement, have students practice pronouncing each of these words, a few words at a time, usually as a closure activity. Most students will enjoy this activity since it is not graded and therefore is nonthreatening. Students who pronounce a word correctly will smile with pleasure at their success. After the class completes pronouncing all twenty-six words, the vast majority of students will be able to pronounce most words they come across in the future when provided with phonetic spellings. They will use this skill many times in future years. Likewise, their understanding of phonetics will transfer to learning and applying specific strategies I have developed to help students improve in spelling.

LESSON PLANNING FOR MIDDLE-SCHOOLERS

The major difference between high-school students and middle-school students is their energy levels. Many middle-schoolers will run instead of walk to a class, especially when a teacher is not monitoring them. Most are very immature, even though many, especially girls, look much older. Chasing one another around a classroom before the bell is usual. A student grabbing the top bar of the door and swinging from it into the classroom is a common sight. Many delight in teasing others, often cruelly, a practice that should earn immediate punishment.

When I taught high school for a period of six years many years ago, I taught grades 9 through 12—the first few years teaching juniors and seniors, and the last teaching freshmen and sophomores. Each level required somewhat different approaches because of variations in student maturity levels. During that period, I use to think teaching middle school—the term then was junior high—would be a breeze in comparison. Not until I became a middle-school teacher did I realize that teaching this age group was far more challenging. While I have also taught sixth and eighth graders, I have found seventh grade the most difficult but also most rewarding level to teach, and I have taught it for fourteen years.

Lesson planning requires variety to hold the attention of middle-school students. Dividing lessons into ten- to twenty-minute segments will result in more learning, because most middle-school students have short attention spans. Instruction will be far more effective through mini-lessons involving students than through workbook pages or spelling tests. Trying to teach just one concept for an entire class period will lose the interest of most and likewise deter learning. Accordingly, the teaching of a spelling concept should last no more than a few minutes, with extended discussions on the next day or later. Often I have felt like a juggler when moving from one activity to the next, a process that requires thoughtful planning but will reap great rewards in student learning.

THE EFFECTIVENESS OF PEER TUTORING AND GROUP WORK

According to Terrell (1983), peer tutoring is another effective approach to teaching spelling. Her research discusses how a systematic study period involving peer tutoring and contractual consequences helped students make substantial increases in unit spelling word accuracy. "Students can help one another at their levels, and self concepts of students may be improved through helping others. Through this interaction, motivation for spelling will be enhanced. Simply stated, pair-learning works!" (Manning and Manning 1981, 20). Allowing students short periods of time to study by pairs should improve performance. Working in groups fulfills students' need for belonging, which Maslow described (1970). Piaget also stressed the value of children teaching one another (Brainerd 1976, 283). Authorities often quote William Glasser's statement (2006), "We learn 95% of what we teach others," when expounding on the value of peer tutoring.

Frequently, I divide students into groups of four to five. Sometimes I organize each group by the current seating chart, other times by compatibility or ability levels. Group work never lasts for more than twenty minutes, with everyone in the group required to produce written work based on the given assignment. Some teachers direct just one student to be the secretary for the group's findings, a practice that discourages individual responsibility. If all members produce some written account of the group's activity, the likelihood is greater that all members will benefit from the activity, since writing produces learning. Again, including some peer interaction during a class period will provide variety and motivate learners, as long as the teacher carefully structures the group activity to be worthwhile.

Topping's *Paired Reading, Spelling, and Writing: The Handbook for Teachers and Parents* (1995) is an excellent resource that provides specifics on grouping students for spelling instruction. Teachers will find the worksheets he provides very helpful.

ENCOURAGE COMPUTER WRITING

In the years following my retirement, I have done a great deal of substitute teaching. Sometimes when teaching a language arts class, students tell me their teacher does not allow them to produce writing on a computer, mostly because the computer can make many corrections, especially in spelling. I couldn't disagree more. Writing with a computer is the way of the modern world, and weak writers should use this tool as much as possible to improve their writing skills. While a computer's spell-check system makes no use of context (Milton 1996, 139), it will usually list numerous approximations to a selected word. A writer still "must have enough underlying spelling knowledge to recognize the correct choice" (Templeton 2004, 58).

As chapter 3, "Using Logic to Spell," will reveal, many weak spellers will find a computer's spell-checker to be of little use unless an attempted misspelling is close to the correct spelling of a word. Learning the logical spelling techniques discussed in that chapter will help such students become what I term "functional spellers," who can correct most of their misspellings by using a computer's spell-check system.

In addition, most students, especially those with keyboarding skills, will write faster with a computer than by hand, helping them to write down thoughts quickly and therefore more fluently. As stated previously, fluency is the first skill a basic writer needs to develop to become a competent writer.

I cannot imagine trying to write without a computer. In the "olden days" of my undergraduate years at Ohio State University, I spent as much time typing a piece of writing as I did composing it. Typographical errors, white ink tape corrections, and misspellings were frequent occurrences that often resulted in a lower grade. Using a computer for compositions required in my graduate level studies dramatically improved my writing, because I could easily make revisions and corrections. Likewise, all students need to learn to use computer word-processing programs when creating compositions, which will foster progressive improvement in writing.

In summary, most of the activities recommended in this chapter will foster not only spelling improvement but also growth in all whole-language facets—reading, writing, speaking, and listening—because spelling instruction is not a separate component but intertwines with each of these communication skills.

3

Using Logic to Spell

Learning to spell English words appears to the casual observer an almost impossible task because English has so many variant ways to spell the same sounds. In 1966, Hanna, Hodges, Hanna, and Rudorf programmed a computer to "analyze the spelling of over 17,000 words to determine how individual speech sounds, or phonemes, are spelled in different positions in the syllables of words" (Hodges 1982, 5–6).

The results, published in *Phoneme-Grapheme Correspondences as Cues to Spelling Improvement*, revealed a surprising amount of consistency in graphemic representations of speech sounds in English. The program demonstrated this consistency by spelling correctly "over 8,000 words, or slightly over 50 percent, misspelling another 37 percent of the words with only one incorrect phoneme-grapheme correspondence" (Hodges 1982, 6). For example, the "only" misspelled part in the word "phony," was the beginning "f" sound, which the computer spelled with its alphabet counterpart, "fony."

The book indicates that weak spellers can spell most parts of a word correctly if they apply sound strategies to spell each syllable. Learning basic sound–letter principles can help weak spellers improve their spelling significantly. Even though Hanna et al. conducted this research over fifty years ago, few if any practical applications are part of current teaching strategies and philosophies. Failure to implement these findings is unfortunate, because of all the data I have collected, I find this work to be one of the most significant studies on the teaching of spelling.

Once during a presentation I delivered to my school system's spelling committee, I held the book by Hanna et al. (1966) and proclaimed in all sincerity, "This is one of the most fascinating books I have ever read!" Expecting nods of agreement, I was shocked that instead the audience laughed heartily. Later I realized that I had probably seemed like a fool, touting the merits of reading the Chicago telephone book for pleasure, because the bulk of the book is composed of extensive word lists. The size of several metropolitan telephone directories bound together, this is an intimidating piece that requires concentrated effort to understand. Most of my listeners couldn't fathom my finding such reading intriguing.

Anyone giving the book a cursory examination will probably miss its importance because of its intermingling of complex language and interminable word lists. Borrowing this book numerous times from the Virginia State Library, I have spent countless hours examining the word lists for practical commonalities. The book was never destined to make a best-seller list; I was the only person to borrow it from the Virginia State Library. Unfortunately, this library has eliminated the book from its collection since then.

I must admit that my interest in this book is not so much in reading the text as in examining and studying the extensive word lists. These lists group syllables in words according to their pronunciations and accompanying spelling patterns that competent spellers learn tacitly. The ones that occur most frequently are the most significant for spelling-deficient students.

The weakest spellers will have great difficulty spelling words given them to copy. They will also produce disphonetic spellings, which show little logical letter correspondence to the word. Following are a few examples of misspellings my students have made:

- "ancer" for "anchor"
- "screse" for "series"
- "dumentry" for "documentary"
- "detion," "detean," and "dectenchon" for "detention"
- "alwrhashion" and "allterkaishon" for "altercation"
- "vowelor" for "valor"
- "gratuoertahs" for "gratuitous"

My files were filled with numerous other examples that any teacher of weak spellers will also encounter.

I call these spellers "Letter Sprinklers," because they put down any letter combinations for a word without considering any sound–letter correspondences. When asked to spell or copy the word again, they will often produce a totally different and equally illogical misspelling.

Such spelling-deficient students can improve their spelling skills significantly if they learn to apply to spelling syllables in words the sound strategies that Hanna et al.'s work describes. I first developed a list of basics from this work to teach strategies that I termed "logical spelling." Excellent spellers have learned these basics tacitly; poor spellers can make significant gains in learning to apply these principles to any word they attempt to spell.

A DIAGNOSTIC TEST

Before discussing the elements of "logical spelling" with my students, I give them a diagnostic test to determine what effective spelling strategies they already possess. I love announcing at the beginning of class that they are to take a spelling test. Most respond in shock with, "What test? You didn't tell us!"

I tease them back with the question, "Do you mean you didn't study for it?" Then I appease them by telling them that the test is a diagnostic tool, not one that they will be graded on for existing knowledge. After I write "diagnostic" on the board, we discuss the meaning of the word, usually relating it to what a doctor does when he or she examines an ailing patient. If time permits, I also write and discuss briefly the word's other forms—diagnose, diagnostician, diagnosis, etc.

Before the test, I tell the students that the words I am going to ask them to spell are multisyllable ones, most of which they don't know the meanings of, some of which even I don't know. I encourage them to make their best effort in spelling each word to reveal what spelling strategies they possess. I also tell them I will grade each student on this diagnostic test only on whether or not he or she checks his or her own paper correctly. Then I dictate the following ten words:

1. degradation
2. sanctimonious
3. endocrinology
4. spurious
5. irrefutable
6. indemnify

    7. contemporaneous   9. elaboration
    8. inexplicable   10. animosity

By this time, I expect all students to have a red pen or pencil for marking; anyone without one loses the right to grade test. I collect these students' test to grade myself, penalizing each student five points for failing to have a grading tool.

Then I show a transparency of these words, revealing one word at a time. I direct students to mark each word in red with an "X" or check mark beside—not through—each number so the mark is clearly visible. Students also need to write the correct spelling for any misspelled words.

Any student who follows these directions will earn 100 or A+ on the test. Poor spellers, however, will flounder in this task because they have never developed the ability to focus on letter patterns in a word to copy correctly.

In addition to placing a number and letter grade on each paper, I carefully analyze each test for misspelled words, placing an "x" over each misspelling in each syllable part that shows the student has not applied a logical spelling principle to that part of the syllable. For example, if a student spells "inexplickable" for "inexplicable," I mark an "X" over "ck" for being a bad guess. Likewise, for "incredulous" spelled "incredulus," I mark an "X" over the "us" as a bad guess. Poor spellers often make several mistakes in attempting to spell a dictated word. For example, one boy spelled "earyfuetabal" for "irrefutable." This misspelling resulted in four "X's"—one over "ea," the next over "y," the next over "ue," and the last over "al." The "X's" I mark go by logical spelling principles that I developed from my research of the book by Hanna et al. (1966), which I describe in detail below.

When returning the diagnostic spelling tests, I explain first that the grade at the top is based on accurate checking, but in the corner is a number indicating the number of mistakes in spelling strategies made on the test. I usually provide a chart of how many students made each number of errors. Table 3.1 is a chart I prepared for honors-level students, whose spelling abilities usually, but not always, range higher than students at lower levels. In some classes, I have had students who made more than thirty errors.

I then translate these numbers into the following ratings:

        0–2: Superior   3–4: Excellent
        5–9: Average   10 or more: Needs Help!

Table 3.1. Example of Number of Errors One Class Made on Diagnostic Test

#Errors	#Students
0	0
1	5
2	3
3	6
4	5
5	2
6	9
7	2
8	3
9	2
10	6
12	2
13	1
17	1
20	1

Next I direct students to write the following on the back of the test in complete sentences:

- A statement of agreement or disagreement with the error assessment.
- If the rating is in the medium to low range, a statement on whether or not they wish to improve their spelling abilities.
- If the rating is in the high range, a statement that gives the reason(s) for their excellent spelling abilities.

When students are finished, I re-collect the papers, which I then return with the post-test on the same words. Data on four years of these test papers appear later in this chapter.

LOGICAL SPELLING PRINCIPLES

I usually present the concepts I teach in my language arts classes in all ways of communication: reading, writing, speaking, and listening. The strategies, activities, and games for spelling improvement given in this book, however, are only a minor component of whole language approaches I try to implement in each daily lesson plan. When beginning a new concept not clearly explained in the students' textbook, I usually prepare and give out a handout to explain and discuss it, along with reading it in class. Likewise, in teaching students to use logic in spelling attempts, I first give them a handout titled "Logical Spelling Principles," at the beginning of which is the following paragraph:

> Weak spellers can improve their spelling ability dramatically by learning and applying the following spelling basics. These principles will teach a poor speller how to make an "educated guess" when spelling an unknown word because they describe what happens MOST OF THE TIME in spelling English syllables. Resulting guesses should be so close to correct spellings that a computer's spelling check system will probably be able to recognize and spell most spelling attempts correctly!

After reading this paragraph aloud, we discuss how making an educated guess is similar to a gambler making bets based on probabilities. We then discuss the following "basics":

- Spell EACH SYLLABLE (WORD PART) logically—count the syllables and guess a logical spelling for each one.
- Guess only ONE VOWEL for each syllable: Always guess one of the major vowels—a, e, i, o, or u.
  - √ Never guess the letter "y" for a vowel sound.
  - √ Never guess combination vowels such as -ea-, -eau-, -aigh-, etc.
  - √ If a vowel sound is long—pronounced as it sounds when saying the alphabet—guess that vowel. For example, when hearing a long "ō" sound as in the word "go," spell "o."
  - √ Guess a corresponding vowel for a short vowel sound. For example, if the vowel part sounds like the "a" in the words "bat" and "mat," guess "a." If it sounds like the "e" in the words "bet" and "let," guess "e." If it sounds like the "i" in the words "sit" and "it," guess "i." If it sounds like the "o" in the words "not" and "tot," guess "o." If it sounds like the "u" in the words "up" and "cup," guess "u."
  - √ If the vowel sound is a schwa sound (ə)—an "uh" sound—guessing any one of the five major vowels—a, e, i, o, or u—would be a good educated guess.

- Spell consonant sounds at the beginning or end of each syllable as they sound when pronounced in the alphabet. One EXCEPTION to this rule is a "K" sound: Guess the letter "C" instead of "K."
- Never guess double consonant letters for any consonant sound. For example, spell an "M" sound in the middle of a word with just ONE "M," not two.
- Guess the usual spelling for common suffixes—word-ending syllables:

For -shən, spell -tion   For -əl, spell -le

For a long -ē or -ī, spell -y   For -əs, spell -ous

For - əs, spell -ous   For -əl, spell -le

- If the last syllable in the word, called a suffix, has a long vowel pattern, add a silent -e. For example, -īt, -ēd, and āt suffixes would be spelled "-ite," "-ede," and "-ate." NOTE: Do NOT add a silent -e to MIDDLE SYLLABLES that contain a long vowel. Spell each word part according to its vowel and consonant sounds.
- NEVER spell a word part with a little word that sounds like that part. For example, spell "for" instead of "four," "ded" instead of "dead," "com" instead of "comb," etc.

Teaching would be easy if a teacher only had to present rules once for instant understanding and application. A great deal of further instruction and drill work will be necessary for students to assimilate this information into permanent memory. As I have stated previously, short mini-lessons will be most effective.

Most middle-school students are adept in counting the number of syllables in a word. Many will start clapping their hands to count each syllable, revealing their learning of this technique in elementary school. Providing some words for the class to analyze will be valuable. "Simultaneous," "snufflelufagous," and "electroluminescence" are good choices, but any list of multisyllable words will suffice.

I always like to relay to my students a writing that a student produced when serving detention, misspelling "detention" as "detion." Writing this word on the board and asking why it is misspelled will quickly bring the response that the misspelling fails to spell the word's middle syllable, leaving no chance to produce a correct spelling. The misspelled word "dumentry" for "documentary" contains the same error. Directing students to think of a logical spelling for each syllable in a word is a helpful strategy

In a quick review, I then illustrate possible syllable combinations by writing the following patterns on the blackboard and provide an explanation for each:

V —syllable that contains only a vowel or vowel combination

CV —syllable that contains a consonant or consonant blend before a vowel or vowel combination

VC —syllable that contains a consonant or consonant blend after a vowel or vowel combination

CVC —syllable that contains consonants or consonant blends before and after a vowel or vowel combination

After presenting these possibilities for syllables, I ask, What is always in an English word syllable, a consonant or a vowel? The answer "a vowel" is obvious. The student who spelled "screse" for "series" failed to provide a vowel for the first syllable, leaving little chance for a close spelling of the word.

In discussing why students should guess only one vowel in each syllable of a word, the concept of frequency cannot be overstressed. For each given part under the vowel section, asking why a speller should guess only one vowel instead of spelling "y" or multiple vowel combinations will bring the repeated response "because most English word syllables contain just one vowel." The student who misspelled "alter-cation" with "allterkaishon" gave a common "-ai-" vowel combination, but not one a student should guess if trying to spell an unknown word.

Spelling vowel sounds is the greatest source of spelling mistakes, because their spellings are so variable.

The Constancy of Consonants

On the other hand, the spelling of consonant sounds has little variation. The work by Hanna et al. (1966) work illustrates this concept, giving frequency of occurrence after listing all words containing a specific consonant, as shown in the following summaries:

Using Logic to Spell61

b—97 percent (733)

d—97.83 percent (756)

f—78.23 percent (768-9)

g—88 percent (778)

h—97.94 percent (782-3)

l—90 percent (853)

m—94.3 percent (878)

n—97 percent (915)

p—95.57 percent (938-9)

r—97.11 percent (982)

s—72.69 percent (1015)

t—96.60 percent (1068)

v—99.53 percent (1082)

w—92.33 percent (1086-7)

z—64.29 percent (1097)

Other Basics

One major variation is the spelling of a "K" sound. "C" spells this sound in English syllables 73.27 percent of the time (Hanna et al. 1966, 820), so a good guess for spelling a "K" sound would be "C." The sounds of "J" and "Q" also have similar variables, but I did not include them in the logical spelling guidelines for the sake of simplicity.

Learning the common spelling patterns of the four given suffixes will also positively affect spelling improvement. Many poor spellers are oblivious to these common patterns. Some students, for example, attempt to spell the suffix "-tion," with "-chon," "-shion," and "-shon," producing the misspellings "dectenchon," "alwrhashion," and "allterkaishon." Likewise, many weak spellers do not know the common suffix spellings "-ous," "-y," and "-le."

Learning that a suffix containing a long vowel usually ends in a silent "e" will also be valuable for students.

When thinking of spelling just one syllable, many students will spell the known spelling of a word that makes the same or similar sound instead of making a good guess about the vowel and consonant sounds in the syllable. The student who misspelled "valor" with the misspelling "vowelor" used this reasoning when making this spelling attempt.

HELPING STUDENTS ACQUIRE AND APPLY
LOGICAL SPELLING BASICS

Over the following weeks in my language arts classes, I emphasize these logical spelling principles in various ways, but only for short periods of time. A reader might think that I only emphasize spelling in my English classes, since this book is devoted to teaching this subject. Although I always include some spelling instruction throughout each week, I do far more in my classroom than teach spelling. I intermingle that teaching with many other facets an English teacher must emphasize to help students improve all their communication skills in reading, writing, speaking, and listening.

A Practice Test

One procedure I use is to have students prepare a sheet of notebook paper to be kept in their notebooks, titled, "Logical Spelling Practice." I then direct them to number their papers to 25, skipping lines, in a single column using both the front and back of the sheet. I then select twenty-five multisyllable words to dictate. Appendix C lists numerous words that I selected from the hundreds of words listed in *Phoneme-Grapheme Correspondences as Cues to Spelling Improvement* (Hanna et al. 1966, 1109–1155).

The dictation of these words extends over many days in mini-lessons. In the first few days, I cover only a few words because many concepts need to be reviewed for each dictated and checked word. As students progress, they are able to do more words in the same amount of time.

Before starting I instruct students that the object of this practice is to make a good educated guess when spelling each word, using the logical spelling principles given them. I first pronounce a word quickly, as it would be said in conversation. Then I pronounce it slowly, articulating each syllable distinctly.

Because many letters sound similar, students need to watch my lips as I pronounce each word to decipher what letter to spell. For example, the pronunciation of the letters "m" and "n" is similar in sound but dramatically different in lip movement. Likewise, pronouncing short vowel sounds can sometimes be hard to distinguish, but is easier when viewing a speaker's lips. Pronouncing "bat" to show a short "a," "bet" for an "e," "it" for "i," "hot" for "o," and "truly" for "u" will help to demonstrate slight differences in lip movements in producing these short vowel sounds.

Students then spell the word with pencil or blue or black ink and correct it with a red pen or pencil. I then reveal the correct spelling of the word on a transparency. As I review the word's spelling, I remind students what letters they should have used to make a good guess, thus reviewing the logical spelling basics—for example, "c" for "k." For a spelling that is a good guess, they make a check mark to the side of the number—not through the number—so the check mark is visible. Likewise, if they have made a bad guess, they mark an "X" beside the number. Hopefully they will understand the reason for the bad guess and be able to avoid making the same mistake in the future.

Good guesses based on the logical spelling basics will not necessarily produce the word's correct spelling. For example, each schwa sound in a syllable can have any of the five major vowels as a good guess. Likewise, short vowel sounds can have acceptable variations. For example, the "i" in the second syllable of "aspiration" might sound like an "a," "u," or "e." To denote these acceptable variations, I underline any letter spelling a schwa sound and list above any short vowel other acceptable vowels, as long as they are single ones in the syllable. I am usually very liberal in accepting other short vowels for a short vowel spelling, since their sounds are often so similar. If a student has guessed just one vowel for the short vowel sound, he or she will most likely be close enough to the word's spelling that a computer could make a correction.

If a student has not spelled the word correctly even though he or she has spelled it with a good guess, he or she then needs to write the correct spelling of the word when I reveal it.

When directing this activity, I assure students that it is risk-free and there will be no penalties for bad guesses. Students find this practice test "fun" when they find out that they are graded down only if they fail to correct their mistakes. This self-correction practice fosters learning.

The continued dictation/correction procedure will bring constant squeals of delight from students pleasantly surprised to find that they can spell complicated words by learning and applying these spelling basics. A teacher's chagrin over having large numbers of disphonetic spellers will change to enthusiasm and excitement when he or she sees results from instructing students with these methods

Games for Learning

Another effective strategy is to direct students in a game based on applying logical spelling basics. Leslie Landin's *100 Blackboard Games* (1956)

provides many ideas for teaching games. Of course, many other games and activities abound; I made copies of those I selected in my original research, which resulted in a thickly bound book.

My last long-term substitute position was for a group of special education learning disabled students, most of whom were disphonetic spellers. A few were avid basketball players, so I purchased a small realistic looking basketball and a wire circular wastebasket weighted with some rocks at the bottom, to use for the game. I then divided the group into two sides, who vied against each other for candy prizes. All students had to produce on notebook paper logical spelling attempts for each multisyllable word I dictated. I also constantly reminded them to produce a logical guess the same way we had been doing on the practice test. Using cards that each had the name of one of the students in the class on it, separated according to each side, I then drew the name of a student to go to the board to spell the word he or she had just written.

If the student produced a good guess for spelling the word, he or she would then be able to "shoot baskets" to earn points for his or her side. I placed lines of masking tape on the floor for two- and one-point shots, with each contender allowed to make two shots at the line of his or her choice. If the student produced an illogical spelling at the blackboard, we discussed the part(s) that made the spelling a bad guess. I then drew a card from the other side, and that student had a chance to correct the spelling and likewise shoot for points.

Once we had analyzed a word on the board together, each of the remaining students judged whether he or she had made a "good guess" for spelling the same word, marking it with a check or "x." If a student had made a bad guess, he or she needed to circle the part(s) that prevented the spelling attempt from being a "good guess." At the end of the game I collect all papers and give credit, again only for following directions.

Such a game is highly motivational and will foster a great deal of learning, especially since everyone will make spelling attempts that each student will assess for good guesses.

This game format is typical of those I use throughout the year to review materials I have taught. Playing tic-tac-toe at the blackboard, with one side taking "X's" and the other "O's" (Landin 1956, 12); "Putt-Putt," putting golf balls into a putting machine; and a form of *Jeopardy* are other formats I have used for learning reinforcement. I usually direct students to produce written responses during the game and allow them to use accompanying notes and handouts. However, each contender may not use his or her written work and notes.

Directing such games is a sneaky way to drill students and highly motivational for students to learn required concepts.

Student Assignment Sheets to Reinforce Logical Spelling Principles

Preparing student practice handouts is another way to reinforce logical spelling basics. See appendix D for two examples. The first assignment requires students to assess mistakes made on the logical spelling pretests. The second lists a variety of misspellings for words given on the diagnostic test that students are to assess for illogically spelled syllables. I have devised similar one-word activities using the words "declension," "detention," and "dictation," but other words would result in an almost interminable list. Again, any one of the words listed in appendix E could be used to design similar activities.

Placing these or similar activities on a transparency is a good closure activity for questioning students in the last few minutes of a period. Reviewing logical spelling principles throughout the entire school year will certainly help students retain this knowledge permanently.

Writing Answers in Complete Sentences to Questions on Logical Spelling Concepts

Another possibility for a homework assignment is to direct students to answer questions about logical spelling principles in complete sentences. Such an activity will not only reinforce logical spelling concepts, but also give students practice in answering questions in complete sentences that repeat information given in the question. See appendix E for an example.

Post-test

After several months of logical spelling practice in short time segments, students are ready for their post-test, which covers the same words given on the diagnostic test. Students self-correct their tests, but this time they mark good guesses as correct. They also give the correct spelling for each bad guess and good guess not spelled exactly right.

I staple each student's diagnostic test to the back of his or her post-test and then return both. Again, I ask students to compare both tests and write honest responses on whether or not the logical spelling procedures have helped them to improve in spelling. At this point I always stress the importance of being truthful in their written evaluations, which help me evaluate the validity of logical spelling instruction.

SCIENTIFIC DATA ON LOGICAL SPELLING TECHNIQUES

While I have given similar diagnostic and post-tests on logical spelling concepts for at least seven years, I have saved sets of tests from only four years—1997–1998, 1998–1999, 1999–2000, and 2002–2003—to develop scientific data on the effectiveness of teaching these logical spelling basics. I produced the first three years of saved tests when I was still a full-time teacher, and the last when I was a long-term substitute for an English teacher on maternity leave.

Evaluating Students' Responses

Reading written evaluations students produce after the post-tests is always interesting and variable. To determine the degree of positive or negative response, I used the following number system:

10: Very Effective   1: No Benefit
7: Helpful   0: No Comment
3: Somewhat Helpful

Refer to table 3.2, which summarizes the total responses of students for all four years.

These data reveal that students' comments were far more positive than negative. Out of the 269 students who wrote a response, a total of 187 students—87 + 33 + 29 + 38—found value in learning the logical spelling principles. In many cases, a student would just write a statement saying the principles were "very helpful," "somewhat beneficial," or "no help

Table 3.2. Summary of All Student Responses for Four School Years

Ratings	1997	1998	1999	2002	Totals
10 Very Effective	70	16	23	25	134
7 Helpful	7	8	4	5	24
3 Somewhat Helpful	10	9	2	8	29
1 No Benefit	12	22	11	2	47
No Comment	6	9	5	15	35
Totals	105	64	45	55	269

at all." On the other hand, some students wrote lengthy comments making various points about these spelling principles. I have selected a few typical comments, of which excerpts follow. First are those that are most positive, all rating "10" for "very effective":

- "Before . . . I was a very poor speller. Now I can spell long words logically." 1997–1998
- "I now listen to what words sound like and then make a good guess." 1997–1998
- "Learning tricks and different ways of figuring out words' spellings' was very helpful in learning new, BIG words. Thank you . . ." 1997–1998
- "[Now] my computer can tell me what I'm spelling." 1997–1998
- "I wish all teachers would use this system." 1997–1998
- "I can [now] spell words my parents can't." 1997–1998
- "It made me think clear when I go to spell a word." 1997–1998
- "Now I don't have to spend hours looking through a dictionary when I'm doing a report." 1997–1998
- "I have learned that sometimes the biggest words can be the easiest." 1997–1998
- "It helped me improve my spelling so much, it surprised me!" 1997–1998
- "These rules would work for anybody who learns to use them properly." 1997–1998
- "[H]elpful to me when I don't have a clue how to spell a word, I sound it out sylable by sylable." 1997–1998
- "[H]elped me spell many difficult words." 1997–1998

Chapter 3

- "I had never learned phonics [in the past] and when I learned them this time I can spell more words." 1997–1998
- "You should give these rules to students for years to come." 1997–1998
- "I can [now] spell big words which helps my self-esteem." 1997–1998
- "I had no idea I could improve so much over such a short time." 1997–1998
- "Now when I hear a word I really listen to specific things that I might have not caught at any time before that." 1997–1998
- "Even though I didn't study the sheet a lot you still taught us the rules in class." 1997–1998
- "[B]ut if you make a good guess then the computer is more likely to pick up the correct spelling." 1997–1998
- "I learned to spell words I couldn't even pronounce." 1997–1998
- "I use to spell words really bad but now I'm closer to the spelling of the word." 1997–1998
- "[H]elpful because sounding them out makes it easier to spell." 1997–1998
- "It has helped me to be clear on the most common mistakes . . ." 1999–1900
- "Now I'm an excellent speller after those strategies . . ." 1999–1900
- "[H]elpful because they made me think more." 1997–1998
- "Now I know which letters or prefixes or suffixes to use in a word." 2002–2003
- "It is helping me to spell better." 2002–2003
- "[W]as very effective and that many English teachers should use on poor spellers." 2002–2003

I have included many more responses from the school year 1997–1998 because I had more students then than in the following years. The reason for the lower teacher–student ratio starting in the 1998–1999 year was that Chesterfield County implemented blocks of one-and-a-half-hour classes for seventh-grade English classes in the middle schools instead of the previous forty-five-minute periods, to include computer instruction in the curriculum. Another reason for the abundance of excerpts from the 1997–1998 year is that I had then numerous highly gifted and talented writers who more aptly expressed their feelings about the value of teaching logical spelling principles.

In addition, I had some students in each of the other years who did not take either the diagnostic or post-test, so I eliminated those papers from the reported data.

Not all the responses were as positive as those listed above. Following are excerpts from selected negative evaluations:

- "I was already pretty good at spelling. The logical spelling strategiers are just one more thing I have to remember and worry about. They are just to confusing." 1997–1998
- "I try to understand [the rules] but there are a lot of rules. I misspelled a word because the rule was not on the page." 1997–1998
- "In fact, I think the logical spelling strategies misguide a person. There are many words that have double vowels, but the Logical spelling strategies say not to guess that. I don't like them . . . , and I don't think they help." 1997–1998
- "All I need is to learn how to spell those words." 1998–1999
- "I think my spelling is pretty good. I really don't think logical spelling helped me." 1998–1999
- "Logical Spelling hasn't helped me at all. It's a waste of my time and paper as well as ink." 1998–1999
- "My spelling ability is excellent. These strategies didn't help me." 1999–1900
- "To be honest, I don't think that this has helped me at all to spell better." 1999–1900

All of the students quoted above made few errors on the diagnostic spelling test, revealing that they already had "Superior" or "Excellent" spelling abilities. As emphasized previously, such students have learned these concepts tacitly and therefore find little value in trying to apply rules to things they already do automatically.

In reviewing the forty-seven evaluations that reported "no value" comments, a total of twenty-eight students made four or fewer errors on the diagnostic test, explaining again why they did not find value in learning information they already had.

Reviewing the total report shows that only 47 of the 234 students who wrote evaluations found the logical spelling principles of no benefit. Subtracting the 28 students who originally scored as "Superior" or "Excellent" spellers leaves only 19 of 234 responders who should have realized some benefit in learning these principles, since their scores on their diagnostic tests showed a need for improvement. Ten of these 19 scored in the "average" range, so maybe these students already tacitly knew many of the taught principles. The remaining nine made at least ten or more errors on the diagnostic test, revealing a definite need for help. Ironically, only one of these 19 negative responders showed no improvement on the post-test; she was frequently absent and probably missed a lot of instruction.

Diagnostic Test versus Post-test Results

Over four years, I saved students' diagnostic and post-tests to analyze and show the value of teaching logical spelling principles. I wanted to supply scientific data to support my excitement and enthusiasm about the value of teaching these strategies. Tables 3.3 and 3.4 reveal the results of all four years of students taking the diagnostic test and the follow-up post-test.

- The first column in both tables gives the number of errors made, labeled "No. of E/DT" on the diagnostic test and "No. of E/PT" for errors on the post-test.
- The columns labeled "No. of Pupils by Years" reveal the number of students who made the number of errors given in the first column. For example, 6 students in the 1999–2000 school year made 10 errors on their diagnostic tests.
- The columns labeled "No. of Errors by Years" show the total number of errors made as listed in column 1 for that year, multiplied by the number of students who made that number of errors in the selected year. For the example given above, the number 6—the number of students—would be multiplied by 10—the number of errors for each students—for a total of 60 errors these six students made.
- The subtotal columns give totals of numbers for each row.
- The final totals reveal that the 269 students made a total of 1,915 errors on their diagnostic tests and that the same 269 students made only 687 errors on their post-tests. In other words, they scored 1,228 fewer errors than they did on their diagnostic tests.

Table 3.3. Error Totals on Diagnostic Tests for Four School Years

#E/DT	# Students by Years				# Errors by Years				Subtotals	
	1997	1998	1999	2002	1997	1998	1999	2002	# Students	#E/DT
0	5	0	0	1	0	0	0	0	6	0
1	5	0	5	1	5	0	5	1	11	11
2	4	6	3	1	8	12	6	2	14	28
3	13	6	6	4	39	18	18	12	29	87
4	15	10	5	6	60	40	20	24	36	144
5	13	4	1	3	65	20	5	15	21	105
6	11	2	8	3	66	12	48	18	24	144
7	9	6	2	3	63	42	14	21	20	140
8	3	6	3	8	24	48	24	64	20	160
9	11	3	2	7	99	27	18	63	23	207
10	6	3	6	0	60	30	60	0	15	150
11	1	4	0	1	11	44	0	11	6	66
12	1	1	2	4	12	12	24	48	8	96
13	3	3	1	3	39	39	13	39	10	130
14	2	2	0	1	28	28	0	14	5	70
15	3	1	0	1	45	15	0	15	5	75
16	0	3	0	3	0	48	0	48	6	96
17	0	1	1	2	0	17	17	34	4	68
19	0	0	0	1	0	0	0	19	1	19
20	0	1	0	0	0	20	0	0	1	20
22	0	1	0	0	0	22	0	0	1	22
23	0	1	0	0	0	23	0	0	1	23
24	0	0	0	1	0	0	0	24	1	24
30	0	0	0	1	0	0	0	30	1	30
Totals	105	64	45	55	624	517	272	502	269	1915

Table 3.4. Error Totals on Post-Tests for Four School Years

#E/PT	# Students by Years				# Errors by Years				Subtotals	
	1997	1998	1999	2002	1997	1998	1999	2002	# Pupils	#E/PT
0	34	7	12	12	0	0	0	0	65	0
1	36	8	7	12	36	8	7	12	63	63
2	11	9	10	6	22	18	20	12	36	72
3	14	6	5	7	42	18	15	21	32	96
4	5	10	2	7	20	40	8	28	24	96
5	3	6	4	3	15	30	20	15	16	80
6	2	5	1	3	12	30	6	18	11	66
7		3	2	4	0	21	14	28	9	63
8		1	1		0	8	8	0	2	16
9		2	1		0	18	9	0	3	27
10		1			0	10	0	0	1	10
11		1		1	0	11	0	11	2	22
13		2			0	26	0	0	2	26
14		1			0	14	0	0	1	14
17		1			0	17	0	0	1	17
19		1			0	19	0	0	1	19
Totals	105	64	45	55	147	288	107	145	269	687

Table 3.5.   **Thirteen Students Made More Errors on Post Test**

#	Year	Gender	#E/DT	#E/PT	Comment
1	1997	Girl	4	6	7
2	1997	Girl	3	4	7
3	1997	Boy	1	3	10
4	1997	Girl	3	5	1
5	1998	Boy	4	13	1
6	1998	Boy	2	6	10
7	1998	Girl	4	7	0
8	1998	Girl	2	5	7
9	1998	Boy	16	17	0
10	1998	Girl	2	5	1
11	1998	Girl	4	6	1
12	1999	Girl	6	7	3
13	2002	Girl	6	7	7

Analyzing these charts should make the reader realize that students made significant improvement in spelling after learning some basic logical spelling principles.

A Few Did Worse

Of the 269 students participating, only 13 made more errors on their post-tests than on their diagnostic tests. Table 3.5 that reveals these results. It lists each of these students along with their scores on the diagnostic and post-tests. Also given are these students' ratings: 10 = very effective; 7 = helpful, 3 = somewhat helpful; 1 = no benefit; 0 = no response.

Of these numbers, the scores of the boy who made 13 errors on his post-test versus 4 errors on the diagnostic test were the most disappointing. His written evaluation is as follows: "My ability to spell is fair, I do need some work and I think that my grades reflect that. These lodgical spelling tips have confused me somewhat. I think I would of done better if I did not think about the rules."

SIGNIFICANCE OF THE DATA

Readers should agree that my experiment in developing and teaching logical spelling principles proved highly successful. I think these results should encourage teachers to use these principles in teaching spelling, especially those who teach in the lower grades. If elementary teachers start young learners listening to the pronunciation of monosyllabic words and making good guesses about their spellings, they can help all of their students acquire the spelling knowledge that excellent spellers "naturally catch as they do singing" (Peters 1985, 24).

For example, a first-grade teacher might explain that a silent "-e" occurs when a word has a long vowel sound. This concept seems to be a natural one, since students are usually adept by this point at reciting the letters of the alphabet. The teacher might then dictate the following words for students to try to make "good guesses" in spelling:

1. date
2. doze
3. fine
4. hate
5. late
6. life
7. more
8. nose
9. pole
10. rate

Such a lesson would set a base for learning to spell a suffix with a long vowel with a silent "-e."

Likewise, teachers could devise other lessons that require students to make "good guesses." The word lists by Hanna et al. (1966) are valuable resources for these. The spelling of two-syllable words would then be a natural progression. Students will probably express the same delight in spelling these words correctly as did my students, especially if teachers direct them in "no-risk" activities.

OTHER PATTERN POSSIBILITIES

When applying the findings of these spelling researchers, which I have presented as logical spelling basics in this chapter, I selected those I felt would be of most value. Teaching other common patterns like the following would also be helpful:

- Spelling the suffixes –ence, –ance, -ive, -ion, -ism, -cial, -ian,
- -ture, -or, -er, and -ture
- Spell a long "e" or schwa sound before a suffix with an "i"
- Spell a "j" sound with a "g"
- Spell a "kw" sound with "qu"

McAlexander, Dobie, and Gregg (1992, 54–56) provide guidelines for other patterns:

-able versus -ible	-ff or -gh
-ary versus -ery	im- versus in- prefix
-cede or -ceed	-ize versus -ise
-ch or -tch	-dge versus -ge
-efy versus -ify	-ck versus -c

Meyers (1998) also supplies rules for learning when to spell the following patterns:

-ai- versus -ia- (2)	-ant/-ance/-ancy versus-ent/-ence/-ency (129)
letters c and g (103)	-ary versus -ery (129)
-able versus –ible (127)	-al versus -el (130)

Again, the lists provided by Hanna et al. (1966) are excellent resources for creating corresponding lists of words for practice. Jo Phenix's books also offer extensive lists of words following spelling patterns as well as methods for teaching spelling (2001, 2003). Of all the recently published books I have examined, Phenix's works are the most practical and informative on the teaching of spelling; most English teachers and/or language arts departments would find them worth purchasing.

COMPATIBILITY WITH INVENTED SPELLINGS

The current thinking of many researchers on teaching spelling to beginning writers is to encourage them to invent spellings as they compose.

"By first grade, if not sooner, almost all children can write with invented spelling" (Wilde 2004, 1). Demanding correct spelling will stymie a child's writing and result in a loss of voice (Laminack and Wood 1996, 8). In addition, "young children using invented spelling employ a considerably greater variety of words in their writing than those encouraged to use only the words they can spell correctly" (Weaver 1996, 5). In Laminack and Wood's book, one teacher notes that when she "valued the children's approximations in spelling, it freed them to take risks and to use more precise interesting words" (1996, 23).

I agree that spelling should not stymie writing, but teaching logical spelling strategies helps students to make closer approximations to correct spellings. Sandra Wilde, a noted authority on the teaching of spelling, points out that "invented spelling is a starting point not a stopping point" (1996, 7). Instructing young children how to make logical guesses will help them make closer approximations. Students who learn to apply these strategies in appropriate mini-lessons will undoubtedly produce improved spellings. Otherwise, students who have not discovered on their own letter–sound patterns will struggle to spell many words and will most likely rely on sprinkling a variety of letter combinations for each spelling.

A FUTURE GOAL

I hope the logical spelling strategies I have described in this chapter will inspire other teachers to create many other effective lessons to teach students how to use their brains when spelling an unknown word. Once students understand and apply logical spelling principles, they will become "functional spellers" who can correct most of their misspellings with a computer's "spell-check" system.

4

Focusing on Letter Patterns

Sounding out the syllables in a word to make a logical spelling guess is an effective strategy when spelling an unknown word. This method, however, will not always result in a correctly spelled word. Many authorities stress the importance of teaching visualization strategies to help writers learn correct spellings (Fisher and Studier 1977, 8, 10).

When I was just beginning my research on spelling, I struggled with understanding why some authorities recommend visualization strategies while others stress auditory strategies for spelling improvement. The two approaches seemed to be contradictory, but I soon realized they were compatible: Auditory strategies help spellers guess spellings of unknown words, and visualization strategies help students learn the correct spellings of words.

VISUALIZATION STRATEGIES GOOD SPELLERS USE TACITLY

Children "need to develop more of a sense of how words look when written. 'Does it look right?' should be heard as often in the classroom as 'Sound it out!'" (Fisher and Studier 1977, 10). In 1986, Sears and Johnson showed the superiority of visual imagery over auditory methods. Their results support Radaker's research, completed in 1963, which stressed visualizing the image of the word displayed on a large outdoor screen, picturing each letter of the word being pasted onto the screen, "nailing each letter in place with fantasy nails" (Sears and Johnson 1986, 231). Evidently, "a mental picture is also worth a thousand pronunciations" (1986, 233).

Self-taught Learners

When they were little, good spellers were especially fascinated with the world of words around them. While any trip presented a multitude of sensory delights, words would often capture much of their interest. Often they would LOOK at a word closely, inspecting each letter. Most likely, an accompanying parent would pronounce the word as they stared at it, and perhaps the child would parrot its pronunciation.

As these word observers grew in language development, they, like most children, learned to read. However, they were not necessarily fast readers, because the various letter combinations in words they saw every day continued to captivate them. Many of these spellers delighted in reading nursery rhymes and other rhymed poetry that drew their attention to how the same sounds in words often have different spellings.

In other words, good spellers used visualization strategies when looking with fascination at various letter combinations in words. They became competent spellers by discovering on their own numerous principles about English spellings. Most superior spellers would be at a loss to explain how they have acquired such spelling skills. A typical response, like Dr. Chandler's in chapter 1, would be, "I don't know. I've just always been a good speller." What most competent spellers do not realize is they have taught themselves how to spell!

A memorable event for me was standing in line at the Virginia Department of Motor Vehicles, memorable first because my fifteen-year-old son was obtaining his learner's driving permit. It was also an unforgettable moment because I suddenly started focusing on unusual letter patterns in words on various signs around us.

I had become familiar with variant spelling patterns by studying word lists developed by a variety of authors. Cootes and Jamieson's book *Spotlight on Spelling* (1985) lists more than 4,250 words according to letter string patterns. Another excellent source is Lillian Devault's *Word Lists for the American English Language* (1973). In preparing a reference text for the Montessori language program, Devault lists numerous example words containing common letter string combinations for each major phonological sound pattern in English.

The best reference text for developing word lists is *Phoneme-Grapheme Correspondences as Cues to Spelling Improvement* by Hanna, Hodges, Hanna, and Rudorf (1966), which has lists developed from 17,320 words arranged according to letter string and pronunciation patterns.

When I observed words on signs at the DMV, I started to do more than just read and understand their meanings; instead, I began focusing on the unusual spelling parts in each, letter combinations that seemed to jump out once I started looking for them. The "-ea-" in "Learner's," "-ia-" in "Virginia," and "-oi-" in "Points" are only a few examples. Practically every sign I viewed contained a number of words with variant spelling patterns.

I continued to observe letter combinations in words after we left the DMV. Even today, I still find myself analyzing letter patterns in words I see during my daily activities. Street signs, store names, department store notices, gas station instructions, and TV commercials are only a few of an almost limitless list of things that contain words in the world around us. Of course, I don't stop to analyze words in a book I am reading unless I encounter a word I don't know. Then I usually stop to try to decipher its meaning from the context as well as noting any unusual patterns in its spelling.

Once I started noting unusual spelling patterns in the words I saw every day, I couldn't fathom how Radaker's visualization strategy could be effective. Instead of imagining the spelling of a word "letter by letter," visualizing a word's spelling by picturing it syllable by syllable, with emphasis on noticing any deviant spellings in each syllable, seemed a better strategy.

Analyzing the spelling of words made me understand how young spellers teach themselves to spell: They learn by closely focusing on letter patterns in words. I hypothesized that if I could get poor spellers to start looking "with interest" at unusual spellings in words, they could make great strides in spelling skills.

Most poor spellers, however, have developed few, if any, visualization strategies. Until they can start analyzing the letter patterns in the words they see, they can make few gains in spelling. In other words, they need to learn HOW to look at a word and note closely WHAT letter combinations the word contains.

A REVIEW OF SYLLABLE PARTS

To help weak spellers learn how to look at words, I gave them the following information in a handout to discuss and use for future practice:
   Most middle-school students understand the meaning of syllables in
words. Likewise, most are familiar with the terms *vowels* and *consonants*
and can give an adequate definition for each. Their tacit knowledge of
language will guide them in correctly analyzing a syllable part when

---

How to Observe and Analyze a Word's Spelling

- Understand the word's meaning and know how to pronounce it.
- Divide the word into its correct syllables. Remember that syllables
  may be one of any of the following patterns: CVC, CV, VC, and
  V—(C-consonant or consonant blend; V-vowel or vowel combination). The syllables in the following three words provide examples
  of these three patterns:

  Chesterfield: Ches ter field (CVC CVC CVC)
  ceremony: cer e mon y (CVC V CVC V)
  curiosity: cur i os i ty (CVC V VC V CV

- All syllables will have at least one vowel or vowel combination:

  (Ch*Es* t*Er* f*IE*ld, c*Er* *E* m*O*n *Y*, c*Ur* *I* *Os* *I* t*Y*)

- Some syllables may be composed of just one vowel:

  (Ches ter field, cer *E* mon y, cur *I* os *I* ty)

- A consonant or consonant blend can occur at the beginning of a
  syllable:

  (*CH*es *T*er *F*ield, *C*er e *M*on y, *C*ur i os i *T*y)

- A consonant or consonant blend can occur at the end of a syllable:

  (Che^S te*R* fie*LD*, ce*R* e mo*N* y, cu*R* i o*S* i ty)

- A consonant or consonant blend can occur at BOTH the BEGIN-
  NING and END of a syllable:

  (*CH*e*S* *T*e*R* *F*ie*LD*, *C*e*R* e *M*o*N* y, *C*u*R* i os *I* ty)

- LOOK at each syllable part for "oddball" spellings—letters or letter patterns that do not follow logical spelling principles:

   (Ches ter fIEld, cer e mon y, cur i os it ty)

- FOCUS on "oddball" parts for memory. Connect the word to other words with the same "oddball" part, a word the speller knows how to spell.

pronouncing it, that is, whether or not the syllable contains beginning and/ or ending consonants as well as the sound of its vowel part.

EXAMPLE LIST OF WORDS WITH DEVIANT LETTER PARTS

Once they have learned and applied the logical spelling principles presented in the last chapter, most students, especially excellent spellers, will be able to identify any illogically spelled consonant or vowel part. Students who have difficulty identifying deviant spellings in words will most likely be poor spellers, who can benefit greatly by learning to use their eyes to note these unusual spellings in words that I term "oddball parts."

As an introduction to the meaning of "oddball spellings," I provide on the back of the same handout a list of examples, shown in table 4.1.

Planet Spellingmess Creatures Reinforce Oddball Pattern Concepts

Each year, the spelling creatures from Planet Spellingmess helped to introduce and reinforce the concept of "oddball" parts in words. Queen Spell, whose headdress contained numerous examples of "oddball spellings," helped to reinforce the concept of deviant spelling patterns. On many days after the initial introduction, I picked at least one word for students to analyze its syllables for logical and "oddball" parts. Sometimes the word was from their reading; other times I asked them to pick a multisyllable word to analyze for the class. Sometimes I developed a word list of multisyllable words to use for a game or quiz.

Table 4.1.   Example of Deviant Syllable Parts

Beginning Consonant Combinations	Vowel Combinations	Ending Consonant Combinations
ch- (chrome)	-ae- (algae)	-bt (debt)
gh- (ghost)	-ai- (rain)	-ck (lock)
gn- (gnat)	-aigh- (straight)	-ct (subtract)
kn- (knit)	-au- (haunt)	-dge (fudge)
ph- (phone)	-augh- (haughty)	-ft (soft)
ps- (psalm)	-aw- (lawn)	-gh (laugh)
rh- (rhubarb)	-ay- (payable)	-gn (sign)
sc- (scent)	-ea- (break)	-gue (tongue)
sw- (sword)	-eau- (beautiful)	-ld (would)
wr- (wrap)	-ei- (ceiling)	-lf (calf)
	-eigh- (freight)	-lm (calm)
	-eo- (leopard)	-mb (comb)
	-eu- (sleuth)	-mn (column)
	-ew- (newness)	-ph (graph)
	-ia- (parliament)	-que (unique)
	-ie- (friend)	-st (wrestler)
	-ieu- (lieutenant	-tch (ditch)
	-igh- (highness)	-tz (waltz)
	-oe- (amoeba)-	
	-oi- (boil)	
	-ou- (found)	
	-ough-(bought)	
	-ow- (low)	
	-oy- (employer)	
	-ue- (blue)	
	-ui- (suit)	
	-ye- (rye)	

At all times, I emphasized that the students needed to start looking closely at the words they saw around them each day, analyzing the ones they focused on for logical and "oddball" parts. Once poor spellers develop this ability, they will be well on the way to spelling improvement, because they will be teaching themselves to spell words in the same way that excellent spellers teach themselves.

VARIANCE OF SPELLING AND PRONUNCIATION IN VOWEL SOUNDS

As stated in chapter 3, the spelling of consonants is very consistent in English words, whereas the spelling of vowel sounds is highly variable.

Single and multiple vowel combinations that have the same illogical letter combinations can have different pronunciations. In turn, single and multiple vowels can have the same pronunciations but different spellings. The following poem by Evelyn Baring, 1st Earl of Cromer (1902), illustrates these spelling differences. In addition, students will enjoy the challenge of reading it aloud without any mispronunciations:

> Our Queer Language
> When the English tongue we speak
> Why is **break** not rhymed with **freak**?
> Will you tell me why it's true
> We say **sew** but likewise **few**?
> And the maker of a verse
> Cannot cap his **horse** with **worse**.
> **Beard** sounds not the same as **heard**;
> **Cord** is different from **word**.
> Cow is **cow** but low is **low**,
> **Shoe** is never rhymed with **foe**.
> Think of **hose** and **dose** and **lose**,
> And think of **goose** and not of **choose**.
> Think of **comb** and **tomb** and **bomb**,
> **Doll** and **roll, home** and **some**.
> And since **pay** is rhymed with **say**,
> Why not **paid** with **said**, I pray?
> We have **blood** and **food** and **good**;
> **Mould** is not pronounced like **could**.
> Wherefore **done** but **gone** and **lone**?
> Is there any reason known?
> And, in short, it seems to me
> Sounds and letters disagree.

Most spelling texts, including the one I was originally required to use, present words that have various spellings for the same sound. Using such a philosophy, the words "bead," "deed," and "suite" from the poem above would be included in a lesson on spelling long "e" words. Such a list will be a nemesis for the weak speller, who most likely would have great difficulty using it, because he or she would have no way to make brain connections to the spelling of words that have such different letter combinations.

The *spreading activation models* described in chapter 1 illustrates how the human brain stores information that connects together. Words with such deviant letter patterns as "-ea-," "-ee-," and "-ui-" have absolutely no commonalities for the brain to group together, even though these letters all sound the same. Spelling requires giving correct letter combinations for syllable sounds, and these sounds often have many different spellings.

Try to imagine tiny little rooms in a brain, each of which contains information that connects to the others. One section might be related to deviant spelling patterns, with each room containing words spelling a pattern such as "-ough-," "-ai-," "ph-," or "-ea-." A spelling list of words containing the same letter pattern, therefore, would be far superior to one based on a common sound. The following is a list of words that all contain the letters "-ough-":

1. although	5. dough	9. ought	13. thorough
2. bought	6. drought	10. rough	14. thought
3. brought	7. enough	11. sought	15. through
4. cough	8. fought	12. though	16. tough

A poor speller has a chance to spell all of these words correctly as long as he or she can remember the "-ough-" letter combination. Notice that "-ough-" does not spell all the vowel sounds in these words. Three of them—cough, rough, and tough—have an "-ou-" vowel spelling and "-gh" for a final consonant "-f" sound. Even so, a student will be able to connect the spellings of these words because they contain the same "-ough-" letter pattern, even though these letters represent both vowel and ending consonants sounds. The "look" of all these words is the same.

LEARNING AND APPLYING COMMON LETTER PATTERNS

Of the students who master logical spelling strategies, many are unaware of acceptable letter sequence patterns in English. For example, writing "wot" for "what" is a logical choice, whereas "waht" is not (Peters 1985, 86). Weak spellers who lack knowledge of common variant letter string patterns need to emulate the strategies of competent spellers, who associate letter strings in unknown words with known words containing the same letter strings (Peters 1985, 44). For example, a speller coming across the word "haughty" might associate its spelling with known words such as "daughter" and "laughter." Good spellers mentally store the spelling of words according to the same letter strings irrespective of sound, as exemplified in the discussion above of "-ough-" words.

In order to learn the spelling of a word that contains deviant patterns, a student must know the spelling of at least a few words that contain the same pattern. Such a brain-processing connection is necessary for learning the spelling of the word. If a speller cannot generate other words with the same pattern, he or she will find learning the spelling of the word difficult if not impossible.

Weak spellers, therefore, should study lists of words organized around the same letter patterns until they learn a base of frequently used words for every letter string pattern that commonly occurs in English. Such an associative learning technique will help weak spellers to remember any deviant letter patterns in a particular word.

TEACHING STUDENTS WITH SPECIAL NEEDS

Educators will find the book *Spotlight on Spelling* a valuable reference tool for individualized teaching of weak spellers. Claire Cootes and Juliet Jamieson wrote this book as a result of a "highly structured intensive" remedial spelling program they developed and used with "excellent results" (1985, 3) for five years in Great Britain. Although placing an inordinate emphasis on teaching explicit phonological knowledge, the book is valuable for its diagnostic test, arranged according to sequential development spelling acquisition patterns. Its greatest value, however, is its reference list of more than 4,250 words, organized according to letter strings for each phonological pattern. Such lists have been helpful to me in developing word lists containing common letter strings. For example, a teacher would probably decide that the student who spells "what" as "waht" needs practice spelling "wh-" words, selecting the following:

whale, what, wheat, wheel, wheeze, when, where, whether, which, while, whine, whinny, whip, whirl, whisk, whisker, whiskey, whisper, whistle, white, why

Once the student masters the "wh-," the teacher might decide he or she needs an exercise that mixes "wh-" words with words starting with a single "w." The following list would then be applicable:

want, was, wax, way, we, went, west, wide, win, wine, wise, won, word

Cootes and Jamieson offer numerous practical suggestions for ways students might study their own individualized word lists:

- Use a particular set of words in their own sentences.
- Write a nonsense story that uses all of the selected words.
- Solve crossword puzzles that use many of the selected words.
- Study a word list, then cover the list, and then try to write as many of the words as possible.
- Dictate the words into a tape recorder to produce a self-directed playback test.

Unfortunately, the cost involved in implementing individualized spelling programs is prohibitive for most public school systems: Most could not support the additional staff, rooms, and needed equipment.

In addition, students concentrating on just one spelling pattern at a time, though a logical approach, seems as slow as chipping small chunks from a stone mountain to tear it down. Perhaps such an approach would be useful for special education, especially educable mentally retarded (EMR), students in small, self-contained classes. Setting up individualized spelling programs is more practicable in classes where the teacher–pupil ratio is low than for the typical language class, which usually has more than 120 pupils. I am not a special education teacher and have little experience with students in a self-contained classroom other than as a substitute teacher, so I do not know for sure that individualized spelling programs would be the best way to teach students with such special needs.

Many of my weak spellers have made great strides in spelling improvement by learning and applying the methods good spellers have used to teach themselves. These learners naturally "caught" spelling abilities by having "the internal structure of words . . . pointed out to them, not only in books, but in the world of words surrounding them, their names, the names of foods and sweets, road signs, street names" (Peters 1985, 24).

These children did not acquire their linguistic abilities by proceeding one pattern at a time, but rather by looking "'with interest' at various syllable parts in words" (Peters 1985, 25).

In other words, poor spellers who learn to start observing deviant patterns in words they see daily do not look for just one pattern at a time. Once students understand logical spelling principles, they can note these different letter patterns in the words they observe. In viewing words "with interest," their brains naturally organize these spelling patterns into related groups.

I remember vividly the praise I received from the mother of one of my students. This student had an IEP—Individual Education Program—to address his special education needs. She remarked, "His spelling has improved so much that I don't think spelling is now one of his disabilities!" I have also worked with many other weak spellers, many labeled learning disabled (LD), who have improved tremendously in spelling.

I especially remember one girl, another special education LD student I had in the 1991–1992 school year. Of all of the students I have taught, I will always recall her as probably the most disphonetic speller I have ever instructed. Following is a list of her attempted misspellings on practice pretests given in November 1991, which illustrates her spelling difficulties:

"declmas" for "decimal,"
"seniecentic" for "scientific,"
"comlon" for "column"
"prilpel" for "principle"
"howlo" for "hole"

In 1991–1992, I was just beginning as a teacher-researcher in continuing my study on the teaching of spelling. What I did then for my students was minimal and hardly effective compared to lessons I designed in later years. In fact, I now shudder when viewing the entire list of words I gave all my students that week, from which this student's misspellings came. I composed a list of multisyllable words similar to the ones I dictated to students to teach logical spelling principles, but grouped around the spelling patterns in my "Spelling Nauncence" game (see chapter 5). Maybe such a list would have been more workable in a class of highly gifted students. I gave these words to my X-level kids. What a dumb, disastrous mistake!

My students had no way to make the necessary brain connections to learn these spellings; most could not make connections to even simple words because they had not stored in their brains memory banks of words with the same letter patterns.

One of the most important concepts I have discovered in my many years as a teacher-researcher is that any list of words a teacher provides for spelling must be those in their students' working vocabulary, words they commonly use in writing, reading, speaking, and listening.

Even though I did not have as many strategies then to help my most disphonetic speller, she was always attentive to any spelling instruction. Frequently, she would stay after school for additional help, which I was always delighted to give her. At the end of the year, she wrote the following remarks in the "Memories of English" assignment that I always directed my students to write on the last day of school:

> Thank you for helping my spelling. You're the frist teacher you really cared. My very greatful.

Although her written evaluation still contains many grammatical errors and misspellings, it reveals her improvement in spelling. Best of all, her eighth-grade teacher reported to me the next year that she didn't feel this student had any major spelling problems.

The successes I have had in helping LD and EMR students improve in spelling lead me to believe that the spelling strategies I have developed would also be effective in self-contained classes for special education students.

WORD LISTS ORGANIZED BY
SOUND-LETTER CORRESPONDENCES

When starting my research, I started developing source lists of words containing "oddball" patterns. Originally, I used these lists in creating the game "Spelling Nauncence." Starting first with Cootes, Jamieson, and Devault's lists, I continued to refine them with lists in *Phoneme-Grapheme Correspondences as Cues to Spelling Improvement*.

Most authors organize word lists by sound-letter correspondences, a phonics approach important in teaching reading. For example, the Houghton Mifflin program often presents spelling lists according to sound-letter correspondences, as the following list from Level 3 of long vowels illustrates (Templeton 1998, 32):

lay	feel	neighbor	speak	clay
seem	leave	paint	green	eight
paid	play	weight	need	

The reader should note the variety of spelling patterns in these long vowel words: "-ay," "-ee-" "-ai-", "-ea-", and "-eigh-."

Pinnell (2003, 108) provides the following "Spelling Sort: The k Sound with Different Vowel Patterns":

kick	clock	smoke	soak	speak	folk
back	neck	bike	cheek	book	hawk
luck	cake	strike	cook	talk	

These words have many spelling patterns for spelling the "k sound": "-ck," "-ke," "-k," and "-lk," Understanding how to read these "k sound" words is an important reading concept but has little value for helping students to spell the "k" parts in words.

Although most writers will group spelling word lists by spelling patterns, they still list these patterns according to sounds. For example, Bolton lists the following words that follow a long e sound:

leave	believe	money	machine	key
meat	every	people	quay	ski

She then states, "The words may then be regrouped according to spelling patterns" (1993, 29). In the list above, however, only two words—leave and meat—share the same pattern and, therefore, such a word sort would have little transfer to a spelling activity.

WORD BANK OF DEVIANT LETTER PATTERNS

At first, I was tempted to organize my lists of deviant spelling patterns according to their pronunciations, because all other authors used this form of organization. As illustrated above, a phonic approach is essential in the teaching of reading but not for teaching spelling.

I finally decided to abandon a similar listing because the human brain focuses on the arrangement of letters in a word to learn spellings, not on the sounds of these letter combinations. Of course, the only words of value to a student will be those in his or her working vocabulary—words he or she can read, write, use in speaking, and understand when listening to a speaker.

Teachers should find this extensive list of example words containing deviant syllable parts a valuable resource, but should also realize it is by no means comprehensive (see appendix F). Chapter 5 offers suggestions for using this word bank to help students improve in spelling.

DOUBLE VISION

While consonants occur singly the majority of time in words, they can occur in doubles in a number of words. Spellers need to focus on double consonants in words to remember their spellings. *Phoneme Grapheme Correspondences to Spelling Improvement* by Hanna (1966) lists these frequencies of occurrence:

b spelled bb—occurs 2.7 percent (733)

d spelled dd—occurs 1.99 percent (756)

f spelled ff—occurs 8.8 percent (768)

g spelled gg—occurs 4.99 percent (778)

k spelled cc—occurs 1.61 percent (820)

l spelled ll—occurs 9.07 percent (853)

m spelled mm—occurs 3.99 percent (878)

n spelled nn—occurs 1.65 percent (915)

p spelled pp—occurs 4.42 percent (939)

r spelled rr—occurs 2.20 percent (982)

s spelled ss—occurs 6.98 percent (1015)

t spelled tt—occurs 2.77 percent (1068)

See appendix G for a word bank of words containing double consonants.

WARNINGS

A number of these listed words containing deviant patterns will not be in many students' working vocabulary. A student must be able to read a word, pronouncing it correctly, and thoroughly understand its meaning, to make it an effective illustration. The word should also be one that a student would use and/or understand in reading, writing, speaking, and listening activities.

Most of this list, however, contains many words that the majority of students can pronounce correctly and know their meanings. I decided to include the more difficult words for future reference. For example, few middle-schoolers will know the following words in the "sc-" pattern words:

adolescent, ascertain, convalescent, descent, irascible, incandescent, reminiscent, resuscitate

At the same time, most will probably recognize the following:

discipline, fascinate, muscle, scene, scent, science

Noticing "with interest" the unusual "sc-" pattern in each of these known words will help a speller build a memory base of words containing "sc-" in his or her brain. When encountering an unknown word containing this same "sc-" pattern, this memory base will help the speller learn the new word's spelling, along with adding the pronunciation and meaning to working memory.

In addition, students need to note double letter patterns in words to memorize their spellings. On the other hand, when guessing the spelling of an unknown word, they need to spell the consonant sound with only one letter, since the vast majority of words have only one consonant.

In turn, teachers can use the word bank to select appropriate examples of words that do not follow logical spelling principles. By carefully observing various deviant spelling patterns in words, students will improve their spelling of these words, as long as teachers direct such activities in enjoyable ways.

Achieving, motivated students are proof of successful teaching. Risk-free practice and games in spelling will encourage students to start teaching themselves to spell by closely looking at the words they see each day. Practically any experience presents a myriad number of words. For example, a trip to the mall, a favorite pastime for teens and preteens, provides thousands of words to view. If weak spellers pick a few of these words to LOOK at carefully, analyzing each word's letter patterns, they will be doing far more toward spelling improvement than they would by performing deadly drills and studying for impossible tests on lists of unrelated words.

5

Eye Openers

Readers should now understand that poor spellers need to look closely at words they see daily to grow in spelling ability. Weak spellers need to learn *how* to observe these words, and teachers need to teach them this skill through enjoyable, risk-free activities. Most readers will probably be asking, "Well, how do I do that?" The ideas in this chapter should be a helpful starting point.

My fascination with the word lists I found inspired me to create my creatures from Planet Spellingmess, spelling their names with as many "oddball spellings" as possible. These word lists also led me to create an original game that emphasized phonetics as well as oddball and logical spellings.

SPELLING NAUNCENCE GAME

Originally, I named this game "Spelling Naughnsceagnce," but I decided to change it to a more decipherable spelling of "Nauncence." My advising professor, Dr. Bill Smith, couldn't even begin to pronounce "Naughnsceagnce," and probably no one else could make a reasonable attempt unless they had also immersed themselves in studying various lists of deviant spelling patterns, as I had been doing.

Using as a guide the common spelling variations Devault lists for key sounds (1973), I developed this game as a way to purposely consolidate initial, medial, and final letter string patterns that have little or no phoneme-grapheme correspondence. Note that *phoneme* refers to the sound a letter or letter string makes, whereas *grapheme* refers to the position of the letter pattern in a syllable. "Ph-" and "gh-" commonly represent the phoneme sound of "f." The "ph" pattern can occur in both beginning and ending positions, as the words "phonics" and "graph" demonstrate, but "gh" occurs only in a syllable ending.

George Bernard Shaw once gave the spelling "ghoti" as a phonetic spelling of "fish" to demonstrate how illogical many English spellings are. As he explained, the pronunciation of "gh" is an "f" sound as in the word "rough," "o" is pronounced as in "women," and "ti" is pronounced as in "nation" (Furness 1977, 80). Shaw, however, ignored rules of English phoneme-grapheme correspondences in his intentional misspelling, because "gh" only occurs at the end of a syllable, and "ti" only at the beginning.

First, I made a "Spelling Nauncence Key," which listed seventy possibilities. Refer to table 5.1, the first five sets of syllable parts, to understand how I structured this key.

The "Spelling Nauncence Key" I created was very similar to table 4.1, "Examples of Deviant Syllable Parts."

For each of these seventy patterns, I constructed a context sentence for the example word that used the word's phonetic spelling instead. An example follows:

2. **–f** as in **k ŏ f** : If your **k ŏ f** doesn't go away soon, you better see a doctor.

Accompanying the game were word lists for each of the seventy patterns. I compiled these lists from Devault's work (1973) as well as Cootes

Table 5.1. First Five Syllable Parts for "Spelling Nauncence" Game

Beginning Consonants	Vowel Combinations	Ending Consonants
1. f- phone (ph-)	1. -a- plaid (-ai-)	1. -d would (-ld)
2. g- ghost (gh-)	2. -a- pause (-au-)	2. -f graph (-ph)
3. g- guess (gu-	3. -e- bread (-ea-)	3. -f cuff (-ff)
4. j- gem (g-)	4. -e- friend (-ie-)	4. -g egg (-gg)
5. k- cat (c-)	5. -e- said (-ai-)	5. -g league (gue)

and Jamieson's text (1985). For example, the PH- category contained a list of the following words:

> phonics, elephant, pamphlet, prophet, graph, sphinx, alphabet, emphasis, geography, hyphen, microphone, nephew, orphan, paragraph, phantom, phase, phrase, pheasant, phony, photograph, physical, physician, physics, prophet, symphony, telegraph, telephone, triumph, phenomenon, philanthropic, philosophy, photo.

In other words, many of these example words are the same as the ones listed after "PH-" in the word bank of deviant letter patterns given in appendix F.

Then I made transparency copies of the context sentences and lists, cut them apart, and placed each in its corresponding envelope, one for each of the seventy patterns. I labeled the outside of each envelope with its code letter and number corresponding to the key. The PH envelope contained the outside label "B2," for the second item under "Beginning Consonants." On the outside of each envelope, I color-coded the letter and number code, using three different colors to differentiate the three sets of syllable parts.

The game starts with a teacher choosing a student to select three envelopes from the stack of seventy—one from the "beginning consonants," another from the "vowel combinations," and the last from the "ending consonants." Students love any activity that involves drawing choices, and the game offers 9,780 possible combinations. The teacher then places all three selected context sentences on an overhead projector for the entire class to view. For example, the following are possible choices:

B2 g- as in **g ō̄ s t** : John dressed as a **g ō̄ s t** on Halloween.
V28 ō as in **h ō̄** : After you till the garden with a **h ō̄**, rake the soil.
E17 –t as in **d ĕ t** : Parents often go into **d ĕ t** to pay for their children's
college tuition.

Students then write the spellings of these three words on their own papers: ghost, hoe, and debt. After spelling each of these words, they circle the oddball sounds in each: "-gh-," "-oe-," and "-bt." They then write the spelling of the produced "nauncence" syllable: ghoebt. Circling these variant letter strings will require them to look "with interest at various syllable parts in words" (Peters 1985, 25).

The resulting "nauncence" spelling of most drawn combinations will probably look as strange as this one. For each resulting "nauncence" spelling, the teacher needs to stress its "oddball" structure, emphasizing that English words rarely have more than one "hard part." If English words had deviant spellings commonly occurring together, spelling would be impossibly difficult. Most parts of words, however, have spellings that follow their pronunciation, as Hanna and his associates clearly demonstrated. Each of the Spellingmess creatures emphasized this fact.

In the next step, students write the phonetic spelling for the "nauncence" syllable by copying each part of the phonetically spelled word that corresponds to the sound its deviant letter string spells. The phonetic spelling for the example above would be g ō t.

After pronouncing this phonetic spelling, students write a logical spelling for it. In this case, "gote" or "got" would be two acceptable answers. "Gote" results if a student views it as an ending word syllable with a long o and would need a silent -e at the end. Another student might justify a "got" spelling by viewing it as occurring in any part of a word other than its end, a part that would not have a silent e. Some students might suggest the spelling "goat," the correct spelling for the animal but not a logical spelling because of its deviant "-oa-" spelling pattern. Explaining accepted possibilities will make a good review of logical spelling principles.

"Spelling Nauncence" is just one game that can help to open poor spellers' eyes to variant English spellings. Most of my students enjoyed playing the game and wrote, "It was fun!" in their written evaluations. While "Spelling Nauncence" is certainly not a panacea for teaching spelling, I think it could be a valuable tool if used throughout the elementary grades and middle school.

POWERFUL MEMORY TOOLS

Carol Scearce, who was Chesterfield County's director of staff development for many years, developed a fascinating presentation titled "Enlightening," a program to instruct teachers how to become more effective in the classroom by using strategies based on how human brains process knowledge.

One of the most memorable strategies was one she termed "mind-mapping." Her research reveals that color and capital letters are powerful memory tools. "Mind-mapping" requires students to record information in diagrams that resemble treelike branches with category labels, each written in capital letters and in different colors to designate groupings. Using this process helps students memorize the "mind-mapped" information, because the resulting diagramed trees reveal how their brains have made connections. By the end of that school year, practically every teacher in the county was directing his or her students to use this memory device.

I started thinking how I could apply capital letters and color to my spelling research to help poor spellers note deviant patterns in words. I had used colors to separate syllable parts in the "Spelling Nauncence" game, but without any reason for each selection, so I decided to choose colors that would logically accompany each of the three possible syllable parts. Green was my choice for beginning syllable patterns, blue for the middle or vowel section, and red for ending parts.

Like traffic signals, in my system green means "go," and therefore the "beginning" of movement; red signals "stop" and the "ending." However, yellow, the middle light on a traffic signal, is not a visible color for a letter, so I decided instead to use blue for vowel sounds. I later applied my color-coding system in a number of other ways.

Open Eyes to Student Names

The spellings of students' names will usually supply a number of deviant syllable patterns, and using names of actual students is an attention-gaining activity (Dean 1979, 2). For one class that had a preponderance of poor spellers, I printed each student's name on a 4-by-6-inch card, placing any deviant spelling in capital letters in the appropriate color code. For example, the name "Chris" would be spelled with the capital letters "CH" in the color green, the name "Sean" would contain the capital letters "EA" in blue, and the name "Donald" would have the capital letters "LD" in red.

At first, I showed a number of cards usually for a closure activity to discuss both "oddball" and logical parts. From time to time, I asked a student to pick a card for discussion of the spelling by questioning reasons for the letters being in capitals and colors. Frequently, we would note that letters spelling a schwa sound would need to be capitalized in blue because this sound is so variable.

Dividing students into groups to produce the spellings of selected names in the same way would also be a valuable activity. Another would be to draw a name of a student to write his or her name on the blackboard, again marking any deviant patterns in capital letters and appropriate color code. Drawing the name of another student to explain the reason for each letter spelling and if the spelling is correct, or to correct any mistakes, is another possibility. Students who give correct answers could then win a chance ticket. Readers should enjoy examining their own names for deviant spellings.

This color-coded spelling system also lends itself to group activities. The key to maintaining interest is variety, so concentrating on the spellings of students' names will be only an occasional activity, perhaps just a starting point to help students look at various deviant spellings. Once students understand the meaning of the capital letters and their colors, they can apply this strategy to other words to memorize their spellings.

CREATIVE USES OF WORD LISTS

Following are suggestions for effectively using the word lists in appendix E. These lists are meant only for reference for both teachers and students, certainly not for memory work.

1. Choose a pattern for students to study example words. Students then close their notebooks and list on paper as many as they can remember. They then reopen their notebooks and make red check marks over correctly spelled words and Xs over any mistakes. After spelling correctly any misspelled attempts, they then copy five more words, also in red, from the list (if there are at least five remaining). In other words, if "mn-" is the selected ending consonant syllable, there would only be five choices.

2. Draw three to five cards that each lists one deviant syllable pattern. Give students approximately five minutes to look at the patterns they have been given. After closing their notebooks, students write as many of these words from memory as they can during a set time—a kitchen timer works well, especially a digital one. When time is up, students correct their papers in red in the manner described in item 1.

3. Divide students into groups and have them open their notebooks to review three sets of syllable patterns—beginning, middle, and ending. Then hold a contest between groups. Each group reviews a selection from a literature text that the class has already read and discussed, searching for words containing the chosen deviant spellings. Everyone in the group records every found word along with its citation—page number, column number, paragraph number, and sentence number. The group with the most correct listings is the winner. As the year progresses, groups can find any word appearing in appendix E and words containing double consonants. Because there are many possible answers, the selected reading should be limited, perhaps to a single page, several paragraphs, an article in a newspaper, etc.

4. Draw a card that contains a deviant syllable pattern and then direct students to list as many words as they can without looking at their word list. Continue drawing cards and having students write example words. After drawing three to five cards, direct students to open their notebooks to their lists. They then place check marks in red above each correct word.

5. Have students review a list containing many unknown words, such as the ones listed for "Y" used as a vowel. Then select words from the list that most students know, with students helping in the selection. Students can circle the selected words to study briefly before a practice test, which they check in the manner described in item 1.

6. As a closure activity, ask a student to come forward to play "I'm thinking of a word that contains the letters ____ (gives a deviant letter pattern) and begins with the letter ____." Other students guess until someone selects the correct word. The student who makes the correct guess is the next student to play "I'm Thinking of."

7. Select a group of words from a list to teach students a common spelling pattern. An elementary teacher in the lower grades, for example, might want students to learn that many simple words have an "-ai-" vowel combination, which would not be a logical guess in spelling an unknown word. Such a teacher might choose commonly known words from the "-ai-" list, such as air, brain, chair, explain, gain, rain, said, train, and wait.

- After emphasizing the spelling of the "-ai-" vowel combination, the teacher could then give a practice test, instructing students to spell each vowel combination with "-ai-." Then the teacher could show a transparency of all the words dictated. Students should use the same self-correction process used on the logical spelling practice test checking, with a red pen or pencil, and write the correct spelling for any misspelled word.

- Students will quickly catch on to spelling these words with "-ai-" in the vowel position. They will also be building a base of "-ai-" words in their brains, to which they can connect when encountering new words that contain "-ai-" spellings.

- After proceeding with dictating other words in the same manner, ask for volunteers willing to take a "Spelling Challenge" to spell correctly another word with the same pattern correctly, for a chance ticket.

- Likewise, teachers could select other patterns to spell in the same risk-free manner. For example, a teacher could direct students to focus on the most common patterns, such as "wh-," "ea-," "ee-," "oo-," "ou-," and "ck-."

These are only a few ways to make use of these word lists. Both teachers and students can probably create many more. All will be effective as long as they are risk-free for students, who learn by self-correcting their own papers. Teachers grade each resulting paper only on whether or not the student has followed directions.

Some readers might think I never give my students any tests, since I have stressed repeatedly the importance of practice tests and student self-correction. Quite the reverse is true. I hold students accountable for a graded test when I feel certain most will perform well on it. If test results prove otherwise, I keep trying different tactics until most students become successful. Experiencing success is highly motivational, especially to a learner used to constant failures.

REASON IN RHYME

Bradley and Bryant's *Rhyme and Reason in Reading and Spelling* (1985) definitely opened my eyes to other possibilities for fostering spelling improvement. Their study observed that a child's rhyming and alliterating ability is highly correlated with his or her spelling ability (116). Such word games are skills that most children acquire naturally and informally before entering school (3). They concluded that "a child's skill in test of sound categorization at the time that he goes to school plays an important part in his learning to read and to spell" (119).

Bradley and Bryant recommended teaching sound categorization to children to help them to "progress in reading and spelling" (1985, 119). Children using rhyming and alliteration games to "group together words that have common spelling patterns and also share common sounds — groups of words like fight, might, light, and sight . . . will help them understand that "the relationship between a cluster of letters like 'igh' and the sound these letters with single sounds is not a simple one." They concluded that word games, especially those involving rhyme and alliteration, should be central to a program for spelling-deficient students, because such activities "give children experience in breaking words up into phonetic segments, and also of grouping together words that are very different from each other but that do have phonetic segments in common" (1985, 117).

Other well-known researchers have also noted the value of students' reading and writing rhymed poetry for spelling and reading improvement. Hodges states that such activities will "foster auditory discrimination . . . [and] can also reinforce word meaning and spelling patterns" (1981, 17). Mapes recommends encouraging students to make lists of rhyming words to use in writing nonsense poetry, a nonthreatening type of writing that most students will be anxious to share (1983, 45). Nurnberg supplies numerous words that students change the spelling of by adding a letter to the beginning based on a definition clue to the new word. For example, "?camper = hurry away in fright" results in the answer "scamper" (1970,

1) and likewise involves students in meanings of words and their rhyming counterparts that contain the same letter patterns.

Rhyming Dictionaries

Since a set of rhyming dictionaries seemed to be a essential to directing rhyming activities, I was able to convince my school system to purchase thirty copies of *Webster's Compact Rhyming Dictionary* (1987) for my use as a teacher-researcher.

Most of my students were unfamiliar with such a dictionary. When I first gave these books to students, I "played dumb" and stated, "I don't understand how these dictionaries organize words. Can you figure it out?" With puzzled expressions, they then started examining the texts, until a few students had an answer. If they had first read the cover of the book—something I can never remember a student doing—they would have learned that the book compiles "50,000 words arranged by their rhyming sound in a single alphabetical sequence for quick and easy use." We then noted that the book is based on vowel sounds and their endings in the usual alphabetizing of vowels—a, e, i, o, u, and y.

Next, we examined the "Pronunciation Symbols" guide near the beginning to note the phonetic symbols used. Since my students had by this time learned basic phonetics, most easily understood this section and how to apply phonetic spellings in trying to find rhyming words.

After this introduction, we tried some practice words to find rhyming counterparts. Students who found a correct list held up their hands. When at least half the class had their hands up, I called on a student to give the page number of the answers. When everyone in the class had turned to this page, we discussed how to find the list and name the words listed. At first, I had students concentrate on finding the correct page and understanding the process for turning to that page.

Once most of the students had caught on to finding a list of rhyming words, we concentrated on a list to examine, eliminating any unknown words. For example, I asked the class to find words that rhyme with "salt." When most had found the list, I asked for the rhyming words that most students would know, remarking that some were unfamiliar, like "smalt," "basalt," and "gestalt." The words "fault," "halt," "vault," "asphalt" "ex-alt," and "somersault" are possible responses. A natural action then was to ask students to note differences in the spellings of these words, noting the oddball vowel pattern of "-au-" in "fault," "vault," and "somersault," whereas the remaining words follow logical letter sequences. This example clearly illustrates how rhymed words can help students understand spelling variations for the same sound.

Once students understand how to find rhyming words, a teacher can use these dictionaries in numerous ways to foster spelling improvement. Following are some ideas:

- Contests are held between groups of students for each to write down rhyming words that the group finds in a set period of time, monitored by a kitchen timer. When time is up, students pass their papers around to check for correct spellings. Everyone in the group must cross off any word that anyone in the group has misspelled. The group with the most correctly spelled words wins the round.
- The teacher gives a "test" on using a rhyming dictionary once students are adept in using them. Students are to look up rhyming words for words the teacher lists on the blackboard, recording the appropriate page number and one of the possible answers. A number of "practice" tests might be necessary until practically all can be successful on a graded test.
- The class is divided into two teams that are to follow a relay format. The teacher gives a word that everyone looks up to generate rhyming words, but without writing them down. Then with dictionaries closed, a student from each side races to the board to write a correct answer. Misspelling any word results in eliminating not only the misspelled word but also one correctly spelled word. For example, the teacher might give and write on the blackboard the word "bleak." Resulting answers will require students to produce words with "-ee-" and "-ea-" vowel patterns as well as an ending "-que" pattern. Student coaching on each side will result in a noisy learning process.
- The major value of these dictionaries is to have students use them in writing rhymed poetry. Writing a personal limerick is an excellent way to start. Each student's limerick should start with, "Once there was a boy/girl named [first name of writer]." Students will enjoy finding words that rhyme with their names as well as words that de-

scribe themselves. Likewise, they will enjoy writing rhymed poetry about other subjects.

A set of rhyming dictionaries in a classroom will be a source of joy and learning, especially for spelling-deficient students. Poor spellers' generating lists of rhymed words will immerse them in noticing different spelling patterns in words that sound the same.

Books of Poetry

Another essential supplement is books containing rhymed poetry, which most students would find pleasurable reading. Ideally, language arts classrooms, especially those with many spelling-deficient students, will have numerous volumes of poetry to be read aloud or silently for enjoyment. Not only can rhymed poetry serve as a writing model, it can also guide students to look at words "with interest."

Teachers will find a wealth of rhyming poems that students will enjoy in works by Ogden Nash, Oliver Wendell Holmes, Daniel Lee, Shel Silverstein, T. S. Eliot, and Roald Dahl, and many others in children's literature.

A teacher can turn the reading of a poem into a spelling lesson by also showing it on an overhead transparency. A few carefully designed questions about the words that rhyme lead students to look closely at the letter patterns in these words. Helping students focus their attention on the "internal structure" of the rhyming words will also guide them to correctly spelling them in the future.

For example, the poem "She Dwelt Among the Untrodden Ways" by William Wordsworth could be used:

She Dwelt Among The Untrodden Ways

She dwelt among the untrodden ways
Beside the springs of Dove,
A maid whom there were none to praise,
And very few to love.

A violet by a mossy stone
Half-hidden from the eye!

Fair as a star, when only one
Is shining in the sky.

She lived unknown, and few could know
When Lucy ceased to be;
But she is in her grave, and oh,
The difference to me!

A teacher might ask students questions like these, to focus on various letter patterns:

1. How many words that end a line are spelled logically? (stone, be, and me)
2. List all the words spelled with an "-ai-" pattern. (maid, praise, fair)
3. List all ending words that contain an oddball letter pattern. (ways, praise, love, eye, sky, know, oh)

For any rhymed poem, a teacher could generate hundreds of similar questions. Asking interminable questions, however, will result in boredom. A teacher only needs to ask a few to help students start looking at unusual patterns in words.

Once students understand the format of questions that require close attention to letter patterns in words, they should be able to make up their own similar questions—creating questions is a higher level thinking skill. Peer questioning will be more motivating than a teacher-directed format.

TONGUE TWISTERS

Reading and writing tongue twisters is an alliterating activity that can help weak spellers learn common initial letter string patterns. Students love practicing tongue twisters, an activity that can easily be turned into a spelling lesson if the teacher also asks questions to direct their attention to spellings. For example, examine the possibilities in the following tongue tangler:

Theophilus Thistle, the celebrated thistle sifter, thrust three thousand thistles through the thick of his thumb.

Besides directing questions to note the initial "th-" consonant blend, the teacher could also draw students' attention to the letter "c-" for the "s" sound in celebrated, the "-ou-" letter string in "thousand," the "-ough" in "through," and even the ending consonant "-mb" for the "m" sound in "thumb." Of course, dwelling on all of these would be deadly dull, but noting a few when practicing tongue twisters can help draw students' attention to variant spelling patterns.

Any tongue twister contains numerous orthographic lessons, and hundreds of tongue twisters abound in our language. I have collected numerous tongue twisters throughout my teaching years, but Charles Francis Potter's *More Tongue Tanglers and a Rigamarole* (1964) arranges them creatively in poetry forms that will bring smiles to readers.

See appendix H for a list of tongue twisters I have collected over my teaching years, organized alphabetically according to beginning consonants. While it is not comprehensive, it is extensive, and both students and adults will enjoy trying to speak these twisters quickly and correctly.

PALINDROMES, RIDDLES, AND SPELLING

Students' reading and creating palindromes—words or phrases whose spellings are the same forward and backward—is another excellent activity to draw students' attention to commonly occurring letter strings within words. Students will enjoy Marvin Terban's *Too Hot to Hoot: Funny Palindrome Riddles* (1985). Middle-school students will delight in the riddles and questions that require palindrome answers. For example, the answer to the question, "What is a flip-flop phrase for a 'snuggly friend'?" is "lap pal" (35). Terban accompanies each question and answer with an illustration that guarantees delight in the reader. Students will enjoy creating similar questions and pictures of their own after reading Terban's book.

Another book students will enjoy reading is *Rainbow in the Sky*, edited by Louis Untermeyer (1963). Besides numerous limericks, this work provides riddles with simple answers that usually have a "twist or trick" to keep the reader from guessing the answer. For example, in the section titled "Twenty-one Old Riddles" is the following:

Tomas a Tattamus took two Ts
To tie two tups to two tall trees,
To frighten the terrible Thomas Tattamus—
Tell me how many T's are in that. (1963, 146)

The answer is "two" because there are only two "Ts" in the word "that,"
but most students will instead try to count all of the "Ts" in the riddle.

CLASSROOM BOOKLETS OF POETRY, TONGUE TWISTERS, PALINDROMES, AND RIDDLES

As part of my original research project, I started looking for rhymed
poetry and wordplay students would enjoy and that would guide spelling
improvement. My efforts resulted in a large volume I titled *Spells for the
Orthographic Demon: Poems, Riddles, and Tongue Twisters to Make
Spelling Fun.* (*Note:* My original title for my book was *Spells for the
Orthographic Demon,* but I was the only one who liked it!) The works I
collected made a lengthy bibliography that included such well-known authors as Roald Dahl, Ogden Nash, and Shel Silverstein. I wanted to have
a collection of material I could use for reference in my classroom. What I
compiled was a lengthy collection that resulted in a thickly bound book.

What I really wanted was class sets of books containing rhymed poetry
and wordplay. The cost of purchasing such sets would be so prohibitive
that I didn't even consider making such a request to the school system.

Far more economical would be to compile this material in pages that I
could easily copy into a class set for my students. Therefore, I produced
thirty booklets titled *For Spelling Improvement* that numbered 106 pages
each on just over 50 sheets of paper. The majority of the booklets contained poems arranged in categories—animals/insects, everyday problems, food, noisy poems, school, story poems, what if's, witches, and
spelling. Also included were riddles, palindromes, tongue twisters, and
homonym riddles.

In preparation for the next school year, I made up these booklets over
the summer of 1989. Having just completed my graduate program in
July, I then had time to prepare them over the rest of the summer. Bind-
ing each with the English department's book-binding machine gave them

a professional look. As the beginning of the school year grew closer, I looked forward with excitement to using them with my students.

Breaking the Law!

Unfortunately, my bubble of excitement quickly burst when I attended an in-service training given by the school librarians on copyright laws. The information they relayed made me realize that I had blatantly broken copyright laws. The owner of the copyright—and practically all of the works in my booklets were copyrighted—has the exclusive right to authorize any reproduction of the work. Of course, I had not obtained permission from any author for the works that I had selected for my class sets. Using this material in an educational setting would not automatically give permission to use copyrighted material. The old adage, "Ignorance of the law is no excuse for breaking the law" certainly applied.

Once I clearly understood the illegality of my booklets, I reluctantly put them away. I certainly did not want to do anything questionable as I continued experimenting with teaching spelling as a teacher-researcher. I resolved that I would try to make my booklets legal by gaining the permission of all the authors involved.

Such a task was certainly not feasible during the 1989–1990 school year as any dedicated English teacher will understand. As a teacher who always strives to make a difference for my students, I spent many hours working beyond the classroom. Work weeks of more than seventy hours were not unusual in trying to implement everything I had learned in my graduate program, and not always with success.

The following summer, I wrote and sent letters to all the publishers and authors of the works I had selected, a task that required researching the addresses of each and took a great deal of time. The responses were very disappointing: Almost all resulted in polite refusals.

ROALD DAHL RESPONDS!

Imagine my shocked delight when I received a personally signed letter from Roald Dahl, one of the world's best-loved authors (see figure 5.1). What a treasure I had received! Not only did Roald Dahl give approval for

GIPSY HOUSE
GREAT MISSENDEN
BUCKINGHAMSHIRE
HP16 0BP

TELEPHONE:
GREAT MISSENDEN 2757

Sally Burkhardt,   6th September 1990
3011 River Hills Lane,
Midlothian,
Va 23113,
USA

Dear Sally B.,

     A copy of your letter to Penguin reached me yesterday so
I will reply to you direct. Whatever Penguin say to you, you
can take it from me that I gladly give you permission free of
charge to reproduce any verses you like from DIRTY BEASTS or
indeed REVOLTING RHYMES or from the latest one RHYME STEW. I
totally agree with you that you can teach children a
tremendous amount of reading and spelling through these comic
verses. When I was seven and eight years old I got hooked on
Hiliare Belloc's CAUTIONARY TALES which are very much the same
sort of thing and very soon I knew every one of them by heart.
I still do. And it was from these that I got the idea of
doing my little things.

     What I cannot give you is permission to include these in
a book which is a serious commercial venture. If that were to
come about, and I hope for yourself it does, then you would
have to come back to us again. In this case you would write
direct to my London agent, Murray Pollinger, 222 Old Brompton
Road, London SW5 0BZ with a copy to me.

                         Yours sincerely,

                         Roald Dahl

Figure 5.1.   Copy of Roald Dahl's Letter to Author

me to use any of his poems from *Dirty Beasts* (1983), *Revolting Rhymes*
(1982), and *Rhyme Stew* (1989), he also strongly supported the value of
using rhymed poetry in the classroom. He agreed with me totally that using poetry can "teach children a tremendous amount of reading and spelling through comic verses." He then recalled that as a child, he became
"hooked on Hiliare Belloc's *Cautionary Tales*," which gave him "the idea
of doing my little things" in composing his poetry.

I had his letter framed, and it hangs on a wall in our home office, where I proudly point it out to any visitor. I also kept the envelope in a pocket on the back.

At the age of 74, Roald Dahl died on November 23, 1990, just a few months after responding to me. He must not have been in good health in September, but he still took the time to respond to me probably because he held the same convictions about the teaching of spelling and reading.

MANY OTHER POSSIBILITIES

While teachers may find some of my ideas applicable to their classrooms, they should also search for or create their own materials to open the eyes of poor spellers and help them start observing words closely. Any selected activity should comprise only a minor part of the curriculum for weak spellers, with the stopping point always being when high pupil interest starts to ebb.

Weak spellers who consistently start looking at and analyzing words they see daily will eventually develop in their brains a comprehensive base of words containing practically all the common spelling patterns in English. Once they absorb these foundation basics, poor spellers will have developed the necessary brain connections to learn the spelling of new words they see in the world around them. Good spellers have tacitly learned these same processes to teach themselves to spell. "Eye openers" will help poor spellers also become their own spelling teachers.

6

Rules Rule

On the blackboard, I wrote the words my "practicum" teacher dictated to give me some practice writing with chalk. The "practicum" was an integral part of one of my undergraduate courses at Ohio State University on the teaching of English. Lasting several weeks, it required an undergraduate to work with an experienced English teacher and helped to prepare English education students for student teaching.

When the teacher dictated the word "beginning." I stopped, struggling whether to spell it with one or two "n's." When I wrote it correctly, the teacher smiled her approval, and I sighed with relief.

At that point, I realized that I had better improve my spelling ability if I wanted to be a competent English teacher. A proficient teacher of English should certainly be able to spell words correctly, especially those written on a blackboard and used in instructional handouts.

Throughout my school years before this point in my life, I had often struggled with spelling words correctly but had little interest in improving. Wanting to be an English teacher certainly motivated me to start paying attention to my own spelling ability. Probably the major reason I became so interested in researching the teaching of spelling is my own struggles with spelling. From that investigation, I discovered that the major reason for my spelling weaknesses related to my rapid reading ability, which never required my paying close attention to various letter patterns in words.

When I became a student teacher of eighth-grade students, my cooperating teacher directed me to teach a unit on basic spelling rules. Though I was the teacher, I probably learned more than my students did. Learning and applying these basic spelling rules helped me correct many of my common misspellings. Likewise, students' learning and applying a few basic spelling rules will have a positive impact on their spelling ability.

SPELLING RULES TO KNOW AND USE

Practically any book on the teaching of spelling will recommend teaching basic spelling rules to help students spell numerous words correctly. Following are those that are usually recommended:

For Forming Plurals:
   Add -s to MOST WORDS
   "S" Sound Ends
      Add -es to words that end in a "s" sound: -s, -sh, -ch, -x, or -z
   "O" Ends
      If the word is a musical term, add s
      If a vowel is before the o, add s
      If a consonant is before the o, add es
   "Y" Ends
      If a vowel comes before the y, add s
      If a consonant comes before the y, change the y to i and add es
   F/FE Ends: Change the f or fe to v and add es
For Forming Possessives:
   If the word is singular, add an apostrophe s ('s)
   If the word is plural and does not end in s, add an apostrophe s ('s)
   If the word is plural and ends in s, add an apostrophe ONLY (')
For Spelling IE/EI Words:
   The majority of ie/ei words are spelled with ie
   If the word is pronounced with a long a sound, spell ei
   If the word had the letter c directly before, spell ei
For Adding Prefixes: Add the prefix and do not change the spelling of the word

For Adding Suffixes: Most words do not change in spelling when add-
ing a suffix
Silent E Ends:
If the suffix begins with a vowel, drop the e
If the suffix begins with a consonant, keep the e
Y Ends
If a vowel comes before the y, just add the suffix
If a consonant comes before the y, change the y to i and add the
suffix
Double the Final Consonant If All Three Are True
The word ends in one consonant
Only one vowel is before the final consonant
The suffix begins with a vowel

USING INDUCTIVE WRITING TO LEARN, AND "WAIT TIME" STRATEGIES

Most middle-school students have difficulty learning and applying these rules even though they have supposedly learned most of them in elementary grades. A deductive presentation of them is the usual format in spelling texts, a process that many teachers use. In other words, the teacher or text first presents the rules, similar to those listed above, after which students do various exercises to apply them. While these approaches are effective for some students, many others still fail to apply these rules to correct their misspellings, as middle-school teachers will often note in student writings. Giving students the list of rules to study therefore will have little impact until students have incentives to learn them.

My own dramatic improvement in spelling from teaching these rules made me realize that students' thoroughly learning and applying them is a worthwhile educational goal. While I knew what spelling rules I wanted my students to learn, trying to think of ways to motivate them to learn the rules eluded me.

As a student teacher, I knew presenting these rules inductively would result in more learning than a deductive approach. For example, in presenting rules on adding suffixes to words ending in "-y," I wrote some example words on the blackboard:

carry	convey
hurry	display
deny	betray
cry	destroy
magnify	employ

Then I asked the following questions:

1. What do all these words have in common? (They all end in the letter "-y.")
2. What kind of letter—consonant or vowel—is directly before the final "-y" in the first-column words? (a consonant)
3. What kind of letter—consonant or vowel—is directly before the final "-y" in the second-column words? (a vowel)

Next I gave the spelling of each of these words when adding the suffix "-ed":

carried	conveyeded
hurried	display
denied	betrayed
cried	destroy
magnified	employed

My next step was to ask if a student could state a spelling rule for adding a suffix to a word that ends in "-y." The expected answer was a statement of the two rules on adding suffixes to "y" end words.

Teaching rules inductively will gain more student attention than deductive approaches. Today, I would add two additional strategies to increase learning. First, I would provide a "wait-time" period, as Madeline Hunter recommends (1990, 61). "Wait-time" will provide all students an opportunity to think of an appropriate answer to a teacher's question. Instead of calling on students whose hands are raised and therefore most likely have the correct responses, I drew a card with a student's name on it to ask for his or her answer to the question. If the student didn't know, he or she had to repeat the question. If the student couldn't do so, he or she was guilty of not listening. Providing "wait-time" in class will foster more learning because students will be more attentive when they are made accountable for listening in class.

The second strategy I used was to direct students to write in their own words a statement of the rule. As a fellow in the 1985 Capital Writing Project at Virginia Commonwealth University, I learned the value of all teachers using writing-to-learn strategies: When students write learned material in their own words, they are far more likely to learn and understand the taught material.

A SPELLING RULES SCIENCE KEY

While using these strategies was far more effective than the usual deductive approach, I still continued to think of other ways to motivate my students to learn these rules. When I remembered the science key my botany professor required us to use when I was a freshman undergraduate, I came up with the idea to create a similar key to help students learn spelling rules.

My professor required all of his students to give both common and scientific names and identifying characteristics of all the trees growing on campus, a considerable task because a variety of trees abounded. To help us acquire this information, he provided a science key that taught us step-by-step a great deal of terminology about all trees as well as a means of accurately identifying any tree we examined. Working in groups with each student having a key, we found this identification process a very enjoyable way to acquire a great deal of highly technical information.

Likewise, learning spelling rules requires understanding complicated information, probably the reason so many students find learning and applying these rules so difficult. I thought a key would be equally helpful in learning these complex rules.

Learning Meanings of Technical Words in the Spelling Rules Science Key

Because students would not be able to use the key until they knew the meanings of all the technical terms in it, I picked the following eight words as necessary for students to know:

1. affix	4. possessive	7. suffix
2. consonant	5. prefix	8. vowel
3. plural	6. singular	

Listing these words on a transparency, I directed students to take a pretest on these terms by copying and defining each in a complete, well-constructed sentence. They also had to write on every other line to leave room to write any necessary corrections. For any term they did not know, they were to copy it, leaving three blank lines for recording the correct answer after the pretest. Once the majority had finished their definitions, I gave them the following answers on a handout to use for self-correction in red:

1. 2. The term consonant refers to any alphabet letter other than "a," "e," "i," "o," "u," and sometimes "y."
3. Plural means a word that is more than one.
4. Possessive refers to a word that shows ownership or belonging to something.
5. A prefix is a word part that is added to the beginning of a word.
6. Singular means a word that is just one.
7. A suffix is a word part that is added to the end of a word.
8. A vowel refers to the alphabet letters "a," "e," "i," "o," "u," and sometimes "y."

After giving students a few minutes to start correcting, I informed them that their homework would be to finish correcting the pretest and then study these terms for a quiz the next day. They would also be accountable for returning their corrected pretests, which would be attached to the quiz and part of the grade. The quiz had definitions worded exactly as in the list above, to ensure that most students would be successful in taking it. See appendix I for the key I created.

The key was definitely a different approach, and most students seemed interested in trying it once they understood how to use it. However, the first exercise I designed, "Spelling Rules Practice One," proved a disaster. Students were to use the key to spell correctly twenty words in four categories—possessives, plurals, ie/ei words, and adding affixes. Before giving the correct spelling of each word, students had to list each number and the letters they followed on the key. For example, making "men" possessive would require the following information: 1A, 5B, 6B, men's. As a result, students focused more on writing the correct numbers and letters than on learning the rules. I decided that this approach was certainly a dumb one and needed revision.

A Different Approach

Remembering how interaction in using the tree key with other students helped my learning, I decided that students using the Spelling Rules Key together in groups would be a superior approach. Instead of giving words representing all four areas, concentrating on one area at a time made more sense. Students were to use the key to spell a list of words and then answer questions on the rules they had examined. Following are the four worksheets I gave on four nonconsecutive days—no more than twice a week. They were to answer the questions, but not in complete sentences.

Spelling Possessives

1. What kind of punctuation mark is used to make a word possessive?
2. How do you make a singular word possessive?
3. How do you make a plural word that does not end in the letter "s" possessive?
4. How do you make a plural word that does end in the letter "s" possessive?

Spelling Plurals

1. How do you form the plurals of most words?
2. How do you form the plural of a word that ends in an "s" sound: s, -sh, -ch, -x, or -z?
3. How do you form the plural of a word that ends in the letter "o" and is a musical term?

(continued)

Spelling Plurals (*continued*)

4. How do you form the plural of a word that ends in the letter "o" with a vowel before it?
5. How do you form the plural of a word that ends in the letter "o" with a vowel before it?
6. How do you form the plural of a word that ends in the letter "y" with a vowel before it?
7. How do you form the plural of a word that ends in the letter "y" with a consonant before it?
8. How do you form the plural of a word that ends in "f" or "fe"?

Spelling IE/EI Words

1. Which combination—ie or ei—occurs more often?
2. Which combination do you use—ie or ei—for a word that has a long "a" sound?
3. Which combination do you use—ie or ei—for a word that has the letter "c" directly before it?

Adding Affixes to Words

1. How do you spell a word when adding a prefix?
2. When adding a suffix to a word that ends in a silent "e," what must be true about the suffix to drop the "e"?
3. If a word ends in a silent "e" and the suffix to be added begins with a consonant, what happens to the "e"?
4. What happens to the silent "e" if the word ends in the letters -ce or -ge and the suffix begins with "a" or "o"?
5. When adding a suffix to a word that ends in a silent "e," what must be true about the suffix to keep the "e"?
6. When a word ends in a SINGLE CONSONANT, two circumstances must be true to double the final consonant when adding the suffix. Explain both:
7. What kind of letter must come before the ending consonant?
8. What kind of letter must begin the suffix?
9. How do you add affixes to most words?

At the beginning of each worksheet were ten words for students to spell correctly by using the key together with students in their assigned groups, in which I purposely mixed weak spellers with competent ones. I warned that students wouldn't be allowed to give correct spellings before going through the steps, because this process would help students learn these rules.

At the end of the spellings and answers to each set of questions were the following homework instructions:

> Homework: Write a well-organized paragraph that explains all the rules on (the selected area). Be sure to title your paragraph — Can you think of a creative one? Begin your paragraph with an appropriate topic sentence. Use controlling sentences to discuss a separate circumstance that each needs example words for illustration. End your paragraph with a suitable summary sentence that "clinches" the information your paragraph has given.

Students will enjoy working together with their keys to spell the given words correctly. Giving short answers to each set of questions will provide all the necessary information they need for their written paragraphs. This writing-to-learn activity will help students commit these rules to permanent memory. Such approaches will result in far more learning than will the usual deductive procedures.

WORD BANKS FOR APPLYING SPELLING RULES

I did not supply the ten words in each of the four worksheets above because I felt they would be a redundant listing of word banks for spelling rules that I have created over the years (see appendix J). Teachers may use these lists, as I always did, to select a variety of spellings for each of the four areas.

Supplying students with a handout that lists spelling rules — such as the one on pages 112–113 — will be of value to them once they have expressed the rules orally and in writing. In addition, they will benefit from receiving a list of words the teacher has selected and put on a handout for them to keep in the English section of a large loose-leaf notebook for all of their classes. Students could use both of these handouts in additional activities that will help to instill learning and application of the rules.

GAME FOR LEARNING BASIC SPELLING RULES

After students have had some experience in learning and applying these rules, a game will help to gel this information in their brains. The teacher will need to do the following:

- Prepare name cards, one for each student in the class.
- Divide the name cards between the two teams who will vie against each another.
- Prepare four colors of index cards. Each color will represent one of the four areas of spelling rules—forming possessives, forming plurals, spelling IE/EI words, and adding affixes.
- Consult the Word Bank for Application of Basic Spelling Rules in appendix J for possibilities, recording one word on each card that matches the color selected for a spelling area.
- Select numerous words for each spelling area, ones that represent various facets of these rules.
- Provide necessities for a chosen game format—chalk for tic-tac-toe, a putter and a golf ball for putt-putt, a ball and basket for basketball, etc.

Rules for the game are as follows:

- Divide the class into two teams that will take turns trying to score points.
- During the game, students may view their list of rules and word banks, but not when they are contenders.
- Draw a name card from the stack for the team to determine each contender.
- A contender may compete more than once as long as his or her name is drawn each time.
- Each contender must spell the word on a selected card correctly, as well as clearly explain the rule for its spelling.
- No coaching is allowed. A team member yelling out answers will disqualify his or her team from that round. The opposite team purposely shouting a wrong answer will cause them to lose a turn.

- If the spelling and explanation are correct, the contender attempts to score a point for his or her team.

I have used this spelling rules game successfully in my classrooms over many school years. The game will motivate students to study their rule sheets and examine word banks in class during the game. It is a devious way to drill students, one they will enjoy. While the system for selecting each contender will not guarantee that everyone in the class gets a turn, drawing a card for the next contender means that everyone must be prepared, not just the student who knows he or she will be next. Most important, such a game will help the weakest students learn and apply these spelling rules.

A WAY TO TEACH OUTLINING SKILLS

Teaching outlining skills to middle-school students is a worthwhile goal that most school curriculums include. Once students learn the correct numbering and lettering of an outline, they need practice in creating one. Converting the list of spelling rules into outline form makes ideal material and serves as a review of these rules as well.

One of the most common mistakes students make in outlining is to have only one item under a category. To teach the concept that any grouping must have at least two points before going on to another grouping, I draw a circle on the blackboard and then tell the class to pretend the circle is a pie. When asking for a volunteer, I have never had any trouble getting a student to the board: Middle-school students love volunteering even when they have no idea what they will be expected to do. I pass my chalk to the volunteer and say, "I want to draw a line in the pie to cut it into one piece."

Of course, the student will be befuddled and will usually respond with, "You can't cut something into one piece." After smiling in agreement, I emphasize this concept to the whole class, stating that once anything, such as a pie is divided, at least two parts will result. Then we relate this concept to creating an outline, summarizing that if a category has only one further point, that point needs to be included in the category and not listed as a separate item under it.

After reviewing the order of Roman numerals, letters, and numbers in an outline, as a class we work together creating an outline of spelling rules. Students need to use their handouts of the word bank in appendix J.

After beginning the outline of spelling rules to illustrate the outlining procedure, students complete it for homework. Some classes, however, might need more modeling of outlining these rules before completing it on their own. When students return with their homework outlines, I show on a transparency the outline given in appendix K, which students will use for self-correcting their created outlines.

Directing students in constructing an outline on spelling rules will thoroughly familiarize them with outlining skills they will be able to use in all of their classes. Rather than producing the given examples in the outline above, students need to search their word banks for choices. I always give students a handout of a list of applicable words to keep for the rest of the school year in the English section of their loose-leaf notebooks for all classes. I select them from those given in appendix J. Having affixes as a fourth category will show students further divisions and their classifications. Making prefixes and suffixes into separate Roman numerals will greatly simplify them.

HOW ABOUT THE SPELLING OF "BEGINNING"?

The "doubling rules" listed above explain only when to double the final consonant in one-syllable words. Until students understand how doubling rules extend to two-syllable words, they will still probably stumble in spelling a word like "beginning," as I did as an undergraduate. Teaching how "doubling rules" apply to two-syllable words will be valuable, but only after students are adept in applying these rules to one-syllable words.

Students need to understand that all three circumstances for doubling final consonants in a single-syllable word still apply:

- The word ends in one consonant.
- Only one vowel is before the final consonant.
- The suffix begins with a vowel.

In addition, the word's accent or stress has to be on its ending syllable to double the word's final consonant. At this point students need a short review of a stressed syllable versus an unstressed one, even though they learned this information when studying phonetics. Using names of students in the class to illustrate the difference will tap their memory and understanding of accented and unaccented syllables.

Activities—worksheets, games, questions in an anticipatory set, etc.— requiring students to add suffixes to words that result in spellings that provide a mix of doubled or single ending consonants will be valuable practice. Refer to the "Double or Not?" word lists in appendix L to select words.

Students who thoroughly understand extensions of the basic doubling rule will gain access to spelling a large base of words correctly. Many middle-school students, however, will probably have difficulty absorbing this material, so teachers should not dwell on presenting these rules. In other words, some activities on these concepts are justified; multiple ones are not. Many students may not be able to grasp these concepts until their high school years and perhaps never will.

WHAT ABOUT EXCEPTIONS?

Anyone thoroughly familiar with spelling rules knows that there are many exceptions to them. For example, multiple words are exceptions to the ie/ei spelling rules, as the list below illustrates. I remember presenting these exceptions to my eighth-grade students during my student teaching experience. At that time, I gave students the challenge to write a set of sentences that used all of these words as a way to remember these spellings. The resulting writings were, of course, nonsensical, and this exercise probably confused the students more than helping them remember the spellings of "ie/ei" words.

For the first few years of teaching spelling rules to middle-school students as a teacher-researcher, I continued requiring my students to learn major exceptions. Besides the ie/ei exceptions, I felt they needed to understand two exceptions for adding suffixes. One was that adding the suffixes -ous and -able to words that end in -ce or -ge would result in keeping the -e.

Another was that adding -ing to words ending in -y preceded by a consonant would result in keeping the -y, not changing it to -i. I soon came to realize that these exceptions further complicate an already complex subject. First learning the simplest spelling rules would still be a challenge for most students.

In other words, basic spelling rules are applications of what happens "most of the time" in English spellings. These basic rules will help students spell an enormous number of words correctly in a similar manner as the application of logical spelling strategies will help students make good guesses when spelling unknown words. The exceptions students misspell, a computer will most likely correct.

While students are in the process of learning these rules, teachers still need to stress that many exceptions exist, and learning these exceptions will require their close attention to the letter(s) in the word that breaches the rule. For example, when encountering the word "financier," a student should note that "-ie-" not "-ei-" follows the letter "c." To me, this spelling seems to coincide with its French origination and the pronunciation of its last syllable. While my analysis of this word might not make sense to others, my observation of these letters has always helped me spell it correctly.

Likewise, students who open their eyes to letters that make a word an exception to a spelling rule will also be committing that word's spelling to memory. Students need to focus on the unexpected letter combinations to learn spellings, and any activity that requires students to look closely at words will be valuable. Visualization of any unusual spelling in the "mind's eye" will help a student commit the word's spelling to permanent memory.

Only after students thoroughly learn to apply basic spelling rules will learning exception rules be of value to them. Over the years, therefore, I did not teach my seventh graders exception rules unless I had a class of gifted learners who had quickly acquired a thorough understanding and application of the simplest spelling rules.

On the other hand, students' learning to apply all these exception rules will give them access to spelling a vast majority of words correctly. High school teachers could probably teach these rules more successfully, since older learners would most likely have developed the abstract thinking skills that Jean Piaget states fully develop around the age of fifteen (Brainerd 1976, 38).

Teachers who feel their students are ready to tackle learning and applying exception rules should first give them a word bank handout of example words selected from those in appendix M. Then they should teach these rules in nonthreatening ways. A practice test on the "-ce," "-ge," and "-ing" endings, which students then correct in red, is one possibility. A game titled "Why an Exception?" is another option.

BASICS FIRST AWARENESS NEXT

This chapter has emphasized the importance of students' learning basic spelling rules thoroughly before any exposure to further complexities. Teachers should not present more complicated rules until the majority of students have acquired these basics and can apply them to their spellings. Teachers will have some classes in which most students will still struggle to learn the simplest spelling rules and therefore should have no exposure to more complex rules and exceptions. For such students, teachers still need to emphasize the existence of many exceptions, and students need to use visualizing strategies to learn these spellings.

At the same time, teachers need to realize that teaching spelling should be only a minor part of a language arts curriculum. They need to teach spelling rules in short time segments, emphasizing them only over a few weeks and then sometimes quickly reviewing one concept occasionally for the rest of the school year. They also need to realize that I used only a few of these approaches each year. If teachers used all of these possibilities to teach spelling, they would spend most of the year just teaching spelling rules.

The focus of the last part of this chapter has been on concepts that complicate these basic rules, and most teachers will use this material for reference. While presentation of these rule complexities will benefit a number of students, others will fail to absorb this information until much later, and in some cases never. Many students will value this information only when its acquisition becomes important, as I did when an undergraduate.

Teachers should encourage their students to make their best attempt when a word's spelling eludes them. If in doubt, they should spell it logically, as chapter 3 describes, and then a computer's spell-check system will usually correct it.

7

Which One?

Chapter 6 ends with the statement "a computer's spell-check system will usually correct" many misspellings, an assertion reiterated in other chapters. Programs with spelling checkers are extremely helpful to weak spellers but not always reliable, as the following poem the computer teacher at my school shared with me shows:

Spellbound

I have a spelling checker
It came with my PC.
It plainly marks four my revue
Mistakes I cannot sea.
I've run this poem threw it;
I'm sure your pleased too no.
It's letter-perfect in it's weigh.
My checker tolled me sew.

"SPELLBOUND," A PLAGIARIZED POEM

When trying to document this poem, I originally attributed it to Pennye Harper, because many Web sites give her credit for authoring it. Later, I discovered Eric Shackle's Web site, which states that Dr. Jerrold Zar, a retired professor of biological sciences at Northern Illinois University, wrote the original poem, titled "Candidate for a Pullet Surprise," in 1992. Shackle states that Zar's poem is "a classic example of intellectual property being stolen on the internet" (2010, 1). Since I had seriously considered majoring in biological sciences instead of English when pursuing my undergraduate teaching degree, I was delighted to discover a scientist who spent time composing poetry, one who most likely has developed "whole brain" thinking skills.

When I e-mailed Dr. Zar for information, he immediately responded, stating that his poem "has appeared literally thousands of times on the Internet." Shackle's site discusses many other venues of the poem: "The original poem has been set to music twice, once by a rapper and in the second case made in a Gilbert & Sullivan-like opera by a music teacher in Bangkok, who had his students sing it at graduation" (2010, 3).

Readers will enjoy checking Dr. Zar's Web site (www.bios.niu.edu/zar/poem.html) to read his original poem, published in the *Journal of Irreproducible Results* in 1994 (13) and reprinted in 2000 (20).

Whichever version readers peruse, it will reveal that writers cannot be confident that spelling checkers will correct all misspellings, because no program can differentiate spellings of homonyms and other commonly confused words.

Edna Furness lists numerous memory tricks in her book, *Spelling for the Millions*, to help readers learn the spellings of selected words (1977, 91–96). I imagine she spent a great deal of time writing them to help spellers learn the spelling of the homonyms and commonly confused words she selected.

Other current spelling researchers also suggest specific memory tricks, rather than giving students the means for creating their own mnemonics for remembering these spelling (Chandler and Mapleton Teacher Research Group 1999, 90; McAlexander, Dobie, and Gregg 1992, 61–63; Topping 1995, 167–169). In *Vocabulary & Spelling in 20 Minutes a Day*, Meyers also emphasizes numerous memory tricks for learning numerous spellings (1998).

Teaching students how to write their own memory tricks, however, is a far superior strategy! We only remember "10% of what we read" but "80% of what we experience" (Glasser 2006). Expressing a concept in writing certainly helps a learner gain "experience." This chapter, therefore, focuses on how to write effective memory tricks to remember spellings of homonyms and words commonly confused, which many students and adults frequently misspell.

SPELLING MNEMONICS

"Mnemonics" is the only word in English that begins with letters "mn-"; it refers to any technique that assists memory. Probably everyone has heard the memory trick to remember the spelling of "principal"—The principal is my pal. This sentence helps students remember the spelling of "principal," but provides little help for remembering the numerous other words that sound the same but have totally different meanings.

On the other hand, examining why this sentence is an effective mnemonic device will reveal what components are necessary to compose a memory trick. First, the connection of the spelling pattern in the homonym to a common word containing the same pattern in a sentence will help a speller remember the word's spelling. Second, the context of the composed sentence must reveal the meaning of the homonym. "The principal is my pal," however, seems at first glance to lack context clues to the meaning of "principal." Quite the reverse is true, since "pal" labels "principal" as a person and therefore separates this word from its homonym "principle," which refers to a rule.

Once I analyzed why this memory trick is a helpful one, I hypothesized that poor spellers could learn the spellings of many homonyms and commonly confused words if they could learn how to write equally effective memory tricks.

As stated previously, competent spellers, when encountering a new word, automatically LOOK at the word closely, observing its spelling patterns and especially any deviant letter combinations. If the word contains all logically spelled parts, it is an easy one to memorize. If not, good spellers concentrate on the hard or differing parts to learn the spelling of the new word. To remember these unusual letter strings, a learner's brain makes a connection to words that contain the same letter pattern. For example:

tournament: our, hour, pout
employee: see, need, fee
whose: hose

Good spellers perform this process so quickly and naturally that they are totally unaware of how easily they are able to learn the spelling of a word, even a complicated one.

The memory trick connecting "principal" and "pal" addresses only one definition—the person who directs a school—and not the meaning of its adjective form—first in importance, a matter or thing of primary importance. Once learners understand the two necessary components of an effective memory trick—connecting meaning and letter pattern—they might compose the following to remember the other meaning of "principal":

Sal is Melvin's principal gal, his main squeeze!

"Sal" and "gal" will help the speller remember the "-al" spelling, and the sentence's context, particularly "main squeeze," will help a speller remember that this meaning of "principal" refers to something of major importance.

Once I understood these necessary components of memory trick writing, I composed the following instructions on a handout for students to use when composing memory tricks for a list of homonyms and words commonly confused:

1. **Define** the meaning of each homonym or word commonly confused.
2. **Focus on the letter pattern** in each homonym or word commonly confused that **causes it to be spelled differently** from its counterpart. Think of a word that contains the same letter pattern **THAT YOU KNOW HOW TO SPELL!** Sometimes you will find a word within the word, sometimes the word will also rhyme, but most of the time it will be a word that just contains the same letter pattern.
3. Write a **sentence** or two that **connects** each homonym or commonly confused word to its **letter string twin and each word's meaning.** UNDERLINE or **HIGHLIGHT** the words containing common letter strings. If you write two sentences for each homonym, they do not need to be connected in meaning, but each sentence needs to make sense. Be sure your sentence(s) contain(s) context clues to reveal meanings of each homonym or commonly confused word.

Of course, a teacher should keep stressing each of these concepts until the vast majority of students understand how to compose a memory trick.

First Attempts

For the first few years that I worked with them on memory trick writing, students compiled word lists from rhyming dictionaries and lists of deviant patterns using dictionaries for definitions. I provided the entire list of homonyms and commonly confused words—forty-nine sets in all—that the county expected all seventh graders to learn. Some of the resulting writings were excellent; others were not. From these, I was able to select examples to illustrate clearly what and what not to do when writing them. I put all of the following on a single transparency and discussed them one at a time. I also presented them in groups by each point they represent. Following are those that met all criteria:

The angel used gel to keep her wings in place.
The statue of an angel in the nativity scene sang the song "Noel" when a button was pressed.
A triangle consists of three angles.

For a memory trick to help a speller remember letter combinations, it must make sense. Following are examples of nonsensical and unacceptable attempts:

The angel could excel because of the angle of the triangle.
The angle and Mr. Rectangle mangled the eagle.
The angel that rebelled spent a night in a hotel while the angle got caught in a tangle right by a triangle.

One student writing illustrated two appropriately connected words but failed to contain context to their meanings:

We went to the Hotel Angel.

In order to write an effective homonym memory trick, the writer needs to make a connection between the spelling of the letter pattern and its meaning. Including a context clue guarantees that the writer is making this association.

These examples helped students understand the expectations they had to meet in their writings, all of which required effort and thought. The memory tricks students wrote kept improving in quality. Over the years, I collected numerous student papers that contained many creative memory tricks, but I must have thrown them out when purging my files upon retiring. I did find one paper from a rather average student who composed her memory tricks in April 1993. Following are some of her more effective ones:

My favorite kind of b<u>erry</u> is strawb<u>erry</u>.
When a man dies of a bad inj<u>ury</u>, people b<u>ury</u> him underground.
I went to the capit<u>al</u> Washington D.C. with my p<u>al</u>.
The capit<u>ol</u> building I saw looked very <u>ol</u>d.
I had to d<u>o</u> s<u>o</u> much homework that it took 5 hours t<u>o</u> complete it.
My report on my tr<u>ue</u> friend is d<u>ue</u> tomorrow.
I have a p<u>air</u> of ch<u>air</u>s that look the same.
I d<u>are</u> my friends to p<u>are</u> a piece of paper into a perfect circle.
Over the y<u>ears</u>, I hated eating p<u>ears</u>, my least favorite fruit.
The st<u>ars</u> in the sky are always station<u>ary</u>, and I wonder why they don't move.
I wrote my friend a nice lett<u>er</u> on my new station<u>ery</u>.
I th<u>rew</u> a seed to the ground, and it g<u>rew</u> into a plant.
My finger went thr<u>ough</u> the d<u>ough</u> when I was making a pizza.

None of these are particularly quotable, but all are typical of those students as well as adults will enjoy writing to remember homonym spellings. More important, their mnemonic writings will help students remember the spellings of the selected homonyms.

A New Approach

After several years of following these procedures, I decided that I was requiring busy work by making my students record definitions and words containing corresponding letter patterns for each set of given homonyms. Most of my students knew the meanings of these words; they just confused their spellings. In addition, almost all of them were familiar with common deviant patterns found in many words and knew how to spell most of them.

Providing my students with a list of homonyms with corresponding definitions and words with matching letter strings that they could use for reference expedited their producing mnemonic writings. In other words, the composed memory tricks, not the search for definitions and corresponding words, helped them to remember these spellings.

From that point on, I selected twenty-seven sets of homonyms that students commonly confused, each of which contained all this reference information. Success was immediate because students produced their mnemonic writings more quickly to easily learn the spellings of these words. Most scored well on the homonym test that followed.

When writing this chapter, I was strongly tempted to just supply my original list with a statement that a book on homonyms should follow the same patterns. I quickly dismissed this idea, because one of my major purposes in writing this book is to provide valuable reference materials for all teachers and students to use, from elementary to adult levels.

With this purpose in mind, I set out to create a list of homonyms that is as comprehensive as possible, examining numerous lists in various books, including those I was required to teach. Current spelling researchers often provide lists of commonly misspelled homonyms and words often confused (see McAlexander, Dobie, and Gregg 1992, 46; Pinnell 2003, Appendix 15). The most extensive one I found was in Jerry Mallett's *101 Make-and-Play Reading Games for the Intermediate Grades* (1976, 279–280). As I continued to work on this project, any time I encountered homonyms I checked my list to make sure they were included, adding them if they weren't there. I may have missed a few, but readers should be able to add them easily.

After each definition is a list of words containing corresponding letter patterns. (Appendix N is a good reference list for all students, as well as for adults who commonly misspell homonyms.) The "Word Bank of Words Containing Deviant Letter Patterns" in appendix F also provides additional choices for common deviant patterns such as "-ai-," "-ea-," "-ee-," "-ew-," "-ow-," "-ou-," and "-ow-."

Once students learn the process for writing effective memory tricks, spellers who have learned to look closely at words and have built memory bases of words following spelling patterns will probably not need to write out the devised trick. Instead, they should be able to process the trick mentally and quickly when checking the list for a troublesome homonym.

OTHER POSSIBILITIES

One of the most delightful books I examined during my research was Marvin Terban's *Eight Ate: A Feast of Homonym Riddles* (1982). Each page is devoted to one homonym riddle and answer, with an accompanying cartoon illustration. Young students delight in reading this book, and I would choose it as part of a class set to be used in numerous classrooms. Following are some of my favorite Terban riddles:

What does a broken window feel? A pain in the pane. (14)
What is perfume that is mailed? Sent scent. (19)
What is a good-looking horse-drawn carriage? A handsome hansom.
   (57)

Terban's book contains riddles and answers for sixty sets of homonyms, an extensive list that can help students focus on their spellings. In addition, the book can serve as a model for students producing their own homonym riddles from ones Terban does not include. Many students would also enjoy creating accompanying illustrations, as Terban did for each riddle.

Games are also a good tool for learning homonyms. Forte and Pangle's *Spelling Magic: Activities, Gimmicks, Games Galore for Making Learning Mean Lots More!* (1976) suggests many possibilities. For example, in "Teakettle," each student in a class writes on a slip of paper one sentence that contains two homonyms. One student then draws from the collected slips and reads the sentence, substituting the word "Teakettle" for each homonym, and other students guess the homonyms. The student who guesses and spells each homonym correctly becomes the next contender (7).

Wagner, Hosier, Mork, and Cesinger suggest a homonym relay, in which a teacher reads a sentence with a homonym for a contender to spell correctly (1972, 40). This format is organized the same as others I have recommended, with points scored by each team playing basketball, putt-putt, tic-tac-toe, etc. This game will generate interest in looking closely at sets of homonyms, especially when the teacher limits the answers to certain sets.

In *Spelling Games and Puzzles for Junior High*, Robert Miller provides a list of sentences with blanks that students need to fill in correctly with the commonly misused sets of "there," "their," and "they're" (1976, 17).

Because most of the sentences in this exercise were unrelated, I decided to compose ones that connect to some facet of middle school to make a more interesting exercise for my students. In addition, I added practice sentences on another problem set, "to," "too," and "two." See appendix O for my version with the answers given, which I show on a transparency for student self-correction. This exercise will give students valuable practice to help them remember the correct form to use.

MEMORY TRICK WRITING FOR WORDS COMMONLY CONFUSED

The English language also contains numerous sets of words that have different spellings and pronunciations but are commonly confused because of similarity in spelling patterns. Ironically, students rarely misuse these words orally. For example, few if any would say the following:

I went to the diary to see cows milked.
My mother bought me some new cloths to wear to school.
Our football team cannot loose the game.

These types of statements are ludicrous mistakes that would cause instant laughter. At the same time, students frequently misspell such words in their writings.

Appendix P lists commonly confused words following the same format I created for the homonym memory tricks in appendix N. Instead of creating a comprehensive list, I included only those sets that I have found troublesome for most middle-school students.

A SIMILAR PROCESS

Learning the spelling of homonyms and commonly confused words involves many of the procedures discussed in chapter 4, "Focusing on Letter Patterns." In order to remember the spelling of any word, students must

- understand the meaning of the word so well that it is part of their working vocabulary

- closely observe all letter patterns in the word, noting both logical and oddball combinations
- focus on any deviant letter patterns in the word, visualizing them in the "mind's eye"
- connect the deviant pattern in the word to other words containing the same letter strings, but only words they know how to spell
- correctly spell the word a number of times to imbed its correct spelling into permanent memory

To memorize the spelling of a commonly confused word, however, the speller must perform an additional step: Just as done for homonyms, the context of the memory trick the speller produces must reveal the meaning of the word commonly confused. In other words, a student must make two connections—to context and to letter patterns—to learn the spelling of homonyms or words commonly confused.

8

Fine Tuning

The question remains: What kind of spelling program schools should implement for students who have "caught" spelling—those who have mastered the first two developmental stages? Students' spelling ability progresses as a direct "consequence of knowing about words in many guises" (Hodges 1982, 12). A plethora of possibilities exists. Since entire books have been written or could be written on most of the categories in this chapter, I discuss only those on which I can supply my own creative slant, most of which will still be cursory description.

SPELLING DEMONS

Learning and applying concepts that will help students spell large groups of words correctly will develop a degree of competence in spelling. Some words, however, elude these generalities. Most authorities refer to these more difficult words as "spelling demons."

The Internet has a wealth of material on words commonly misspelled, some with diagnostic tests to assess spelling ability. One study I find fascinating is by Cornell Kimball (2006), who analyzes words by frequency of misspellings. He describes a good number of words that Internet news groups commonly misspelled. At the end of his study, he lists various sources of lists that include from 50 to more than 800 difficult-to-spell words.

Table 8.1. First Five Words from Edna Furness's List
of 605 Most Frequently Misspelled Words in English

Word	Hard Spot(s)	Words Minus Hard Spots
ab**ey**ance	ey	ab___ance
ab**sc**ess	sc	ab___ess
absen**ce**	ce	absen___
absolut**e**ly	e	absolut___ly
abs**urd**	urd	abs___

Generating lists of spelling demons is easy; how students should study these words is illusive. Of all the authorities I have researched who discuss difficult spelling words, Edna Furness is the only one who attempts to provide strategies for learning to spell 605 of the most frequently misspelled words in the English language. For each word listed, she gives the correct spelling in the first column, underlining and placing in boldface type the hard spot(s) in the word. In the second column, she lists the hard spot(s) in the word. The last column is for practice in spelling the word; filling in the missing letters in the blank(s) will help a student remember the word's spelling (1977, 175). Table 8.1 shows the first five words.

Furness provides an analysis of each word in an attempt to help students focus on the hard components that make spelling the word difficult. Learners definitely need to concentrate on these difficult spots for correct spelling. Visualizing these parts in the mind's eye will certainly help them develop a spelling memory of the word.

A Better Strategy

As noted in chapter 5, "Eye Openers," using colored capital letters to denote the hard parts in a word is a powerful memory tool. My own experiments have proven the value of such a system. Placing the deviant parts of students' names in colored capitals helped my students focus on these parts. Likewise, I often used flashcards of words with these unusual patterns in colored capital letters.

I also used this technique with a student I tutored one summer. He was extremely bright, but struggled with the spelling program that his private school required. Students were expected to learn the spellings of ten words each week, and from that point on they had to spell them correctly forever. All teachers in the school, even in science and math, severely penalized the misspellings of any previously presented word in any class.

The words students were to remember consisted of a variety of spellings with no attempt to organize them according to patterns. My student had not developed memory bases of words containing common letter strings and would often spell the same word a variety of ways. Consequently, he failed miserably in spelling.

In order to help him, I first worked on teaching him logical spelling techniques. Next, I analyzed the full list of words he was accountable for spelling, looking for those containing deviant patterns. Grouping together words with common letter strings, I made an index card for each group and then listed all the words containing this letter string. At the top of each card, I wrote the deviant part in the appropriate colored capital letters—green for beginning consonants, blue for vowels, and red for ending consonants in a syllable. For example, on the "QU-" card I listed the following words: question, quiet, quite, and require. After each listed word, I spelled it again, capitalizing and coloring in green the "QU-" parts.

We used the resulting cards for drill. He would first study the card for the noted pattern and then focus on each word. I also placed other deviant patterns in a word in colored capital letters. For example, the first "e-" in the word "effect" is in a capital letter colored blue because it has a schwa sound; the "-ct" at the end is in red capital letters to denote its ending pattern. My student improved in the school's spelling program, no doubt from focusing on words with common letter patterns. His mother said he earned an "A" in spelling during the first grading period after the summer of my tutoring.

Even though he showed improvement, I knew he still had many problems in spelling. A few weeks of effective instruction cannot turn a poor speller into an excellent one, because developing competent spelling skills is always a slow, gradual process.

Since using colored capital letters to emphasize the difficult spelling parts in a word seems to be an effective way to help spellers focus on these parts, I think lists of spelling demons should follow the same pattern. Such lists would be far more helpful than the lists of numerous spelling demons most authorities provide.

A Sample Spelling Demon List

Kimball's (2006) list concentrates on thirty-six words that are most frequently misspelled. The frequency of misspellings for these words ranges from 68 to 10 percent of the times they were used in the writings he evaluated. His list therefore represents difficult spelling demons, the reason I chose it to adapt to my colored capital letter system. Table 8.2 shows how I organized these thirty-six words into four columns.

The first column shows the correct spelling of the word.
The second column shows the word's spelling divided into syllables.
The third column shows the syllables, with difficult parts in capital letters.
The fourth column shows the phonetic spelling of the word.

Originally, I added a column that listed how frequently writers misspelled the word in writing, but I eliminated it because this information does not correlate to learning the word's spelling.

I decided to provide each word's syllabication to help students think of each of these parts. As I have emphasized previously, poor spellers frequently misspell a word when they fail to give a spelling for each syllable in a word. Students therefore need to think of each syllable in a word and an appropriate spelling for it to spell the word correctly.

At first, I color-coded the deviant part(s) in each word, using the green, blue, and red system described in chapter 5. Remembering the kinesthetic value of tracing over capital letters, however, I decided that providing the word's parts with capital letters in black would be better; in studying the word, students would then trace over these deviant parts using the appropriate color.

For example, the letters "a-," "-cc-," "-mm-," and "-o" are capitalized in spelling the word "accommodate" in the fourth column. A student studying this word would then trace over the letter "a-" in blue, since it is a vowel or middle syllable part, "-cc-" in green because it is a beginning consonant blend, "-mm-" in red because it is an ending consonant blend, and "-o-" in blue because it is a vowel or middle syllable part. Following such a study system would require practice. Tracing over each capitalized part(s) in the appropriate color would most likely help a student focus on

Table 8.2. **Richard Kimball's Spelling Demon List Converted into an Example Spelling Demon Study List**

Word	In Syllables	Hard Spots	Phonetic Spelling
minuscule	min u scule	min **U** scul**E**	min´s•kyül
millennium	mill enn i um	mi**LL** e**NN** **I** **U**m	mə •len´ē• əm
embarrassment	em barr ass ment	em ba**RR** a**SS** ment	im•bar´əs•mənt
occurrence	o ccurr ence	o **CCuRR** ence	ə•kər´əns
accommodate	a ccomm o date	**A** **CC**o**MM** **O** date	ə•käm´ə•dāt
perseverance	per se ver ance	per s**E** v**E**r **A**nce	per•sə•vir´əns
supersede	su per sede	su per **S**ede	sü•pər•sēd´
noticeable	no tice a ble	not **I** **CE** ble	nōt´ə•sə•bəl
harass	ha rass	h**A** ra**SS**	hə´ras
inoculate	in oc u late	**I**n **O**c **U** late	in•äk´yə•lāt
mischievous	mis chie vous	mis **CHIE** vous	mis´chə•vəs
occurred	o ccurred	o **CCuRR**ed	ə•kərd´
embarrass	em barr ass	em ba**RR** a**SS**	im•bar´əs
indispensable	in dis pen s able	in dis pen s**A** ble	in•dis•pen´sə bəl
privilege	priv i lege	priv **I** le**GE**	priv´ə•lij
questionnaire	quest ion naire	q**UE**s tion n**AI**r**E**	kwes•chən•na(ə)r´
pastime	pas time	pas time	pas´tīm
separate	sep a rate	sep **A** r**A**t**E**	sep´ə•rət
preceding	pre ce ding	pre **C**e ding	pri•sēd´ing
definitely	def I nite ly	def **I** n**I**t**E** ly	def´ə•nət•lē
gauge	gauge	g**AU**ge	gāj
existence	e xis tence	e xis t**E**nce	ig•zis´təns
publicly	pub li cly	p**U**b li cly	pəb´li•klē
weird	weird	w**EI**rd	wērd
misspell	mis spell	mis spe**LL**	mis´spel
grammar	gramm ar	gra**MM** **A**r	gram´ər
miniature	min ia ture	min **IA** ture	min•yə•chər´
precede	pre cede	pre **C**ede	pri•sēd´
rhythm	rhy thm	**RHY** t**HM**	rith´əm
conscientious	con sci en tious	con **SCI** en tious	kän•chē•en´chəs
hierarchy	hi er ar chy	hi **E** rar **CH**y	hī´ə•rär•kē
calendar	cal en dar	cal **E**n d**A**r	kal´ən•dər

each word's difficult parts to commit the word's spelling to permanent memory.

In addition, I would instruct students to note silent letters in purple—a procedure that I had not used previously but that seemed necessary to help a speller note these silent letters. Students, therefore, would trace over in purple the capitalized "E" in the "miniscule," "noticeable," "privilege," "questionnaire," separate," and "definitely."

Following this system would probably be particularly valuable for students just beginning to learn how to spell words correctly, especially for special education students. A learner could first look at the word's spelling, then its syllable division, and finally concentrate on the hard parts in capital letters, tracing over in the appropriate colors. A student could use the phonetic spelling in the fourth column for self-testing by covering the other columns.

On the other hand, competent spellers would more than likely learn the spelling of a difficult word by closely observing all of its deviant patterns to memorize its unusual spelling quickly.

I must admit that I have never presented such lists of spelling demons to my students, because I never focused on students learning the spellings of difficult words. I therefore have no data on the effectiveness of this system. Perhaps others would like to test its value.

SPELLING STUDY PROCEDURE

When I was first researching the teaching of spelling, I found that several authors recommended a "Test-Study-Test with Self Correction" procedure (Henderson 1985, 90; Allred 1977, 25). In addition, others recommended students follow "Study Steps" for memorizing spellings (Hanna, Hodges, and Hanna 1971, 124). At that time, I was still following the required spelling texts, which presented miscellaneous groups of words for each lesson. I developed a spelling study procedure to help my students learn these words, one that required students to self-correct their practice test and then recopy in capital letters each word missed to help them study for the final test. Then they were to cover the word and try to spell it. If they missed it again, they repeated the recopying. Most students improved using this procedure.

If I were to provide lists of unrelated, difficult words today for students to study for a test, I would change this study procedure by first supplying the list of words in the format used in table 8.2. After allowing students to focus on each of these words, I would dictate a pretest on them for students to self-correct. For each missed word, they would be expected to copy the lowercase and capital letters and then trace over the capital letters with the appropriate colors before attempting to spell the word correctly.

These visualization and tracing procedures are kinesthetic strategies that are particularly effective for learning disabled (LD) and educable mentally retarded (EMR) students (Furness 1977, 45). I would insist that students who have performed poorly on previous tests follow this copying procedure, giving them the incentive to learn these spellings just with the visualization strategies most competent spellers would use to learn these spellings. Again, such a spelling study procedure needs testing.

WORD ETYMOLOGIES

Learning the history of English by focusing on word etymology would be one interesting "guise" for advanced spellers. Most students would find other historical facts about words fascinating. A few possibilities follow (Hodges 1982, 35–45):

- Learning how acronyms are formed
- Discovering how many English words have been borrowed from other languages
- Learning how onomatopoeic words have entered our language
- Finding out how many words in our language have been created by writers, inventors, scientists, and others
- Learning how many words are the result of shortening a longer one
- Discovering how sounds and meanings of two or more words sometime merge to form a new word

Practically "every word in our language is a frozen metaphor, a frozen picture," and it becomes a treasure hunt for students to find its origin (Furness 1977, 111). For example, when working with the student I tutored one summer, we tried to figure out the reason for the unusual spelling pattern in the word "Wednesday." Discovering that the name of this day comes from the Old English *Wodnesdæg*, meaning the day of the Germanic god Woden, helped to explain its strange spelling pattern.

Many students become fascinated with word derivations once they have been introduced to the etymological information most dictionaries supply. Finding words interesting is synonymous with spelling improvement. See appendix Q for a list of words with intriguing etymologies that I collected during my high school teaching years. Teachers of students who have higher level English skills might find it a valuable reference.

A suggested etymological activity is to have each student in a class research one word and then do an oral presentation on its history. The teacher designing a writing assignment for students is another possibility. The teacher should first give students their own written model so they understand what is expected of them. Of course, each student must use a different word. One way a teacher could assign a word to each student would be to place the words on index cards for students to draw out of a box.

Another possibility is to assign a number of words to a group, who then would explain each of their words while standing in front of the class, a less intimidating approach for students who are afraid to be an only speaker.

VIVID LANGUAGE

Another way to interest students in words is to direct them to using vivid picture-making words. I use a color activity during the first days of school each year to start students thinking about using words that build pictures in the minds of their readers. I begin by showing the list of basic colors on a transparency, with each color's name highlighted in its color, telling students that their color choice will supposedly reveal their personality. With these descriptions covered, I then direct students to pick their favorite color from the list and answer with it when I called their name from the class roster. When we are finished, I unveil the descriptions to see if they match the students' personalities:

Red: You do things on the spur of the moment. Your energy is endless, and you are always enthusiastic. You often change your mind when on the way to success.

Orange: You love to tell and make jokes. Your warm nature makes you a sought-after friend. You are always encouraging others to do their best. In any project, you are a popular and effective leader.

Blue: You are extremely patient, dignified, poised, and protective of your loved ones. You reach goals by trying your best and making good decisions.

Yellow: You like to think about ideas. Most of the time you would rather be alone. You are successful in thinking of creative and artistic ways to do things.

Purple: You are very sensitive, and your feelings are easily hurt. You have excellent taste, and you set high standards for yourself and others. You enjoy devoted circles of close friends.

Green: Your appreciation for tradition and respect for authority make you a solid citizen. You want to make significant contributions to society and be admired by many people.

After going over these personality types, many students agree with their assessments, but others do not. This is an excellent bonding activity, one of many I use at the beginning of the year to develop a comfortable classroom atmosphere, so necessary for effective teaching, especially for an English teacher who implements a whole-language approach, intermingling various ways of communicating—reading, writing, speaking, and listening.

The next day I present an entirely different list of colors, directing students not to choose a basic color but instead a vivid or more descriptive related color to answer when I call the roll. Before we start, I emphasize that selecting specific, picture-making words is something they need to practice, especially when composing. Of course, we then mention using an English thesaurus for help: Most students are familiar with its use. Following are examples of picture-making color words:

Blue: sapphire, aqua, violet, indigo, royal blue, turquoise
Brown: copper, cinnamon, chocolate, sandy, muddy, tan, bronze
Green: celery, mint, lime, emerald, olive
Red: scarlet, crimson, cardinal, maroon, raspberry, ruby, rose
Purple: lavender, lilac, orchid, plum

White: snowy, milky
Yellow: canary, chartreuse, butter, mustard, banana, gold, blond
Black: midnight, ebony

Whenever a student named an ordinary color, I stopped and reminded the entire class that they were to focus on choosing picture-making words instead of ordinary ones. The next day we continued the same activity, but only after several students could explain the directions and the reason for doing it.

The Spellingmess creature that appeared each year emphasized the vivid color activity when describing her appearance. For example, the creature might declare, "Others rave about my chartreuse complexion, my ebony lips, and crimson eye brows." Of course, the descriptions changed each year with each new combination of colors, but still illustrated the use of vivid colors in descriptions.

One of the creatures, Ms. Vividia Diction, whose Planet Spellingmess's spelling was Voiveidaeo Daickshien, appeared one year to emphasize that using vivid, specific words that appeal to the five senses produces picture-making writing.

The color-naming activity is just the start of my continued emphasis throughout the year for students to use vivid picture-making words when speaking or writing. Students enjoy activities that require them to use a thesaurus to find vivid words for specific situations—for example, instead of "said," they should describe the senses, ways to walk, ways to express feelings, etc. Hopefully, they will enjoy using a thesaurus to search for vivid words so much they will make its use a lifelong habit.

Dramatics for Emphasizing the Use of Picture-making Words

Middle-school students love dramatics, and frequently my English class included "Acting Lessons," always a favorite activity. The actor or actress comes to the front of class and draws from a set of cards, each of which lists one of the following words:

amble	drag	jog	march	slither	stumble
bike	gallop	jump	prance	soar	tiptoe
crawl	glide	leap	roll	stagger	trot

| creep | hobble | limp | skate | stroll | trudge |
| dance | hop | lumber | skip | strut | wander |

Through acting out these verbs, students illustrate to others their picture-making qualities and encourage finding and using them in speech and writing.

Writing Assignment on Picture-making Verbs

Students can also use the above list of vivid verbs as a source for a "Writing Charades" assignment, in which they write a paragraph containing many clues to the chosen word, for which a blank is provided in the last sentence. Other students then try to guess the word. Following is a model paragraph I wrote for students:

> The day was beautiful for the walk the lovers intended. What a perfect day to be alone at last. The woods shone with crimson, golden, and copper colored leaves of the autumn day. Squirrels scurried through the trees so unlike the way the two moved. They both hated the thought of their soon parting so they just _____ down the path. (strolled)

Most students will enjoy searching for vivid picture-making words; using them will improve their compositions.

DENOTATION VERSUS CONNOTATION

Another concept advanced spellers need to understand is the difference between denotation and connotation. *Denotation* refers to a word's actual or literal meaning, whereas *connotation* refers to any negative or positive emotions or feelings a word can arouse. The difference is difficult for most students, even high-schoolers, to understand.

To help them to comprehend the difference, I created the character I named Maude Mudwunkle. I drew her picture on the blackboard. A stick figure would suffice, but if teachers prefer, they can download my drawing of Maude from my Web site (braintospell.com), to copy and place on a transparency for the class to view.

Under Maude's feet, I wrote two descriptions of her: tall and under-weight. Then I explained that Maude affected people in two ways—they either loved her or hated her. We then listed words that each group might use in describing her, listing them on either side of the drawing.

Students delighted in making suggestions. "Loving" descriptions used the words "thin," "trim," "lean," "slim," "slender," "tiny," and "petite" to describe her underweight condition and "stately," "statuesque," and "regal" to describe her tallness. Maude's detesters described her being un-derweight with such words as "anorexic," "pencil-stick," "skinny," "twig bones," "Depression baby," "toothpick," and "bird legs," and her tallness with "bean pole," "the giraffe," "lanky," and "the tower."

Once we finished with our lists, I explained that all of these words had basically the same denotations for the two descriptions. Only the neutral descriptions—underweight and tall—lacked connotative meanings. All words, therefore, have a denotative meaning, but many words also have positive or negative connotations in greater or lesser degrees.

Describing Maude Mudwunkle helped my students understand the dis-tinction between the denotation and connotation of words. Teachers will find many other valuable activities to help students understand underly-ing meanings of words. One way is to supply students with excerpts from literature, newspapers, magazines, editorials, advertisements, etc., that contain words with strong connotations for students to analyze. Many other possibilities exist.

Leading students to evaluate the "slanted" words in writings will help them judge the writer's bias and discern the validity of the work. Once a person has the ability to "read between the lines," he or she should be able to make objective judgments about the truth in editorials, political speeches, advertisements, and other persuasive writings and speeches that often are scams to take advantage of the ignorant.

VOCABULARY WORDS IN CONTEXT

Humans learn new words through all means of communication—speak-ing, listening, writing, and reading. Creating interest in attending closely to new words used in any of these four modes will help learners to enrich and extend their command of language.

Learners need to understand how to make use of context clues in a writing to discover the meanings of words by making logical guesses. One thing I like about *Literature and Language* (Applebee 1994), the texts Chesterfield County adopted for all English classes in the middle schools in the county, is the manner in which they present vocabulary words in context. Each vocabulary word in a selection is underlined, with a footnote below labeled "Words to Know and Use." In this section, the word is listed along with its phonetic spelling, part of speech, and definition. Before reading any selection, I went over these words with my students for their beginning understanding.

After completing the reading, we then discussed the context of each word, picking out surrounding context clues that hint at the meaning. A culminating activity was for students to copy all information about each word, after which they then composed their own original context sentences for it, on which they were tested.

Write Source 2000 supplies a superlative list of examples of context clues that my students and I read and discussed in class. The list gives specific example sentences of ways context clues can appear in a text:

- Through **synonyms** and **antonyms**
- Through **association** with other words in the sentence
- From **comparisons** and **contrasts**
- With an accompanying **definition** or **description**
- By placement in a **series**
- From the **tone and setting**
- Clues derived from **cause and effect** (Sebranek, Meyer, and Kemper 1995, 370)

See appendix R for the student worksheet I created for guessing the meanings of vocabulary words used in context.

The purpose of such an exercise is for students to discover the meaning of each word from its context. Requiring them to also describe the method used in each example would be of little value. While I might mention the means of context used in each sentence when discussing resulting definitions, students need not make such a technical analysis. The model sentences supplied in *Write Source* will help them compose their own effective context sentences. Assignments that teach students how to make use of context clues will be helpful for student understanding; composing their own context sentences will help them learn the meanings of assigned vocabulary words. The lowest level of learners should especially have a great deal of practice in guessing meanings of unknown words used in context and also in writing their own sentences that reveal meanings for given vocabulary words.

Such activities will be invaluable if students continue to make guesses about meanings encountered in life. If they attempt to apply context clues to unknown words when reading, they will often correctly guess close definitions. Listening actively to words heard in conversations and on various TV and radio programs—newscasts, commercials, oral discussions, etc.—and then guessing meanings from each word's context will broaden their vocabularies. Once a learner thoroughly understands the meaning of a word as well as the word's grammatical components, he or she should then be able to use it correctly in all modes of communication.

SUFFIX SENSE

Emphasizing how words change in grammatical form by adding different suffixes cannot be overstressed with higher-level students. Many will misuse a new word when placing it in a context sentence if they fail to understand how the word must function according to its part of speech. Students therefore need to understand how words work in a sentence, concepts that are difficult for most to grasp. To develop suffix sense, students need to have knowledge of four parts of speech, not all eight: nouns, verbs, adjective, and adverbs. Almost all new vocabulary words will occur in one of these forms. I give my students the following information on a handout to help them understand these four forms:

Understanding Nouns, Verbs, Adjectives, and Adverbs

Nouns—name persons, places, things, ideas, etc.
  Persons—**girl, student, typist**
  Places—**school, home, beach**
  Things—**pencil, shoe, bread**

Verbs—show action or existence
  Action verbs—**laugh, skip, walk**
  Existence verbs—**is, am, seems, become, appear**
Adjectives and Adverbs Are Describers
  Adjectives—describe nouns
    Describe persons—**beautiful** girl, **excellent** student, **expert** typist
    Describe places—**superior** school, **comfortable** home, **sunny** beach
    Describe things—**lead** pencil, **old** shoe, **moldy** bread
  Adverbs—describe action verbs, adjectives, and other adverbs
    Describe action verbs—laugh **heartily**, skip **merrily**, walk **slowly**
    Describe adjectives—a **very** beautiful girl, an **unusually** excellent student, an **abnormally** expert typist
    Describe other adverbs—laugh **very** heartily, skip **most** merrily, walk **too** slowly

Using the same example words helps students grasp the interrelationships among these four parts of speech. Most books treat them separately. While these descriptions will be helpful, most students will need continued teaching before they can use vocabulary words correctly in writing. Of course, many will tacitly understand these concepts without much explicit instruction.

In addition, students need to have the lists of suffixes, their definitions, and example words for reference (see appendix S). This list is a daunting one and not appropriate for students to memorize definitions, because so many are the same or similar. Instead, students should use these lists as a valuable reference tool when completing exercises that require them to change a word to various parts of speech.

The word "beauty" is an excellent example, since it can occur in multiple forms—e.g., beauty, beautification, beautician, beautify, and beautifully. List each of these words on the blackboard to demonstrate the various forms of "beauty." Then give the part of speech for each, followed by a corresponding definition, as a valuable starting activity:

beauty, noun. Something that is pleasant to the senses. A person who is lovely to view.

beautification, noun. The act of making something that people will admire.

beautician, noun. A person who makes another as pleasant looking as possible.

beautify, verb. To make something or someone lovely to view.

beautifully, adverb. In a manner characteristic of exciting aesthetic pleasure.

This activity will probably include the use of dictionaries to produce definitions that do not repeat any form of the word "beauty." When composing these definitions, students need to be aware that they have to state a definition according to the word's part of speech. Referring to the corresponding suffix in appendix S and copying an applicable part of the definition will demonstrate how to compose such a definition.

After this point, students will need an abundance of practice applying the same information to other words that can occur in multiple forms. Give one or two sets for students to complete as homework and show the answers the next day for student self-correction; this will help students comprehend how definitions must change according to a word's part of speech. Refer to appendix T for a list of words having a minimum of four grammatical forms.

I dread the thought of how some teachers might use the words listed in appendixes S and T to give numerous, never-ending homework assignments that would be tedious drudgery for students to complete. Instead, teachers should use them only for reference, utilizing the lists in various enjoyable ways. One might be placing each set on index cards for students, in teams, to draw in playing a game, playing tic-tac-toe, putt-putt, basketball, etc. Maybe at the start, naming the part of speech of each word would be enough for a student to try to score points for his or her team.

Games could progress to requiring giving more information. As always, students would be allowed to use their corresponding handouts, but not while being contenders. Students could also draw index cards for a closure activity to win a piece of candy.

I have also used these lists to make up a "Spinner Practice" sheet, on which the first word is defined appropriately, with its other parts numbered. Since my spinner wheel had forty-four numbers—just like the lotto—I had the same number of counterparts on a practice sheet that all students had to use. For example, the spinner dial landing on the number 34 might refer to the following word and its counterparts:

> 34. Organizational, adjective. Having an orderly structure in which all parts relate to the whole
>   1. organization 2. organize 3. organizer 4. organizationally

Before spinning, we selected one of the four numbers to give information about. If our choice was number 3, the contender then gave the part of speech and corresponding definition for the word "organizer." The correct response would be "Noun, a person who places something in an orderly structure in which all parts relate to the whole."

Students also love to play "Stump the Student" at the end of a class, and this material is easily adapted to such a game. A student volunteers to come to the front of the class, and the other students try to stump him or her with questions. In this case, the questioner states a word, and the student then has to give all the other parts of speech to keep his or her position. If the student is "stumped," the questioner replaces him or her with someone who can answer correctly.

Such activities are a nonthreatening ways for students to learn without the need for constant testing. Students will enjoy even the beginning homework assignments as long as teachers grade these for making reasonable attempts and then on accurate self-correcting in class.

Using "Jabberwocky" to Develop Suffix Sense

Lewis Carroll's poem "Jabberwocky"(1923) will delight the vast majority of students of any age group, particularly if read dramatically, as I love to do:

Jabberwocky

Twas brillig and the slithy toves
Did gyre and gimble in the wabe;
All mimsy were the borogroves
And the mome raths outgrabe.

"Beware the Jabberwock, my son!
The jaws that bite, the claws that catch!

Beware the Jubjub bird, and shun
The frumious Bandersnatch!"

He took his vorpal sword in hand;
Long time the manxome foe he sought
So rested he by the Tumtum tree,
And stood awhile in thought.

And as in uffish though he stood,
The Jabberwock, with eyes of flame,
Came whiffling through the tulgey wood,
And burbled as it came!

One, two! One, two! And through and through
The vorpal blade went snicker-snack!
He left it dead, and with its head
He went galumphing back.

"And hast thou slain the Jabberwock?
Come to my arms, my beamish boy!
O fabjous day! Callooh, Callay!"
He chortled in his joy.

Twas brillig and the slithy toves
Did gyre and gimble in the wabe;
All mimsy were the borogroves
And the mome raths outgrabe.

While students will find the sounds of the nonsense words in Carroll's poem amusing and memorable, they should also find analyzing their grammatical forms entertaining. Using the handout (see table 8.3)—without the marked answers, of course—for students to complete in groups will be more effective than assigning it for homework, since students can help one another make accurate answers.

Because many of these nonsense words do not contain the common suffixes listed in appendix S, students will have to decide on each word's form by its position in each sentence. Some will have difficulty with this task and will need the help of others, even the teacher as a final resource.

After students make self-corrections when they regroup as a class to review their answers, the teacher should remark that none of these words

Table 8.3. Analyzing the Parts of Speech of Words in "Jabberwocky"

DIRECTIONS: Work as a group to decide the part of speech for each word listed below. Indicate your selection by checking the block under the selected part of speech. Each person must complete this sheet according to how the group decides.

WORD	NOUN	VERB	ADJECTIVE	ADVERB
brillig			√	
slithy			√	
toves	√			
gyre		√		
gimble		√		
mome			√	
raths	√	√		
outgrabe				
Jabberwock	√			
frumious			√	
Bandersnatch	√			
vorpal			√	
manxome			√	
uffish			√	
whiffling	√	√		
tulgey			√	
burbled				
galumphing		√		
beamish			√	
frabjous			√	
chortled		√		

functions as an adverb. Asking students how to turn the adjectives into adverbs should bring the response, "By adding the suffix '-ly' to each." Then directing students to write the resulting forms in the "Adverb" column should result in the following changes—brilligly, slithily, momely, frumiously, vorpally, manxomely, uffishly, tulgeyly, beamishly, frabjously.

Show these answers on a transparency for student correction as a review of the spelling rule for adding the suffix "-ly" to adjectives and verbs to change them to adverbs.

A "Jabberwocky" Writing Assignment

The "Jabberwocky" activity is an introduction to a writing assignment that will tickle students' brains. Requirements are to make up a nonsense word and give at least four different forms for it, then identify each form's part of speech and provide a corresponding definition. In addition, students must also compose a context sentence for each word form. For all writing assignments, I give students detailed instructions as well as a checklist of requirements they must follow before turning in their completed writing. I give students the following model to help them understand this assignment on using suffixes correctly:

1. **galumph**, verb. To stamp feet noisily. The teacher told the class to **galumph** around the room, with high marching steps and slamming their shoes on the floor.
2. **galumphist**, noun. One who stamps feet noisily. A **galumphist** entering the classroom when students are writing will probably cause everyone to stop working because of the noise.
3. **galumphiness**, noun. The state or quality of stamping feet noisily. The **galumphiness** of the aerobic dancers was so loud that the observers couldn't even hear the beat of the accompanying music.
4. **galumphially**, adverb. In the manner of stamping feet loudly. The Dutch girl dressed in wooden shoes raced **galumphially** down the hall.
5. **galumphious**, adjective. Stamping feet noisily. Before going to the library, the teacher warned the class not to do any **galumphious** walking in the halls to keep from disturbing other classes.

Such an assignment will be difficult for most students. The following excerpts from student writings illustrate their confusion about how to use a word correctly according to its part of speech, the same kind of mistakes students make when writing a context sentence for a vocabulary word:

ballesness, noun. The state of being sad. The **ballesness** boy could not do the happy part of the play.

stumpher, noun. One who drags their feet. She walked **stumpher** like as she droopily went to bed.

sodyizally, adverb. The action of drinking loudly, nonstop, or all the time. The two brothers were mad at each other, so one decided to be **sodyizally**.

Some students will produce an excellent piece, such as the following, which a superior student composed:

1. **shalopist**, noun. One who sneezes loudly. In the car, the **shalopist** sneezed so loudly that he blew the driver's wig off.
2. **shalopness**, noun. The act of sneezing loudly. All this **shalopness** is spreading many germs, so cover your nose when you sneeze.
3. **shalopful**, adjective. Sneezing to its loudest extent. That's one of the most **shalopful** sneezes I've ever heard that I had to cover my ears!
4. **shalopfully**, adverb. In the manner of sneezing loudly. He sneezed so **shalopfully** that he scared the whole crowd.
5. **shalopify**, verb. To sneeze loudly. You may **shalopify** outside when alone, but inside cover your mouth when you sneeze so you don't disturb others with the noise.

A student who can produce the above writing will have few problems using new vocabulary words correctly. Understanding how to use transitive and intransitive verbs correctly will extend this ability, a subject I could expound on at length but will only mention in passing because it involves complicated grammatical concepts that would require almost an entire book to explain.

While some students develop a tacit understanding of how words work, most will need a great deal of practice to develop suffix sense. If all teachers—elementary through high school—would emphasize in enjoyable ways how suffixes affect the meanings and grammatical usage of words, most students would probably become adept in using a new vocabulary word correctly in speech and writing. Students who fail to understand how words work in English will most likely misuse new vocabulary words in speech and writing.

When Hanna, Hodges, Hanna, and Rudolf analyzed errors made by the computer they programmed in 1966, they found that most of the incorrectly spelled words could have been spelled correctly if the computer had been able to couple knowledge of sound–letter correspondences with a knowledge of the characteristic word-building and word-borrowing patterns of our language. "Later research that encodes morphological and contextual clues into a future computer spelling program will certainly reduce the number of computer misspellings" (1971, 96).

MEANINGS OF PREFIXES AND ROOTS FOR VOCABULARY DEVELOPMENT

Learning the meanings of prefixes and roots in an enjoyable manner is an excellent way for students to access new words. James I. Brown is well known for his "Master Word" table of fourteen words whose twenty prefixes and fourteen root elements pertain to over 14,000 words in *Webster's Collegiate Dictionary* and a projected 100,000 words in an unabridged dictionary (Shaughnessy 1977, 213).

Teachers will have no problem finding lists of prefixes and roots that are valuable for students to learn. Chesterfield County Schools in Virginia, the system in which I taught middle school, provides lists of prefixes and roots for each grade level that students are responsible for learning. Although the list for seventh grade does not include all of Brown's prefixes and roots, many are the same. Tables 8.4 and 8.5 show how I used this seventh-grade list to illustrate how any teacher could adapt it to other lists of prefixes and roots.

Before giving students these lists of prefixes and roots to memorize, I direct them to work in groups to look up meanings and example words for each of the prefixes and roots the county requires them to learn. Students use *Write Source 2000* handbooks, which the school system provides for middle-school classrooms. For example, after writing the prefix "anti-, ant-," students would record "[against] anticommunist, antidote, anticlimax, antacid" (Sebranek, Meyer, and Kemper 1995, 374).

After students complete and self-correct their worksheets, I provide them with the lists for study that are shown in tables 8.3 and 8.4. From

Table 8.4. Chesterfield County Public Schools' Seventh-Grade List of Prefixes and Meanings

Number	Prefix(es)	Meaning(s)	Word Example(s)
P-1	anti-, ant-	against	antinuclear, antacid
P-2	auto-	self	autobiography, automatic
P-3	bene-, bon-	good	benefit, benign
P-4	circum-, circ-	around	circumference, circulate
P-5	de-	undo, opposite	deactivate, deform
P-6	dis-, dif-, di-	opposite, apart, away	disagree, different, disarm
P-7	epi-	upon, at, beside	epidermis, epitaph, episode
P-8	in-	not	ineligible, inaccurate
P-9	inter-	among, between	interrupt, interpret, intervene
P-10	magni-	great, big, large	magnify, magnificent
P-11	multi-	many, much	multicolored, multiply
P-12	neo-	new	neoclassic, neon, neophyte
P-13	omni-	all, everywhere	omnibus, omnipresent
P-14	peri-	all around	perimeter, periscope
P-15	re-	back, again, back again	redo, rewrite, repay, reclaim
P-16	semi-	half	semiannual, semicircle
P-17	syn-, sym-, sys-	with, together	synchronize, sympathy
P-18	un-	not, opposite, reversal	unhappy, unable, undo

Table 8.5. Chesterfield County Public Schools' Seventh Grade List of Roots and Meanings

Number	Root	Meaning(s)	Example Words
R-1	-act-	do	action, react
R-2	-aqua-	water	aquarium, aquatic
R-3	-ced-, -ceed-, -cede-, -cess-	move, yield, go	proceed, recede, recess
R-4	-duc-, -duct-	lead	induce, viaduct
R-5	-grat-	pleasing	congratulate, gratitude
R-6	-ject-	throw	project, eject
R-7	-mal-	bad, evil	malignant, malformed
R-8	-man-	hand	manual, manufacture
R-9	-miss-, -mit-	send, remind, warn	missile, transmit
R-10	-mon-	advise	monument, premonition
R-11	-nat-	born	prenatal, native
R-12	-ped-	foot	pedal, pedestrian
R-13	-pend-, -pens-	hang	pendulum, suspend
R-14	-port-	carry	transport, portable
R-15	-reg-	kingly, guide	regal, regulate
R-16	-sed-, -sess-, -sid-	settle, sit	sediment, preside
R-17	-spec-, -spect-, -spic-	look	spectator, retrospective
R-18	-ten-, -tin-, -tain-	hold	tenant, detention, abstain
R-19	-tend-, -tent-, -tens-	stretch, strain	extend, pretend, tense
R-20	-voc-, -vok-	call, voice	vocal, advocate, revoke

that point, drill work is done, and any of the games I have suggested previously would help to instill these principles.

PLAYING BINGO

Students will particularly enjoy a game of bingo using flash cards that they will make for all the listed prefixes and roots. The game is played in the following manner:

1. Use index cards or small sheets of paper.
2. Place your initials in the upper left-hand corner of BOTH sides of each.
3. Place the code of the prefix or root—given in the first column under "NUMBER"—in the lower right-hand corner of BOTH sides of each card or paper.
4. On one side of each card, write the prefix or root.
5. On the other side, write the definition.
6. After the definition, give at least one example word.

Figures 8.1 and 8.2 are examples of both sides of a card.

Prefix and Root Bingo Directions

Throughout the year, I cut up paper into quarter sheets—usually out of scrap paper that is blank on one side—and give the sheets to students

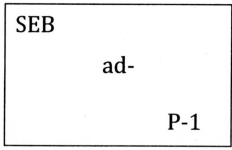

Figure 8.1.   Example of Side One of a Prefix/ Root Bingo Card

> **SEB**
>
> **to, toward, near.**
>
> **(advance)**
>
> **P-1**

Figure 8.2. Example of Side Two of a Prefix/Root Bingo Card

to use in various ways. After passing out these quarter sheets, I show the following directions on a transparency:

1. Select nine cards from your flash cards for prefixes and roots.
2. Place these cards in three rows of three, with the prefix or root side up.
3. Write the order and the code of these cards on a quarter sheet of paper—see figure 8.3.
4. When a definition is called, turn over the appropriate card—you may peek if you need to!
5. Call "Bingo" when you have turned over three definitions in any row, horizontally, vertically, or diagonally.
6. Another student will check your quarter sheet when you call the code numbers.
7. Students who have failed to record their initials and code numbers on their flash cards may not win!

Some students will have failed to make flash cards or to complete them correctly. They should work on correcting and/or composing these while others play. Exclusion from the game will encourage such students to have a complete set by the next time a game of "Prefix/Root Bingo" is played.

Word Webs Generated from Common Roots and/or Prefixes

As discussed in chapter 1, the human brain stores information into interconnected parts that interweave according to structural and functional

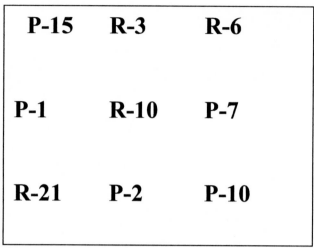

P-15	R-3	R-6
P-1	R-10	P-7
R-21	P-2	P-10

Figure 8.3. Example of Recorded Nine Cards Selected for Playing Prefix/Root Bingo

characteristics. As the brain assimilates new information, it must clearly connect to supporting bases, which must be strong enough to hold each addition. Selecting words that connect to one another will help students grow in vocabulary development.

Building a word web based on words containing a common root and/or prefix is an excellent approach for students for vocabulary development. Appendix U provides examples of words generated from the roots "-spec-," "-spect-," and "-spic-." This list is an excellent model for students' creating other numerous word webs throughout the school year. In addition, it is a valuable vocabulary list for students to learn to use the meanings of each listed word.

Studying words that have a common root will help students remember meanings, unlike the lists of unrelated, difficult words that many vocabulary books present. Teachers should look for vocabulary books containing words that build on students' knowledge of prefixes and roots. Ida Ehrlich's *Instant Vocabulary* (1968) is an excellent example. Using material she developed as an eighth-grade English teacher, she arranges words around 259 "Keys," each of which examines words based on a prefix or root.

The series of books titled *Vocabulary for the High School Student* by Harold Levine, Norman Levine, and Robert Levine (1989, 1994) is also excellent. In addition to giving words based on Latin and Greek prefixes and roots, the authors organize words according to everyday situations: skill, poverty, wealth, fear, courage, concealment, disclosure, agreement, eating, size, quality, weakness, strength, neglect, care, residence, disobedience, time, and necessity (Levine, Levine, and Levine 1989, viii-ix).

When the Spelling Committee for Chesterfield County Public Schools in Virginia, of which I was a member, met to choose new spelling books for all the middle schools in the county, members recommended that the Levine texts be adopted. Higher authorities denied our proposal because of the phrase "For the High School Student" in the title. One would think that the authors might have been willing to change the title, since Chesterfield County purchasing these books would have resulted in a highly lucrative order for at least a thousand books.

Recently I tried ordering several of these texts, since my own copy had fallen apart from overuse. I was disappointed to discover they are out of print, but I was able to obtain some used copies. Hopefully, current vocabulary texts will also present words in interconnected ways.

MAGNILOQUENCE AWARDS

One of my favorite end-of-the-year activities was giving "Magniloquence Awards." In other words, I made up a list of positive descriptions, each on an official looking certificate, to award to each student in all of my classes. See appendix V for the words or phrases I selected.

After receiving awards, students clamored for dictionaries to find out the meaning of the descriptions. Their cries delighted me, since productive activities are a rarity in most classrooms on the last day of school. Of course, I supplied a class set of dictionaries. I imagine that each student still remembers his or her descriptive word or phrase.

In later years, I changed the strategy to have students working in groups use the "Magniloquence" list to describe all the other members in the class except those in their group. Each member wrote on his or her own sheet of paper the complete list of descriptions and the selected students. In addition, they recorded the phonetic spelling of the word or phrase and a definition. Before collecting these papers, which I would check only for completion, we reviewed each listing, with students from each group giving the name(s) of students they thought the word or phrase aptly described. If nobody had selected a particular description, I relayed the meaning.

The "Magniloquence" activity utilizes vocabulary words that connect in a topic and gives students a purpose for using them. Once students have reasons they value for learning information, especially information connected to themselves, they will be highly motivated to acquire that information.

A NEVER-ENDING PROCESS

A child's first word is the start of his or her quickly learning thousands of common words from speaking situations. Developing reading skills will add to a child's word base, words whose meanings are often deciphered from context. Formal vocabulary instruction will also add many more words, especially if they are grouped around common roots. Formal schooling usually adds many more words, many from direct vocabulary instruction.

If learning new words has always been a joyful experience, students should continue for the rest of their lives to discover new words in everyday situations. As these lifelong learners unearth new words and uncover their meanings, their speaking and writing vocabularies will grow.

Unfortunately, students who become avid lifelong learners are not the norm in our modern society. An educational goal should be to increase these numbers, an objective obtainable only by making learning enjoyable for students in school.

CONCLUSION

As mentioned in chapter 2, Mina Shaughnessy is well known for *Errors and Expectations* (1977), which describes students' writing errors falling into predictable patterns that often result from students' misconceptions of formal written language.

Students' spelling errors will also fall into foreseeable patterns, each of which this book addresses. Students who produce disphonetic spellings, such as "flghighting" for "fighting and "kickt" for "kicked," need to learn to apply the logical spelling strategies discussed in chapter 3, "Using Logic to Spell." Once students become skilled in applying these simple concepts, they will make notable gains in spelling. Teachers' frustration should turn to excitement once they realize they can have the greatest impact on their lowest level spellers in teaching them how to spell words logically.

Most likely this same group of students will pay little attention to spelling words with correct deviant letter patterns. Examples, again all from student writings, are spelling "gole" for "goal," "sead" for "said," "broak" for "broke," and "expeiramentation" for "experimentation." Teachers should recognize that such spellers need to open their eyes to common deviant patterns in words, as recommended in chapters 4 and 5.

A teacher of such poor spellers will probably focus spelling instruction for the entire school year on teaching students logical spelling principles and helping them observe deviant letter patterns in words. In addition, such students will need to develop memory bases of words containing these unusual spelling patterns to connect the appropriate pattern to each new word they learn to spell. The major goal in teaching such weak spellers is to convince them they can learn to spell by looking closely at words they see in everyday life. Once students start analyzing both the logical and deviant spellings in words, they will be well on their way to teaching themselves to spell.

Another pattern of spelling error is found in such misspellings as "calfs," "beleive," and "writeing." Such "Rule Eluders" would benefit from learning and applying the spelling rules given in chapter 6.

Likewise, those who write about a "grate day," "riding a hoarse," and "eating to much" would benefit from learning how to write the memory tricks presented in chapter 7, "Which One?" to remember the spellings of homonyms and words commonly confused.

Before students can understand and apply basic spelling rules and write effective memory tricks, they need to know how to spell unknown words logically as well as to develop memory bases of common deviant patterns.

These basic writers will benefit from discovering meanings of words from context, discussed in chapter 8, "Fine Tuning." Directing them to produce context sentences for selected known words is a valuable exercise. They should also learn to make intelligent guesses about the meanings of unknown words from context.

Common spelling demons that are problematic for advanced spellers should also be a concern for English teachers. Using the study procedure suggested in chapter 8 is a viable way to learn spellings of difficult words.

Teaching English would be easy if all the students in a class had the same needs. Any class—even those labeled supposedly "honors level"— will contain students with disparate abilities, especially in spelling. The majority will only need basic instruction, which usually is a quick review of concepts taught in previous years; others will need further training.

An ideal goal is to develop enjoyable computer programs that concentrate on teaching various areas of spelling and other areas of writing. After identifying a pattern of error a student needs to correct, the teacher could recommend a specific program for the student to hone a particular skill. The availability of appropriate computer programs in a classroom would help teachers individualize instruction easily.

TO BE "PRETINUED"

This book begins with my first son, Doug, saying his first word "bur," so ending it with an expression from my second son, Brad, is fitting.

Brad's first word, which I don't remember, was slow in coming, no doubt a result of some medical problems I had during my second month of pregnancy. As a result, his language development was dramatically slow compared to his older brother's.

When Brad began speaking, only our immediate family knew what he was communicating. He started talking clearly around the age of four, and others could understand his speech. When we watched a TV program that at the end stated that it would be continued later, Brad would yell out, "Oh no! It's a "pretinued." To this day my husband and I utter the same expression when viewing a show's episode that leaves the viewer hanging.

While "to be pretinued" is not an appropriate expression, "to be continued" is. Hopefully those who have read my book, including volunteers who enjoy tutoring students to help them reach their highest levels of achievement and adults who enjoy working with children, such as leaders of Boy Scout or Girl Scout groups, will implement my ideas when relating to the youngsters in their lives, such as pupils, children, and grandchildren.

A future educational goal should be that by the time they reach middle school, almost all students will be competent in the initial and intermediate spelling developmental stages Charles Read (1975) first described. Abandoning the boring, senseless drills of traditional spelling programs will be necessary. If teachers implement logical spelling and visualization strategies in the elementary grades, the vast majority of students should be able to "catch spelling." Language arts teachers in higher grades could then focus on advanced spelling activities, especially vocabulary development.

A child's first word is the beginning of his or her language development, a complex process with which spelling intertwines. When starting my research on the teaching of spelling, I was determined to understand all orthographical aspects and theories thoroughly so that I could apply them in practical ways in my own classroom.

The orthographic demon proved to be a formidable foe, a monster whose innumerable, complex tentacles constantly intertwined with one another. Understanding one appendage often required comprehending how that part related to all others, at times a seemingly impossible task. The discoveries I have made have only slightly subdued this demon.

If highly creative teachers in our schools today extend my research to develop successful spelling programs, they will finally enchant this orthographic demon into total submission. If all teachers of all subject areas, including professors at the highest levels of learning, would apply similar strategies, our nation's educational systems would improve dramatically, with the majority of students attaining the highest learning level they are capable of achieving. No longer would we have so many youngsters dropping out of school.

If all educational systems in the world would develop similar philosophies that also insist on tolerance for those who differ in race, gender, and/ or religious beliefs, we could create a utopian world no longer filled with so much hate and constant wars, a world that could continue ad infinitum.

A

Richard L. Gentry's List of 500 Words Most Frequently Used in Children's Writing, Reorganized by Patterns

See page(s) 39–40.

The following words from Gentry's original list are organized by patterns—see chapters 3 and 4 for detailed explanations. The listing is based on the assumption that students have been thoroughly versed in the logical spelling principles discussed in chapter 3. Words containing two or more patterns are duplicated accordingly. For example, the word "knew" occurs in two places—under its beginning consonant pattern "kn-" and also under its deviant vowel pattern "-ew-."

When presenting words in the deviant letter pattern list, teachers should color-code and capitalize the deviant patterns in each word to help their students visualize and memorize the selected letter combination. Placing each of these words on a separate flash card to show to students is an effective strategy.

LOGICAL SPELLINGS

a	ate	bring	cut	Father	gas
after	baby	bus	Dad	find	gave
ago	bad	but	did	fire	get
almost	be	by	dog	first	gets
also	bed	came	dogs	fish	girl
an	before	can	end	five	girls

and	being	candy	even	fix	go
any	best	car	ever	fun	God
anything	big	cars	every	game	going
at	both	cat	fast	games	got
grade	it	made	only	she	try
grader	its	man	or	ship	trying
had	job	many	over	shot	united
hard	jump	me	parents	sister	until
having	just	men	park	sit	up
he	lady	Mom	party	so	upon
help	land	more	planet	sport	very
her	last	morning	problem	sports	want
him	later	most	put	start	wanted
hit	let	music	ran	started	war
home	life	my	red	states	water
horse	live	name	rest	stop	we
horses	lived	named	ride	store	went
hope	lives	never	riding	story	win
hot	long	no	run	time	winter
I	lost	not	same	times	wish
if	lot	ok	scared	told	with
important	lots	old	set	top	yard
in	mind	on	seventh	trip	yes

Long vowel/silent e in a suffix: ate, came, fire, five, game, gave, grade, home, horse, hope, life, live (long i), made, more, name, ride, same, state, store, time

Long e or i spelled with -y suffix: baby, candy, every, family, finally, funny, happy, lady, only, ready, really, story, try

K sound spelled C: call, called, came, can, candy, car, care, cars, cat, cut

LOGICAL SPELLING EXCEPTIONS

K sound spelled k: ask, asked, back, bike, black, book, books, broke, homework, keep, kept, kids, killed, kind, like, liked, likes, look, looked, looking, make, making, park, pick, sick, take, talk, talking, think, took, walk, walked, walking, week, weeks, woke, work

-ER sound spelled -or: work, world

Silent -e after a short vowel: some, someone, something, sometimes, where, favorite

DEVIANT LETTER PATTERNS

Beginning consonants: CH-: school, schools, **KN-:** knew, know, **WH-:** what, where, which, while, white, who, whole, why

Vowel combinations: -AI-: afraid, air, hair, said, **-AL-:** animal, finally, **-AU-:** because, **-AUGH-:** caught, **-AW-:** saw, **-AY-:** always, day, days, Friday, may, maybe, play, played, playing, say, stay, today, way, **-EA-:** bear, clean, dream, each, earth, eat, great, head, heard, lean, leave, mean, read, ready, real, really, reason, sea, speak, teach, teacher, teachers, team, year, years, **-EAU-:** beautiful, **-EE-:** been, feel, keep, need, see, seen, sleep, street, three, tree, trees, week, weeks, **-EI-:** their, **-EIGH-:** eighth, **-EO-:** people, **-EW-:** few, knew, new, **-EY-:** money, they, they're, **-EYE-:** eye, **-IE-:** believe, died, field, friend, friends, tried, **-IGH-:** fight, high, might, right, **-OA-:** boat, **-OE-:** doesn't, goes, **-OU-:** about, around, could, couldn't, country, found, four, ground, group, hour, house, mouse, our, oust, out, outside, should, without, would, wouldn't, you, your, you're, **-OUGH:** enough, thought, through, **-OW-:** down, grow, how, now, own, show, snow, **-OY-:** boy, boys, **-UI-:** build, **-UY-:** buy

Ending consonants: -CE: since, **-CK:** back, black, pick, sick, **-GE:** charge, **-LD:** world, would, wouldn't, **-LK:** talk, talking, walk, walked, walking, **-PT:** except, kept, **-TCH:** catch, watch, **-WO-:** two

Double letter pattern words: -DD-: sudden, suddenly, **-EE-:** been, feel, feet, free, keep, need, see, seen, sleep, street, three, tree, trees, week, weeks, **-FF-:** different, off, stuff, **-LL-:** all, ball, balloon, baseball, call, called, fell, finally, football, hill, killed, really, small, still, tell, well, will, **-MM-:** summer, swimming, **-NN-:** dinner, funny, running, **-OO-:** balloon, book, books, door, food, football, good, look, looked, room, roost, root, school, school, soon, too, took, look, looked, room, school, schools, soon, too, took, **-PP-:** happened, happy, stopped, **-SS-:** class, miss, **-TT-:** better, getting, little, pretty

OTHER PATTERNS

Capitalized words: America, Christmas, Dad, Father, Friday, God, I, I'd, I'm, Mom, Mr., Mrs., Thanksgiving

Contractions: can't, couldn't, didn't, doesn't, don't, he's, it's, I'd, I'm, let's, that's, they're, wouldn't, you're

Schwa spellings: another, become, Christmas, circus, come, comes, coming, done, front, love, responsibilities, some, someone, something, sometimes, the, upon, won

Z sound spelled s: as, has, his, he's, games, kids, was, wasn't, years

B

Example Words Illustrating Multiple Spellings of the Schwa Sound

See page(s) 44–48

A: About, bAnanA, cAnal, zebrA, buffAlo, washAble
AI: villAIn, certAIn, mountAIn, reconnaissance, RenAIssance
E: cohErent, legEnd, corrEspondent, squirrEl, vaEntine compEtent
EA: pagEAnt
EI: soverEIgn, forfEIt
EO: pigEOn, bludgEOn
I: anImal, busIly, candIdate, dilIgent, eligIble, invIsible, maxImum, purIfy, qualIfy regIment sensItive terrIble unanImous vehIcle
IA: parlIAment
IE: ancIEnt conscIEnce deficIEnt efficIEnt impatIEnt proficIEnt sufficIEnt quotIEnt
IO: admissIOn additIOn
O: bishOp, carrOt, develOp, ebOny, fathOm, gruesOme, hammOck, lemOn, methOd, periOd, secOnd, wisdOm
OI: porpOIse, tortOIse
U: albUm, calciUm, facUlty, maximUm, sUbmerge, sUbscription, thesaurUs, ukUlele
Y: analYsis, ethYl, methYl, phYsician

173

C

A Source List of Multisyllable Words
for Further Logical Spelling Practice

See page(s) 57–61.

abdication	ambiguity	crocodile	formulate	micrometer
abdomen	animosity	delectable	heterogeneous	monotonous
ability	antagonism	deplorable	hospitable	nonconformist
abnormality	arbitration	diplomatic	impudent	obliterate
abominable	arsenic	disparity	indoctrinate	orthopedic
abomination	aspiration	domesticate	instantaneous	palpitate
absorption	benediction	economist	juxtapose	pantomime
acrobat	carnivorous	elaboration	lubricate	pestiferous
adaptability	contemporaneous	entomology	malnutrition	propaganda
administration	contemptible	exonerate	memorandum	prosperous
adversity	convocation	forensic	meritorious	rendition
reputable	scrupulous	terminology	unanimity	viscosity
revocation	soporific	transfiguration	verisimilitude	voluminous
salamander	strangulation	trigonometry	vindication	vulnerable

D

Student Assignment Sheets to Reinforce
Logical Spelling Principles

See page(s) 62–63.

LOGICAL SPELLING PRACTICE

Directions: Following are twenty words from your Logical Spelling Practice Test. The first word in each numbered item is the word's correct spelling, and the rest are its misspellings, which are poor guesses. For each illogically spelled guess, circle the part(s) in the word that make(s) the word a wrong guess. If the poor guess fails to have a spelling for a syllable, place an "X" where the syllable should have been. Be ready to explain your reasons for circled parts and X's.

1. magnanimous: magnanuhmous magnanomus magnaenimous magnannimous
2. declamatory: dauclametory declametoree duklamitory daclamitorie
3. indefatigable: indafatugabul indofatygable indufaitigable
4. criminology: krimanology crimiknology crimanaloge
5. interpretation: inturpruhtation interpratashun intirprataytion inturpration
6. combustible: cumbustable comebustoble combusstible
7. meritorious: maruhtoreous marutoreus marritoreous
8. adversary: adversary adversairy addversary

177

9. contemptible: kuntemptoble contemptuhble contemptabal
10. aspiration: aspearation aspperation asperaition aspirashun
11. ambiguity: ambagooity ambiguatee ammbiguoty
12. pestiferous: pestiferous pestiferous pastiferous
13. delectable: delektible delecble dalectabul
14. animosity: anuhmosaty animosity animositie anmosity
15. benediction: benydiction bennidiction benadicsion benaydiction
16. contemporaneous: chuntemporaneous contemporaneous cuntempouraneous conteimporaneous
17. abnormality: abbnormaluty abnoarmality abnormaliaty abnorrmalutee
18. heterogeneous: heturogeaneous heturrogenious heterohgenious heturogeneus
19. luciferous: lusifurus lusifferous luceofurous
20. arbitration: arebatration arbitraytion arbitrashun arbitration

SPELLING "ALTERCATION"

Directions: Place a check mark in the blank if the spelling of "altercation" is a good guess; place an "X" in the blank if the spelling is a bad guess. For each "bad guess," circle each part in the word that makes the spelling a bad guess.

1. _____ alterecayhshoin
2. _____ allterkation
3. _____ altercation
4. _____ allterkation
5. _____ allterkaishon
6. _____ altercation
7. _____ aliterkation
8. _____ alltercashen
9. _____ alterkation
10. _____ alturkation
11. _____ alturcashun
12. _____ alwrhashion
13. _____ aultercation

14. _____ altercation
15. _____ allterkation
16. _____ artarkation
17. _____ aulterkation
18. _____ altercation
19. _____ alturcation
20. _____ altercaition

E

Student Assignment for Answering Questions on Logical Spelling Principles

Directions: Answer each of the following questions in COMPLETE SENTENCES. Turn each question into a STATEMENT and REPEAT ALL INFORMATION given in the question. Give the correct answer in each sentence you compose. You may use your handout on "Logical Spelling Basics."

1. What is/are the maximum number of vowel(s) a student should guess when spelling a syllable logically?
2. What letter in English can sometimes act as a vowel but should never be guessed when logically spelling a vowel sound?
3. What does a straight line mean when placed directly over a major vowel? How should a vowel with a long mark over it be logically spelled?
4. What specific letters of the alphabet would be good guesses for spelling the schwa sound—an "uh" sound?
5. What letter should a student spell for a "K" sound?
6. What are four common suffix patterns that we have studied?
7. How is a long vowel consonant pattern spelled when it is the ending syllable in a word?

Bonus: How are the strategies we have learned to spell words logically similar to the strategies used by a successful gambler?

F

Word Bank of Words Containing
Deviant Letter Patterns

See page(s) 81–82.

BEGINNING SYLLABLE CONSONANTS

CH-: chagrin, chaos, character, chef, chemical, chivalry, chloride, choral, chord, chorus, christen, chrome, chute, machine, parachute

CZ-: czar

GH-: ghost, ghastly, ghetto, ghoul, spaghetti

GN-: gnash, gnat, gnaw, gnome, gnarl, gnu

GU-: guarantee, guard, guerrilla, guess, guest, guild, guillotine, guilt, guise, guitar

KN-: knack, knapsack, knave, knead, knee, kneel, knew, knickers, knife, knight, kneel, knit, knob, knock, knot, know, knowledge, knuckle

LL-: llama

MN-: mnemonics

PH-: alphabet, elephant, emphasis, geography, hyphen, microphone, nephew, orphan, pamphlet, phantom, phase, pheasant, phenomenon, philanthropic, philology

philosophy, phone, phonics, phony, photo, photogenic, photograph, phrase, physical, physician, physics, prophet, sphinx, symphony, telephone

PN-: pneumonia

PS-: psalm, pseudo, pseudonym, psychic, psychiatry, psychology

PT-: ptomaine

QU-: acquit, banquet, conquest, inquire, lacquer, liquid, liquor, quack, quad, quadruple, quail, quaint, quake, quake, qualify, quality, qualm, quantity, quarantine, quarrel, quart, quarter, queen, queer, quell, quench, query, quest, question, quick, quiet, quill, quilt, quip, quit, quite, quiver, quiz, quota, quotation, quote, request, require, squabble, squad, squalid, square, squash, squat, squeak, squid, squint, squirm, tequila

RH-: rhapsody, rhetoric, rheumatic, rhododendron, rhinoceros, rhubarb, rhinestone, rhomboid, rhyme, rhythm

SC-: adolescent, ascend, ascertain, conscious, convalescent, descend, discipline, fascinate, incandescent, irascible, luscious, muscle, obscene, reminiscent, resuscitate, scene, scenery, scent, scepter, science, scientific, scientist, scintillating, scissors, unconscious

SCH-: scheme, scholar, scholastic, school, schooner, Schnauzer, schwa

SW-: answer, sword

TH-: thyme

TW-: two

WH-: whack, whale, wharf, what, wheat, wheel, when, where, whether, which, while, whim, whine, whip, whirl, whisk, whisker, whiskey, whisper, whistle, white, whiz, who, whole, whom, whose, why

WR-: wrack, wrangle, wrap, wrath, wreath, wreck, wren, wrench, wrestle, wriggle, wring, wrinkle, wrist, write, wrong, wrote, wrought, wrung

VOWEL COMBINATIONS

-AE-: aesthetic, algae

-AI-: abstain, afraid, again, aid, aim, air, appraise, avail, bail, bait, bargain, braid, brain, certain, chain, chair, chaise, claim, cocaine, contain, curtain, detail, detain, drain, entertain, exclaim, explain, fail, faint, fair, flail, fountain, frail, gain, gait, grail, grain, hail, hair, jail, laid, maid, mail, main, maintain, mountain, nail, obtain, paid, pain, paint, pair, plain, porcelain, praise, quaint, raid, rail, rain, raise, remain, refrain, said, sail, saint, slain, snail, sprain, staid, straight, stain, stair, strain, strait, tail, taint, trail, train, trait, vain, waif, wail, waist, wait, waitress, waive, villain

-AIGH-: straight

-AU-: applaud, auction, audible, audio, audit, aunt, author, auto, autopsy, autumn because, cauliflower, cause, caution, cautious, clause, exhaust, faucet, fault, fraud, gauge, gaunt, gauze, haul, haunt, jaunt, laugh, launch, laundry, maudlin, maul, nautical, pauper, pause, plausible, saucer, sauce, sausage, taunt, taut, thesaurus, vault

-AUGH-: caught, daughter, distraught, fraught, haughty, (laugh), naught, naughty, slaughter, taught

-AW-: awful, claw, bawl, brawl, brawn, crawl, dawn, drawl, draw, fawn, gawk, gnaw, hawk, jaw, law, lawn, pawn, raw, saw, scrawl, shawl, straw, thaw, yawn

-AY-: always, away, bay, clay, day, dismay, gay, hay, lay, may, pay, play, pray, ray, repay, say, spray, stay, sway, today, tray, way

-EA-: already, beach, bead, beak, beam, bean, bear, beast, beat, bleak, bleak, bread, break, breast, breath, clean, clear, creak, cream, crease, dead, deaf, deal, dealt, dear, dread, dream, dreamt, each, ear, earl, early, earn, earnest, earth, east, eat, fear, feast, feat, flea, gear, gleam, glean, grease, great, head, heal, health, heap, hear, heard, hearse, heart, hearth, heat, heathen, heave, instead, jealous, lead, leaf, leak, lean, leap, learn, lease, least, leather, leave, meal, mean, meant, meat, near, neat, pea, peace, peak, pear, pearl, peat, plea, plead, please, pleat, read, real, reap, rehearse, scream, sea, seal, seam, search, seat, smear, sneak, speak, spear, spread, steady, steak, steal, steam, streak, stream, swear, sweat, tea, teach, teak, tear, tease, thread, threat, tread, treasure, treat, veal, weak, wealth, wean, weapon, wear, weave, weave, wheat, yea, year, yearn, yeast

-EAU-: beau, beautiful, beauty, bureau, plateau, tableau, trousseau

-EE-: agree, bee, beef, beep, beer, beet, bleed, breed, breeze, career, cheek, cheer, creed, creek, creep, deed, deem, deep, deer, eel, eerie, engineer, exceed, fee, feed, feel, feet, flee, fleet, free, freeze, geese, glee, greed, green, greet, heed, heel, jeep, jeer, keen, keep, leer, meek, meet, need, peek, peel, peep, peer, peeve, queen, queer, reed, reef, reek, reel, screen, see, seed, seek, seem, seen, seep, sheer, sixteen, sleep, sleet, sleeve, sneer, sneeze, speed, spleen, spree, steed, steel, steer, street, succeed, sweep, sweet, tee, teeth, tree, tweed, tweeze, wee, weed, week, weep, wheel, wheeze

-EI-: beige, caffeine, ceiling, conceit, conceive, deceit, deceive, either, foreign, heir, leisure, neither, perceive, protein, receipt, rein, seize, their, veil, vein, weird

-EIGH-: eight, eighteen, freight, height, neigh, neighbor, sleigh, sleight, weigh, weight

-EO-: jeopardy, leopard, people, theory, yeoman

-ET-: ballet, beret, bouquet, buffet, crochet, croquet, gourmet, ricochet

-EW-: blew, brew, chew, curfew, dew, drew, few, flew, grew, hewn, lewd, mildew, new, pew, screw, sew, slew, stew, threw

-EU-: amateur, chauffeur, deuce, entrepreneur, eugenics, eulogy, feud, feudal, grandeur, maneuver, neutral, neutron, rheumatic, saboteur, sleuth, therapeutic

-EY-: alley, chimney, convey, donkey, grey, hockey, honey, jockey, journey, key, kidney, money, monkey, obey, osprey, parsley, prey, survey, they, trolley, turkey, valley, volley

-EYE-: eye

-IA-: parliament, Pennsylvania, Virginia

-IE-: believe, brief, chief, die, field, fiend fierce, friend, grief, grieve, lie, niece, pie, piece, pier, pierce, priest, relieve, relieve, retrieve, shield, shriek, siege, thief, tie, yield

-IEU-: adieu, lieu, lieutenant

-IGH-: blight, bright, delight, fight, flight, fright, knight, high, light, might, night, plight, right, sigh, sight, slight, thigh, tight

-OA-: bloat, board, boast, boat, broad, cloak, coach, coal, coarse, coast, coat, coax, float, foal, foam, gloat, goal, goat, groan, hoarse, hoax, load, loaf, loan, moan, moat, oaf, oak, oar, oat, oath, poach, roach, road, roar, roast, soak, soap, soar, throat, toad, toast

-OE-: canoe, doe, foe, hoe, roe, shoe, toe, woe

-OI-: boil, broil, choice, choir, coil, coin, disappoint, exploit, foil, hoist, join, joint, moist, oil, point, poise, poison, soil, spoil, tabloid, toil, toilet, voice, void

-OO-: blood, bloom, boo, boob, book, boom, boost, boot, booth, booze, brood, brook, broom, choose, cook, cool, coon, coop, crook, doom, drool, droop, flood, food, fool, foolish, foot, gloom, good, goof, goose, groom, hood, hoof, hook, hoop, hoot, look, loom, loop, loose, loot, maroon, mood, moon, moose, nook, nook, noon, noose, oops, ooze, poof, pool, poor, proof, roof, room, roost, root, school, scoop, shook, shoot, snoop, snoot, snooze, soon, soot, spook, spool, spoon, stood, stool, stoop, swoon, swoop, too, took, tool, toot, tooth, troop, wood, woof, wool, zoo, zoom

-OU-: amour, boulder, bounce, bound, bout, cloud, clout, couch, could, count, countess, countless, country, couple, coupon, course, court, cousin, crouch, devour, double, doubt, dour, flour, flourish, foul, found, four, gourmet, gout, ground, group, hound, hour, house, joust, loud, mould, mound, mount, mourn, mouth, noun, nourish, ounce, our, oust, out, pound, pour, pout, proud, rouge, round, route, scour, scout, should, shoulder, shout, snout, soul, sound, soup, sour, spout, sprout, stout, touch, tour, trouble, trout, vouch, would, wound, you, young, your, youth

-OUGH: although, bough, bought, brought, cough, dough, drought, (enough), fought, ought, plough, (rough), sought, though, thorough, thought, (tough), through, wrought

-OW-: allow, arrow, below, bellow, blow, blown, borrow, bow, bowl, brow, brown chow, clown, cow, crow, crown, down, drown, elbow, fellow, flow, flown, flower, follow, fowl, frown, glow, gown, grow, growl, grown, hollow, how, howl, know, known, low, meadow, mellow, mow, now, owl, own, pillow, plow, prowl, row, scowl, shadow, show, shown, slow, snow, sorrow, sow, sparrow, stow, swallow, throw, tomorrow, tow, town, vow, wallow, willow, widow, window, wow, yellow

-OY-: annoy, boy, convoy, coy, deploy, destroy, employ, enjoy, joy, loyal, ploy, toy

-UE-: avenue, blue, clue, construe, cue, due, flue, fondue, glue, hue, pursue, rescue, revue, subdue, sue, true, value

-UI-: biscuit, bruise, build, circuit, cruise, fruit, guide, guild, guilt, guitar, juice, nuisance, pursuit, suit

-UO-: buoyant

-UY-: buy, guy

-Y-: abyss, acronym, amethyst, analyze, antonym, asylum, bicycle, chrysanthemum, crypt, crystal, cycle, cyclone, cymbal, cynic, cypress, cyst, dehydrate, dynamic, dynamite, dynamo, dynasty, dysfunction, enzyme, gym, gymnastic, gypsy, gyrate, gyroscope, homonym, hyacinth, hybrid, hydra, hydrant, hydrochloric, hydrogen, hydroplane, hygiene, hymn, hypercritical, hyphen, hypnosis, hypothetical, hysterical, lymph, lynch, lynx, lyre, martyr, myopia, myriad, mystery, mystic, myth, mythology, nylon, nymph, oxygen, papyrus, paralyze, physical, physics, pseudonym, psychiatry, psychic, psycho, pygmy, python, rhyme, rhyme, rhythm, style, stylus, syllable, syllabus, symbol, symmetry, sympathize, sympathy, symphony, symposium, symptom, synonym, syntax, synthesis, synthetic, syrup, system systemic, thyme, thymus, thyroid, type, typhoid, typhus, typical, typify, tyranny, tyrant, vinyl, zygote

-YE-: bye, dye, lye, rye

ENDING SYLLABLE CONSONANTS

-BT: debt, doubt, subtle

-CCH: saccharin

-CE: ace, advice, dance, device, face, mice, nice, pence, place, police, practice, price, race, space

-CHE: cache, mustache

-CHT: yacht

-CK: attack, back, black, block, brick, buck, bucket, check, chick, clack, click, clock, cluck, cock, crack, crick, crock, deck, dock, duck, flack, fleck, flick, flock, hack, hick, jack, kick, knock, lack, lick, lock, luck, mock, muck, neck, nick, pack, peck, pick, pluck, pock, prick, prick, rack, rack, rock, rock, sack, shack, shock, shock, sick, slack, slick, smack, smock, snack, sock, speck, stack, stick, stock, struck, stuck, suck, tack, thick, tick, track, trick, truck, whack, wick, wreck

-CT: duct, indict, fact, pact, tact, tract, subtract, strict

-DGE: badge, bridge, budge, dodge, dredge, edge, fudge, grudge, hedge, judge, ledge, lodge, nudge, pledge, ridge, smudge, wedge

-FT: adrift, bereft, cleft, craft, deft, draft, drift, gift, left, lift, loft, often, raft, rift, shaft, shift, soft, soften, swift, theft, thrift

-GE: binge, cringe, fringe, hinge, lunge, plunge, singe, twinge

-GH: laugh, rough, tough, cough

-GM: diaphragm, phlegm, paradigm

-GN: align, assign, benign, cologne, design, feign, malign, reign, sign

-GUE: harangue, meringue, plague, tongue

-LD: bald, bold, child, cold, could, fold, held, hold, meld, mild, mold, old, scald, scold, should, sold, told, weld, wild, world, would

-LK: balk, calk, chalk, stalk, talk, walk, yolk

-LM: balm, calm, palm, salmon

-MB: bomb, climb, comb, crumb, dumb, jamb, lamb, limb, plumb, numb, thumb, succumb, thumb, tomb, womb

-MN: autumn, column, condemn, solemn, hymn

-PH: enough, epitaph, graph, laugh, paragraph, rough, tough, sophomore, telegraph, triumph

-PT: accept, adept, concept, crept, except, inept, interrupt, kept, precept, rapt, receipt, script, slept, swept, wept

-QUE: antique, baroque, brusque, burlesque, clique, critique, grotesque, mosque, oblique, opaque, physique, picturesque, pique, plaque, statuesque, technique, torque, unique

-SP: raspberry

-SS: bass, bless, bliss, boss, brass, chess, class, crass, cross, dress, floss, fuss, glass, gloss, grass, gross, hiss, kiss, less, loss, mass, mess, miss, moss, muss, pass, press, puss

-ST: apostle, bristle, bustle, castle, chestnut, christen, fasten, glisten, gristle, hustle, listen, mistletoe, moisten, rustle, thistle, whistle, wrestler

-TCH: ditch, etch, fetch, hatch, hatchet, hitch, hutch, itch, kitchen, latch, match, notch, patch, pitch, ratchet, satchel, scotch, scratch, sketch, snatch, stitch, stretch, switch, thatch, twitch, watch, witch, wretch

-TZ: waltz

-ZZ: buzz, fuzz, jazz

G

Word Bank of Words Containing Double Consonants

b spelled bb—occurs 2.7 percent of the time (733)

abbey	dabble	hubbub	rabble	shrubbery
bobbin	dribble	jabber	ribbon	stubble
cabbage	ebb	lobby	robber	tabby
chubby	flabby	nibble	rubbish	wobble
cobbler	gobble	rabbit	scribble	

d spelled dd—occurs 1.99 percent of the time (756)

add	fodder	muddle	riddle	sudden
addict	giddy	odd	rudder	swaddle
additive	goddess	paddle	ruddy	toddle
bladder	griddle	paddock	saddle	waddle
coddle	haddock	peddle	shoddy	
daddy	huddle	pudding	shudder	
eddy	ladder	puddle	sodden	
fiddle	meddle	riddance	straddle	

f spelled ff—occurs 8.8 percent of the time (768)

affair	affront	cliff	effusive	official
affection	bluff	cuff	fluff	puff

affiliate	buff	diffuse	guffaw	skiff
affirm	buffet	efface	huff	staff
affix	chauffeur	effect	off	stiff
afford	chiffon	efficient	offend	stuff
suffice	suffix			

g spelled gg—occurs 4.99 percent of the time (778)

aggressive	dogged	jagged	luggage	smuggle
aggrieve	doggerel	jigger	maggot	snuggle
aggravate	druggist	joggle	nugget	stagger
baggage	egg	joggle	rigging	straggle
baggy	giggle	juggle	rugged	struggle
beggar	goggle	juggler	shaggy	wiggle
chigger	haggard	laggard	sluggard	
dagger	haggle	legging	shaggy	

k spelled cc—occurs 1.61 percent of the time (820)

acclaim	accord	accuracy	occasion	stucco
acclimate	accordion	accuse	occupant	succor
accolade	accost	broccoli	occur	succumb
accommodate	account	buccaneer	piccolo	tobacco
accompaniment	accrue	hiccup	raccoon	
accompany	accumulate	impeccable	staccato	
accomplish	accursed	moccasin	streptococcus	

l spelled ll—occurs 9.07 percent of the time (853)

all	allegory	alley	allot	allusion
allay	allegro	allied	allow	ally
allegation	allergy	alligator	allude	appall
allegorical	alleviate	allocate	allure	appellate
armadillo	cellular	dollar	gallant	jelly
artillery	celluloid	drill	gallantry	jolly
ball	cerebellum	droll	galleon	kill

ballistics	challenge	dull	gallery	knell
balloon	chancellor	dwell	gallon	knoll
bell	chenille	ebullient	gallop	mall
belle	chill	ellipse	gill	malleable
bellicose	chlorophyll	elliptical	gorilla	mallet
belligerent	collaborate	embellish	grill	marshmallow
bellow	collapse	enroll	gull	maxilla
belly	collate	enthrall	hall	medallion
bill	collateral	fall	hello	mellow
brilliance	colleague	fallacious	hill	miller
bull	collect	fallible	holly	millennium
bullet	college	farewell	idyllic	millionaire
bulletin	collegiate	fellow	ill	mollify
call	collide	fill	illuminate	mollusk
calligraphy	collision	fillet	illustrate	nullification
cancellation	constellation	follow	illustration	nullify
cell	cotillion	folly	infallible	nutshell
cellar	disillusion	frill	install	pallet
cello	distill	full	intellect	pallor
cellophane	doll	gall	intelligence	parallel
pellet	rebellion	skillet	swollen	vanilla
penicillin	rill	skull	syllable	vaudeville
pillow	roller	small	syllabus	villain
pollen	satellite	smell	tall	volley
pollination	scallop	spell	tally	wall
propellant	scroll	spill	tell	wallet
propeller	sell	stall	toll	wallop
pull	shall	stallion	tranquility	wallow
pullet	shallow	stellar	trellis	well
pulley	shell	still	trillion	will
quell	shilling	sullen	trolley	yell
quill	silly	surveillance	umbrella	yellow
rally	skill	swell	valley	

m spelled mm—occurs 3.99 percent of the time (878)

accommodation	commencement	commission	community	hammer
ammonia	commensurate	committee	commuter	hammock
ammunition	comment	commode	dilemma	immaculate
backgammon	commentary	commodity	excommunicate	immense
clammy	commerce	commotion	flammable	immerse
comma	commerce	commune	gimmick	immigration
commandeer	commercial	communicable	glimmer	imminent
commander	commingle	communication	grammar	immolate
commemoration	commiserate	communion	grammarian	immortal
immunity	mammal	recommend	stammer	summon
immutable	mammoth	rummage	summarize	symmetrical
inflammable	persimmon	scrimmage	summer	symmetry
inflammation	plummet	simmer	summit	

n spelled nn—occurs 1.65 percent of the time (915)

annex	banner	connive	innovation	skinny
annihilate	cannibalism	connoisseur	innuendo	spinner
annihilation	cannon	connote	kennel	sunny
annotate	cayenne	cranny	mannequin	tennis
announcement	centennial	cunning	mannerism	tunnel
annoyance	channel	dinner	mayonnaise	uncanny
annuity	cinnamon	flannel	penniless	whinny
annual	colonnade	funnel	personnel	zinnia
annul	comedienne	inner	pinnacle	
antenna	connect	innocence	reconnaissance	
bandanna	connection	innocuous	reconnoiter	

p spelled pp—occurs 4.42 percent of the time (939)

appall	appellate	appertain	applicable	apposition
apparatus	appellation	appetite	application	appraisal
apparel	appendage	applaud	apply	appreciable
apparition	appendicitis	applause	appointment	appreciation
appeal	appendix	apple	apportion	apprehend
appearance	apperception	appliance	appose	apprehension
apprentice	frippery	opposite	snappy	suppose

approach	grapple	opposition	strapping	supposition
appropriate	guppy	oppressive	supper	suppress
approval	happy	pepper	supplant	upper
approximate	hippopotamus	poppy	supplement	zipper
approximation	opponent	poppy	supplementary	
appurtenance	opportune	puppet	supplication	
cripple	opportunity	slipper	supply	
flippant	opposable	slippery	supporter	

r spelled rr—occurs 2.20 percent of the time (982)

abhorrence	barrier	correlate	ferret	irrelevant
arraign	berry	correlate	flurry	irresolute
arrangement	bizarre	corridor	garrison	irritate
array	borrow	corrosive	garrulous	marriage
arrear	burr	corrugate	herring	marry
arrest	carriage	corruption	horrendous	merriment
arrival	carrion	currant	horrible	merry
arrogance	carrousel	current	horrid	morrow
barrack	cherry	curriculum	horrify	narrate
barrage	concurrence	derrick	horror	narrative
barrel	corral	deterrent	hurricane	porridge
barren	correct	embarrass	incorrigible	recurrence
barrette	correction	erratic	interrogate	resurrection
scurrilous	sorrow	surround	terrible	warranty
serrated	sparrow	terrace	territory	warren
sherry	squirrel	terrain	terror	warrior
sierra	stirrup	terrapin	unerring	worry
sorrel	surrender	terrestrial	warrant	

s spelled ss—occurs 6.98 percent of the time (1,015)

abyss	assertion	bliss	connoisseur	dissolution
access	assessment	boss	countess	distressful
accessible	assignation	brass	crass	dress
across	assignment	caress	cross	duress
actress	assimilation	casserole	cutlass	egress
address	assistance	cessation	delicatessen	embarrass

admissible	associate	cesspool	demitasse	embassy
aggressive	association	chess	discuss	emboss
albatross	assorted	classification	dismissal	empress
ambassador	assuage	colossal	dissection	enchantress
assailant	assault	colossus	dissent	essay
assassin	assume	commissary	dissertation	essential
assassinate	assumption	commission	dissident	expressive
assassination	bass	compress	dissident	finesse
assay	bassinet	compress	dissipated	floss
assemble	bassoon	confess	dissipation	fossil
assent	bless	congress	dissociate	fossil
fricassee	impassable	missile	passage	profess
fuss	impossibility	molasses	passive	puissant
glass	impress	moss	permissible	recessive
gloss	kiss	mussel	pessimism	reconnaissance
gossip	lass	narcissism	pessimistic	sassafras
grass	less	necessary	possess	stress
gross	loss	necessitate	possessive	submissive
harass	mass	opossum	possibility	successful
hassock	massage	oppressive	possible	suppress
hiss	messenger	ossify	potassium	transgress
trousseau				

t spelled tt—occurs 2.77 percent of the time (1,068)

acquittal	attire	battle	cattle	ditty
admittance	attitude	betterment	chattel	embattle
attach	attorney	bitter	cigarette	flutter
attack	attract	blotter	clatter	gazette
attainable	attraction	bottle	clutter	ghetto
attempt	attribute	bottom	committee	gutter
attendance	attribute	brittle	confetti	intermittent
attention	attune	butter	cottage	jettison
attenuate	barrette	buttock	cotton	kettle
attest	battalion	button	cutter	kitten
attic	batter	buttress	dilettante	latter
lattice	petticoat	rattle	settle	spatter
little	pittance	rebuttal	shatter	splutter

matter	platter	regatta	shutter	squatter
mattress	poinsettia	remittance	shuttle	statuette
mettle	pottage	rosette	skittish	tattoo
operetta	prattle	roulette	smitten	throttle
pattern	pretty	settee	spaghetti	transmitter

Words containing two or more double consonants:

accessible	appall	commissary	connoisseur	oppressive
accommodate	appellate	commission	embarrass	possessive
address	assassin	commission	millennium	reconnaissance
aggressive	barrette	committee	oppressive	suppress

H

List of Tongue Twisters in Alphabetical Order According to Each Twister's Beginning Consonant

See page(s) 105–106.

1. "Bad Blood"—Say it ten times very quickly.
2. Banishing blight brings bliss beyond belief.
3. Beatrice baked the beans in Betty's brown bowl.
4. Better buy the bigger rubber baby buggy bumpers.
5. Betty Botta bought a bit o' butter. "But," said she, "this butter's bitter. If I put it in my batter, it will make my batter bitter." So Betty Botta bought a bit o' better butter and put it in her bitter batter, which made Betty Botta's bitter batter a bit better.
6. Big black bug bit big black bear; big black bug made big black bear bleed.
7. Big blue beans in a brown blown bladder.
8. Bill Bord had a board bill and a billboard. Both the board bill and the billboard bored Bill Bord. So Bill Bord sold the billboard to pay his board bill and now neither the board bill nor the billboard will bore Bill Bord.
9. Bleak breezes blighted the bright blossoms.
10. Bloom, beauteous blossoms, budding bowers beneath.
11. Blushing Barbara booed boisterously while blind Bobby brought brilliant birds bright barbs.
12. Two bootblacks, one white and one black, were standing on the corner doing nothing with the white bootblack agreeing to black

the black bootblack's boots. The black bootblack was willing to have his boots blacked by his fellow bootblack, and the bootblack who had agreed to black the black bootblack's boots that blacked his boots.

13. Did you copper-bottom 'em sir? No, I aluminumed 'em, mum.
14. Hang the tablecloths close to the clothes and close the clothes basket.
15. The chop shop stocks chops.
16. Dainty Dora dawdles dreamily down the deck.
17. Double bubble gum bubbles double.
18. Fairy frolics fret foolish frumps for frightened frowns.
19. Fanny Finch fried five floundering fish for Francis Fowler's father.
20. I never felt felt feel flat like that felt felt.
21. Flesh of freshly fried flying fish.
22. The gasping gorilla, going on the gondola grasped the glossy gourd of goulash.
23. Give Grimes Jim's great gilt a gag whip.
24. Let the little lean camel lead the lame lamb to the lake.
25. Paula paid Polly a penny for a piece of peach pudding.
26. The proud protector protects proper property, providing publicity for the prudent.
27. Nine nimble noblemen nibbling nuts.
28. Round and round the rugged rocks the ragged rascal ran.
29. The scampish scalawag seldom scurries starboard.
30. The sea ceaseth and sufficeth us.
31. Seven shell-shocked soldiers sawing six slick, slender, slipper, silver saplings.
32. She sells seashells, sherry, and sand shoes by the sea shore.
33. She's so selfish she could sell shellfish shells; shellfish shells seldom sell.
34. Short, sharp, shock.
35. Shy Sally saw six Swiss wristwatches.
36. Silent Sue sees Sammy Sightless sounding simpering somethings.
37. Sinful Caesar sipped his soda and slippery syrup, seized his snoot, and sneezed.
38. Seated serenely on a satin sofa, Sister Susie sews silk socks and shirts for soldiers.

39. Sister Susie went to sea to see the sea you see. So the sea she saw you see was a saucy sea, a saucy sea saw she.
40. Mr. Shott and Mr. Nott agreed to fight a duel. Nott was shot and Shot was not, so it is better to Shott than Nott. Shott and not Nott shot the shot that shot Nott. If the shot that Shott shot, which shot Nott had shot Shott and not Nott, Shott instead of Nott would have been shot, and Nott would not.
41. He shouted short shrill shrieks, which shattered the shadowy night.
42. A skunk stood on a stump. The stump thunk the skunk stunk, but the skunk thunk the stump stunk.
43. This sixth sheik's sixth sheep is sick.
44. Six, slick, slim, slender silver saplings.
45. Sixty-two sick chicks sat on six slim slick slender saplings.
46. Slippery sleds slide smoothly down the sluiceway.
47. Some shun sunshine when the sun shines on shop signs and shabby shop windows.
48. Strange strategic statistics.
49. Strict, strong, Stephen Stringer slickly snare six sickly sill snakes.
50. Swan, swim over the sea. Swim, swan, swim. Swan, swim back again. Well swum, swan!
51. Two twin-screw steel cruisers.
52. Ten tiny toddling tots testily trying to train their tongues to trill.
53. Theophilus Thistle, the celebrated thistle sifter; thrust three thousand thistles through the thick of his thumb.
54. Theyssian Thyssel is a successful thistle sifter. He sifts sieves full of three thousand thistles through the thick of his thumb. If those thistle sifters who sift sieves of thistles think of Theyssian Thyssel, the successful thistle sifter, they will be successful at sifting thistle sieves.
55. Thomas Tattertoot took taut twine to tie ten twigs to two tall trees.
56. Tight Tommy toddled toward two towns.
57. A tutor who tooted the flute tried to tutor two tooters to toot. Said the two to the tutor, "Is it harder to toot or to tutor two tutors to toot?"
58. If to hoot and to toot and Hottentot tot were taught by a Hottentot tutor, should the tutor get hot if the Hottentot tot should hoot and toot at the tutor?

59. A tree toad loved a she-toad that lived up in a tree. She was a three-toed she-toad. The two-toed toad tried to win the she-toad's friendly nod, for the two-toed tree toad loved the ground the three-toed she-toad trod.

60. Washington's washwoman washed Washington's wash while Washington watched Wilson.

61. What whim let Whitey White whittle whistle, whisper, and whimper near the wharf where a whale might wheel and whirl.

62. Wondering Will wandered wearily while Watson wistfully whistled.

1

Spelling Rules Science Key

See page(s) 115–119.

1. Do you wish to make the word possessive?
   A. Yes—go to number 5.
   B. No—go to number 2.
2. Do you wish to make the word plural?
   A. Yes—go to number 7.
   B. No—go to number 3.
3. Do you wish to spell a word with -ie- or -ei-?
   A. Yes—go to number 14.
   B. No—go to number 4.
4. Do you wish to add a prefix?
   A. Yes—go to number 23.
   B. No—You must want to add a suffix! Go to number 16.
5. Is the word singular?
   A. Yes—add apostrophe s ('s).
   B. No—go to number 6.
6. Does the plural word end in the letter -s?
   A. Yes—add an apostrophe ONLY (').
   B. No—add apostrophe s ('s).
7. Does the word end in an "S" sound: s, -sh, -ch, -x, or -z?
   A. Yes—add the letters -es.
   B. No—go to number 8.

8. Does the word end in the letter -o?
   A. Yes—go to number 9.
   B. No—go to number 11.
9. Is the word a musical term?
   A. Yes—add the letter s.
   B. No—go to number 10.
10. Is there a vowel before the -o ending?
    A. Yes—add the letter s.
    B. No—there's a consonant! Add the letters -es.
11. Does the word end in the letter -y?
    A. Yes—go to number 12.
    B. No—go to number 13.
12. Is there a vowel before the -y ending?
    A. Yes—add the letter -s.
    B. No—there's a consonant! Change the -y to -i and add -es.
13. Does the word end in the letters -f or -fe?
    A. Yes—change the -f or -fe to -v and add -es.
    B. No—add the letter -s. Most plurals are formed this way!
14. Does the -ie-/-ei- combination have a long "A" sound?
    A. Yes—spell the word with -ei-.
    B. No—go to number 15.
15. Does the -ie-/-ei- combination have a letter "C" before it?
    A. Yes—spell the word with -ei-.
    B. No—spell the word with -ie-. More words use -ie- than -ei-.
16. Does the word end in a silent -e?
    A. Yes—go to number 19.
    B. No—go to number 17.
17. Does the word end in the letter -y?
    A. Yes—go to number 20.
    B. No—go to number 18.
18. Does the word end in ONE consonant?
    A. Yes—go to number 21.
    B. No—go to number 23.
19. Does the suffix begin with a vowel?
    A. Yes—drop the -e and add the suffix.
    B. No—go to number 23.

20. Does a consonant come before the ending -y?

    A. Yes—change the -y to -i and add the suffix.

    B. No—go to number 23.

21. Does the word have only ONE vowel before the ending consonant?

    A. Yes—go to number 22.

    B. No—go to number 23.

22. Does the suffix start with a vowel?

    A. Yes—double the final consonant and add the suffix.

    B. No—go to number 23.

23. Do not change the spelling of the word. Just add the affix. Most words are formed this way!

J

Word Bank for Application of Basic Spelling Rules

See page 119.

FOR FORMING POSSESSIVES

- **Singular words:** baby, beach, Bess, buffalo, calf, Carlos, chimney, Chris, church, city, class, donkey, Douglas, furnace, James, knife, library, patio, Phyllis, piano, scarf, secretary, soprano, thief, tomato, valley, wolf
- **Plural words:** babies, beaches, buffaloes, calves, children, chimneys, churches, cities, classes, donkeys, furnaces, knives, libraries, lice, mice, oxen, patios, pianos, scarves, secretaries, sopranos, thieves, tomatoes, valleys, wolves, women

FOR SPELLING PLURALS

- **-s ends:** arch, beach, box, bus, bush, buzz, church, class, crash, dish, fox, furnace, gas, glass, loss, mass, match, sandwich, tax, watch, wish
- **-o ends:** alto, banjo, buffalo, cameo, canto, cargo, concerto, contralto, echo, hero, mosquito, patio, piano, potato, radio, rodeo, solo, soprano, stereo, tomato, tornado, trio, volcano

- **-y ends:** activity, alley, army, baby, berry, chimney, city, country, cry, democracy, diary, donkey, duty, entry, family, fly, hobby, horse-fly, jury, key, lady, library, monkey, party, penny, pony, Saturday, secretary, sky, story, toy, treaty, turkey, valley
- **-f/fe ends:** calf, elf, half, knife, leaf, life, loaf, scarf, self, shelf, thief, wife, wolf

FOR SPELLING IE/EI WORDS

- **"i" before "e" in most words:** achieve, believe, brief, chief, die, field, fierce, friend, grief, grieve, handkerchief, hygiene, lie, mischief, niece, pie, piece, pier, priest, relief, relieve, retrieve, reverie, shield, shriek, siege, thief, tie, yield
- **"ei" after "c":** ceiling, conceit, conceive, deceit, deceive, perceive, receipt, receive
- **"ei" when sounds like the letter "A":** beige, eight, freight, heir, heiress, heirloom, neighbor, reign, rein, reindeer, sleigh, vein, weight

FOR ADDING PREFIXES AND/OR SUFFIXES

- **Prefixes:** ad-, de-, en-, il-, im-, in-, ir-, mis-, re-, un-
- **Suffixes:** -able, -ance, -ation, -ble, -ed, -ence, -er, -ful, -ible, -ily, -ing, -ion, -ior, -ist, -le, -less, -less, -like, -ly, -ment, -ness, -ous, -sion, -tion, -y

FOR ADDING A PREFIX AND/OR SUFFIX TO BASE WORDS

- **Silent e ends:** absolute, accuse, advantage, age, arrange, arrive, bake, behave, bite, blame, calculate, care, change, chase, charge, circle, close, combine, commence, come, courage, curve, decide, define, divide, drive, excite, explore, extreme, figure, grade, guide, hide, hope, invite, large, like, lone, love, manage, make, move, name, noise, notice, pale, peace, place, pleasure, polite, prepare, preserve, price, produce, promise, pronounce, propose, prove, provide, pure, purpose, race, raise, reduce, require, response, ride, ripe, rose, salute, salvage, save, score, separate, service, severe, shake, shape, shine, side, slide, slope, smile, sincere, snake, state, store, strike, stone, take, time, trace, trade, trouble, use, wave, write

- **Y ends:** apply, betray, bury, buy, carry, clarify, classify, clumsy, colony, cry, deny, delay, employ, empty, enjoy, falsify, fly, friendly, fry, fury, glory, happy, holy, hungry, hurry, identify, imply, magnify, marry, modify, noisy, notify, occupy, personify, play, plenty, pray, prey, portray, purify, qualify, rely, silly, spray, specify, story, study, supply, thirsty, vary, worry

K

Basic Spelling Rules in an Outline Format

See page(s) 121–122.

I. Forming Possessives
   A. Singular words, add an apostrophe before the -s (-'s).
      1. dog, dog's
      2. girl, girl's
   B. Plural words
      1. Those that end in "-s," add an apostrophe only (-s').
         a. teachers, teachers'
         b. boys, boys'
      2. Plural words that don't end in "-s," add an apostrophe and an s ('s).
         a. children, children's
         b. women, women's
II. For forming plurals
   A. Add "-s" to most words.
      1. card, cards
      2. book, books
   B. For "S" sound ends—s, -sh, -ch, -x, or -z—add -es.
      1. class, classes
      2. wish, wishes
      3. sandwich, sandwiches
      4. box, boxes
      5. buzz, buzzes

    C. For "O" end words

        1. If the word is a musical term, add -s.

            a. piano, pianos

            b. solo, solos

        2. If a vowel is before the -o, add -s.

            a. radio, radios

            b. patio, patios

        3. If a consonant is before the -o, add -es.

            a. buffalo, buffaloes

            b. cargo, cargoes

    D. For "Y" ends

        1. If a vowel comes before, add -s.

            a. monkey, monkeys

            b. toy, toys

        2. If a consonant comes before, change the -y to -i- and add -es.

            a. hobby, hobbies

            b. lady, ladies

    E. For "F" and "FE" end words, change -f- or -fe- to -v- and add -es.

        1. calf, calves

        2. half, halves

III. For spelling IE/EI words

    A. Most use -ie-.

        1. believe

        2. brief

    B. If a long A sound, spell -ei-.

        1. beige

        2. ein

    C. If after letter –c-, spell -ei-.

        1. receive

        2. ceiling

IV. For adding affixes

    A. When adding a prefix, do not change the spelling of the word.

        1. mis- + spell = misspell

        2. il- + legal = illegal

B. When adding suffixes
1. Most added suffixes do not change the spelling.
    a. equip + -ment = equipment
    b. depend + -able = dependable
2. When adding to silent e ends
    a. If the suffix begins with a vowel, drop the -e.
        (1) age + -ing = aging
        (2) use + -able = usable
    b. If the suffix begins with a consonant, keep the -e.
        (1) lone + -ly = lonely
        (2) advertise + -ment = advertisement
3. Adding to Y end words
    a. If a vowel comes before the -y, just add the suffix.
        (1) betray + -ed = betrayed
        (2) spray + -ing = spraying
    b. If a consonant comes before the -y, change the -y to -i- and add the suffix.
        (1) study + -es = studies
        (2) worry + -ed = worried
4. Three requirements for doubling a final consonant
    a. Word ends in a single consonant.
    b. A vowel immediately precedes the final consonant.
    c. Suffix begins with a vowel.
    d. Examples
        (1) trim + -er = trimmer
        (2) shop + -ing = shopping

L

Word Bank for Application of Spelling Rules for Doubling a Final Consonant

See page(s) 122–123.

Following are words in which spellings will result in doubling the final consonant when adding certain suffixes:

admit: admittance, admitted, admitting; allot: allotted, allotting, allotter; annul: annulled, annulling, annullable

begin: beginner, beginning

cancel: cancelling, cancelled, cancellation; commit: committable, committed, committing; compel: compelled, compelling, compellable; confer: conferred, conferring; control: controlled, controller, controlling

defer: deferred, deferring

infer: inferred, inferring; inter: interred, interring

kidnap: kidnapped, kidnapper, kidnapping

occur: occurred, occurring, occurrence; omit: omitted, omitting

patrol: patrolled, patroller, patrolling; prefer: preferred, preferring

recur: recurred, recurrence, recurring; refer: referred, referring; regret: regrettable, regretted, regretting; repel: repelled, repellent, repelling

submit: submitted, submitter, submitting

transfer: transferred, transferring

Students need to understand that the last syllable must continue to be stressed in the newly formed word to result in the final consonant doubling.

Adding the suffix -ence to the words "confer," "prefer," "refer," and "transfer" does not result in doubling their final consonants, because in each outcome the accent changes to the first syllable. "Preference," "reference," "conference," "transference" are, therefore, the correct resulting spellings for these words. The following words also do not produce doubled final consonants because the final syllable in each is not stressed:

develop: developed, developing
envelop: enveloped, enveloping
favor: favored, favoring, favorite; focus: focused, focusing
jewel: jeweled, jeweler
offer: offered, offering; order: ordered, ordering
pardon: pardoned, pardoning
suffer: suffered, sufferer, suffering
wallop: walloped, walloping; worship: worshiped, worshiping

A "Double or Not?" exercise should also include words that do not fulfill one of the three basic requirements for doubling a final consonant. One would be adding a suffix that begins with a consonant:

allot: allotment; annul: annulment
commit: commitment; compel: complement; confer: conferment
defer: deferment
inter: interment

Including several words that do not have a single vowel before the final consonant would also make students attend to the three basic requirements for doubling a final consonant:

afford: afforded, affording; appear: appearance, appeared, appearing
despair: despaired, despairing
earn: earned, earner, earning; equal: equaled, equaling
furnish: furnished, furnishing
intend: intended, intending
join: joined, joiner, joining
mail: mailed, mailer, mailing
open: opened, opener, opening

paint: painted, painter, painting; pick: picked, picker, picking
relent: relented, relenting; repeal: repealed, repealing
scream: screamed, screamer, screaming; sink: sinker, sinking; sleep: sleeper, sleeping; smash: smashed, smashing; squirt: squirted, squirting; stick: sticker, sticking
treat: treated, treating
wander: wandered, wanderer, wandering; work: worker, worked, working

For doubling the final consonant: bag, ban, bet, bid, big, bud, bug, cut, dip, drip, drop, drum, fit, flat, fur, grab, grin, hit, hop, hug, jog, mat, mop, mug, net, plan, pop, run, sad, set, ship, shop, slam, step, stop, swim, tap, thin, top, trap, trim, trip, tug

M

Word Bank of Exceptions to Basic Spelling Rules

See page(s) 123–125.

- **For forming plurals of words with -o ends:** autos, chefs, echoes, heroes, memos, pimentos, pros, potatoes, vetoes
- **Use the apostrophe and -s ('s) for plural forms of capitals and lowercase letters**—i's, o's, a's, u's; **for numbers**—1900's, 100's, three's; **for abbreviations followed by periods**—etc.'s, ibid.'s; **for words referred to as words**—and's, ain't's, plus's
- **Irregular plurals not formed by adding -s or -es:** alumna, alumnae; alumnus, alumni; analysis, analyses; criterion, criteria, data, datum, deer, deer; goose
- **IE/EI rules:** counterfeit, either, financier, foreign, forfeit, heifer, height, leisure, neither, protein, science, seize, sheik, species, their, weird. Spell ie after c if a "shən" sound: ancient, conscience, efficient, sufficient

FOR ADDING SUFFIXES

- **-E endings:** abridgment, acknowledgment, acreage, argument, awful, doubly, duly, horribly, incredibly, judgment, truly, mileage, ninth, possibly, singeing, terribly, truly, wholly, width, wisdom

219

- **Words ending in -ce or -ge, keep the -e when adding the suffixes -able or -ous:** advantageous, changeable, chargeable, courageous, knowledgeable, marriageable, manageable, noticeable, outrageous, pronounceable, replaceable, serviceable, salvageable, traceable
- **-Y endings:** daily, laid, paid, said. Keep the -y when adding the suffix -ing: applying, beautifying, burying, busying, carrying, clarifying, classifying, crying, drying, emptying, hurrying, identifying, implying, justifying, lying, magnifying modifying, notifying, occupying personifying, purifying, qualifying, relaying, relying, specifying, studying, supplying, varying, worrying

N

Source List for Writing Memory Tricks
for Spellings of Homonyms

See page(s) 129–133.

ail—to suffer ill health; to give physical or emotional pain: avail, bail, detail, fail, flail, frail, grail, hail, jail, mail, nail, pail, rail, sail, snail, tail, trail, wail

ale—an alcoholic drink; a type of beer: bale, dale, gale, hale, pale, sale, scale, shale, stale, swale, tale, vale

air—the mixture of invisible, odorless, tasteless gases that surrounds the earth: chair, fair, flail hair, pair, stair

heir—one who inherits property: beige, caffeine, ceiling, conceit, conceive, deceit, deceive, either, foreign, leisure, neither, perceive, protein, receipt, rein, seize, their, veil, vein, weird

aisle—passageway between seating areas, as in an auditorium or passenger vehicle or between areas of shelves of goods, as in stores: appraise, praise, raise, waist

I'll—contraction for "I will": he'll, it'll, she'll, we'll

isle—a small island: aisle, is, let, sled, sledge, slender, slew, rule, crumple, disciple, example, maple, multiple, participle, apple, scruple, simple

allowed—let have: bellow, fellow, follow, hollow, mellow, pillow, swallow, wallow, willow, yellow

aloud—using the voice; not silently: cloud, loud, proud

ant—social insect living in organized colonies; characteristically the males and fertile queen have wings during breeding season; wingless sterile females are the workers: can't, want, debutant, chant, grant, slant, gallant

aunt—the sister of your father or mother; the wife of your uncle: gaunt, haunt, jaunt, launch, laundry, taunt

ate—take in solid food by mouth: crate, date, grate, hate, state, create, cremate, rate, locate

eight—the cardinal number that is the sum of seven and one: beige, caffeine, ceiling, conceit, conceive, deceit, deceive, either, foreign, heir, leisure, neither, perceive, protein, receipt, rein, seize, their, veil, vein, weird

aye—an affirmative vote: bye, dye, eye, lye, rye
eye—the organ of sight: aye bye, dye, lye, rye
I—the nominative case of the pronoun of the first person; the word with which a speaker or writer denotes himself or herself

bail—to clear water from a boat by dipping with a container and throwing overboard; money given to release a prisoner and guarantee his or her court appearance: ail, avail, detail, fail, flail, frail, grail, hail, jail, mail, nail, pail, rail, sail, snail, tail, trail, wail

bale—large bundle of goods, such as a "bale" of hay; closely pressed package of merchandise, such as a "bale" of paper: ale, dale, gale, hale, pale, sale, scale, shale, stale, swale, tale, vale

bare—denuded of clothes, leaves, etc.: blare, dare, fare, hare, mare, pare, rare, spare, square, stare, ware, aware, compare

bear—massive carnivorous or omnivorous mammal with long shaggy coat and strong claws: clear, dear, ear, earl, early, earn, earnest, earth, fear, gear, hear, heard, hearse, heart, hearth, learn near, pear, pearl, rehearse, search smear, spear, swear, tear, wear, year, yearn

bazaar—a sale of miscellaneous items; often for charity: bazooka, azalea, azure

bizarre—conspicuously or grossly unconventional or unusual: sizable, civilizable, fertilizable, recognizable

be—to have the quality of being: he, she, bet, bed, because, become, below, bend

bee—any of numerous hairy-bodied insects, including social and solitary species: beef, beep, beer, beet, fee, glee, see, tee

beat—a stroke or blow: eat, feat, great, heat, heathen, leather, meat, neat, peat, pleat, seat, teak, threat, treat, wheat (See -EA- list)

beet—round, red root vegetable: feet, fleet, greet meet, sleet, street, sweet, teeth

berry—fruit: blackberry, cherry, error, ferry, merry, mulberry, strawberry

bury—to dig a hole, place something in it, and cover it: jury, fury, plural, rural, cur, fur, spur, occur

berth—a bed on a ship or train, usually in tiers: pertinent, fertile, assertive, inert, pert, alert, convert, expert, invert, extrovert

birth—the event of being born: girth, flirt, shirt, skirt, bird, third, twirler, girl

billed—having sent an itemized statement of money owed for goods shipped or services rendered: filled, milled, skilled, willed, grilled, spilled

build—to order, supervise, or finance the construction of: biscuit, bruise, circuit, cruise, fruit, guide, guild, guilt, guitar, juice, nuisance, pursuit, suit

blew—caused to move by means of an air current: flew, slew lewd

blue—the color of the clear sky in the daytime: avenue, clue, construe, cue, due, flue, fondue, glue, hue, pursue, rescue, revue, subdue, sue, true, value

boar—a male hog: aboard, boarder, board, coarse, hoarse, oar, roar, soar

bore—to pierce a hole with a twisting or turning movement of a tool; a person who evokes boredom; tiresome: chore, chore, core, lore, more, sore, spore, store, swore, tore, wore, ashore, bedsore, before, galore

board—a flat piece of material designed for a special purpose: aboard, boarder, coarse, hoarse, oar, roar, soar

bored—having made a hole with a pointed power or hand tool; being uninterested in a subject: cored, gored, pored, scored, snored, stored, adored, deplored

boarder—a pupil who lives at school during term time; a tenant in someone's house: aboard, board, coarse, hoarse, oar, roar, soar

border—a strip forming the outer edge of something; a line that indicates a boundary: order, recorder, reorder

bolder—more fearless and daring: bold, old, told, sold, older, holder, smolder, colder

boulder—a large, smooth mass of rock detached from its place of origin: could, foul, mould, should, shoulder, soul

born—brought into existence: corn, horn, morning, scorn, sworn, thorn, torn, worn, acorn, adorn, forlorn

borne—having taken on as one's own the expenses or debts of another person; moved while holding up or supporting: ornery, net, neon, new

bough—any of the larger branches of a tree: although, bough, bought, brought, cough, dough, drought, enough, fought, ought, plough, rough, sought, though, thorough, thought, tough, through, wrought

bow—a stroke with a curved piece of wood with taut horsehair strands that is used in playing stringed instruments; a curved piece of resilient wood with taut cord to propel arrows: arrow, elbow

brake—a restraint used to slow or stop a vehicle: bake, cake, flake, lake, make, sake, shake, snake, stake, take, wake, awake

break—some abrupt occurrence that interrupts; to separate into pieces or fragments; to destroy the integrity of; usually by force; to cause to separate into pieces or fragments: beak, bleak, break, creak, feat, peak, sneak, speak, steak, streak, teak, weak

bread—food made from dough of flour or meal and usually raised with yeast or baking powder and then baked: knead already, bead, dead, dread, head, lead, plead, spread, steady, thread (See –EA- list)

bred—having impregnated an animal to produce a special lineage: red, bed, bled, fed, fled, led, pled, shed, shred

bridal—designed for a bride; of or relating to a wedding: cymbal, medal, metal, principal, pal, gal, fatal, pastoral, corral, tidal, vassal, dalliance, Dalmatian

bridle—headgear for a horse; includes a headstall and bit and reins to give the rider or driver control: idle, meddle, sidle

Britain—a monarchy in northwestern Europe occupying most of the British Isles, divided into England and Scotland and Wales and Northern Ireland: abstain, contain, curtain, detain, entertain, maintain, mountain, obtain, taint
Briton—a native or inhabitant of Great Britain: ton, won, tone, upon, on, baton, garcon, moron

but—to the contrary: cut, glut, gut, hut, jut, nut, rut, shut, slut, smut, strut, smut
butt—the thick end of the handle; the fleshy part of the human body used for sitting: mutt, putt, mutter, putter, butter, clutter, shutter, stutter, utter, cutter

buy—obtain by purchase; acquire by means of a financial transaction: guy
by—so as to pass a given point; in reserve; not for immediate use: cry, dry, fry, my, ply, pry, shy, sky, sly, spy, sty
bye—advancement to the next round in a tournament without playing an opponent; a farewell remark: dye, lye, rye

cannon—a large artillery gun that is usually on wheels: annual, planned, annoy, annul, cannot
canon—a collection of books accepted as holy scripture, especially the books of the Bible, recognized by any Christian church as genuine and inspired; a complete list of saints that have been recognized by the Roman Catholic Church: candy, can, cancan, anonymous, anon, anorexia, another, canopy, canonize

canvas—heavy, closely woven fabric (used for clothing, chairs, sails, tents, etc.): vase, vascular, Vaseline
canvass—to make an inquiry into public opinion, conducted by interviewing a random sample of people: assist, bass, brass, class, crass, glass, grass, lass, mass, pass

capital—money, securities; a city serving as the seat of government; an alphabet letter in upper case: gal, pal, banal, moral, plural, oral frugal, brutal, canal, fatal, final, formal, frontal, legal, local, mental, moral, mortal, classical, comical, hospital, moral, musical

capitol—a building or group of buildings used to conduct government business: old, patrol, protocol, alcohol, aerosol, told, fold, mold, cold, sold

carat—a unit of weight for precious stones = 200 mg: rat, bat, brat, cat, chat, drat, flat, frat, gnat, hat, mat, pat, sat, scat, slat

carrot—orange root; important source of carotene: arrow, rot, blot, cot, dot, got, hot, lot, pot, shot, slot, tot, trot, carry, arrest, arrogance

caught—having obtained an object with the hands: daughter, distraught, fraught, haughty, laugh, naught, naughty, slaughter, taught

cot—a small bed that folds up for storage or transport: rot, blot, cot, dot, got, hot, lot, pot, shot, slot, tot, trot

cell—(biology) the basic structural and functional unit of all organisms: cellar, cellophane, cellular, cellulite

sell—to persuade someone to buy: seller, select, self, Ellen, ellipse

cent—a coin worth one-hundredth of the value of the basic unit: decent, innocent, recent, centennial, century, center, central, centipede, century

scent—an odor left in passing by which a person or animal can be traced: scene, scenery, scepter, science, scintillating, scissors, scoff, scold, scope, ascent

sent—caused or enabled to go or be conveyed or transmitted: bent, cent, dent, gent, lent, rent, spent, tent, vent, went, absent

cereal—a breakfast food prepared from grain: deal, dealt, heal, health, jealous, meal, seal, steal, veal, wealth

serial—of or relating to the sequential performance of multiple operations: Virginia, Pennsylvania, dahlia, California, via, diamond, diatribe, parliament, Pennsylvania, serious

chew—to bite and grind food in the mouth so it becomes soft enough to swallow: blew, brew, chew, curfew, dew, drew, few, flew, grew, hewn, lewd, mildew, new, pew, screw, sew, slew, stew, threw

choose—to pick out, select, or choose from a number of alternatives: goose, loose, moose, noose, caboose, footloose, mongoose

chord—a combination of three or more notes that blend harmoniously when sounded together: chore, choreograph, chortle, chorus, horde, horn, hornet, horizon

cord—a line made of twisted fibers or threads: ford, lord, sword, accord, record, order, cordial, cordless, corduroy, ordinary

cite—to refer to for illustration or proof; to quote, restate, or paraphrase; to give an exact source for a quote or piece of information by giving the title, author, page number, sometimes the column number, paragraph number, and sentence number: bite, malachite, mite, socialite, stalactite, write

sight—something that is viewed, spectacle; vision: blight, bright, delight, fight, flight, fright, knight, high, light, might, night, plight, right, sigh, sight, slight, thigh, tight

site—a place in a piece of land that is usually intended for building: sit, situated, bite, malachite, miswrite, mite, socialite, write, situation, sit

close—to shut; bar access to: rose, chose, hose, nose, pose, depose, expose, suppose, decompose

clothes—items made of fabric, worn to cover the body; what people wear for covering: the, these, he, thesis, lot, lotion, other

coarse—rough in texture: oar, boar, board, hoard, keyboard: board, hoarse, oar, roar, roast, soar (See -OA- list)

course—plan of study; path followed for racing: amour, devour, dour, flour, flourish, four, gourmet, hour, mourn, nourish, our, pour, scour, scout, sour, tour, your

colonel—a commissioned military officer in the United States Army, Air Force, or Marines who ranks above a lieutenant colonel and below a brigadier general: lone, lonely, colony, colonial, colon

kernel—the choicest or most essential or most vital part of some idea or experience; a single whole grain of a cereal: kerosene, mantel, boatel, hotel, compel, dispel, expel, excel, impel, lapel, motel, noel, pixel, rebel, repel

complement—something added to complete or make perfect: crumple, disciple, example, maple, multiple, participle, apple, scruple, simple, rule

compliment—a remark (or act) expressing praise and admiration: pliant, pliers, plink

council—a group of people who meet regularly for a common purpose or goal: nil, until, illegal, cilantro

counsel—to recommend, advise, or caution; lawyer, mediator; advice, opinion: gel, dispel, excel, expel, hotel, impel, lapel, noel, rebel, repel, seldom, sell, self, select, seltzer

consul—a diplomat appointed by a government to protect its commercial interests and help its citizens in a foreign country: consult, insult, sulk, sulfur, sullen, tulip, gulf, bulk, hulk, bulge, divulge, indulge

core—the center of an object: bore, chore, fore, gore, lore, more, ore, pore, score, shore, snore, sore, spore, swore, tore, store, swore, wore, yore, adore, ashore, bedsore, before, galore

corps—an army unit, usually consisting of two or more divisions: pseudo, pshaw, psychic, Psalms, psychosis

creak—a squeaking sound; to make a high-pitched, screeching noise: beak, bleak, break, creak, leak, peak, sneak, speak, spear steak, streak, weak

creek—a natural stream of water smaller than a river (and often a tributary of a river): cheek, leek, meek, peek, reek, seek, week

crews—teams of men who man ships, aircraft, or other vehicles; organized groups of workers: brews, chews, curfews, dew, drew, few, flew, grew, hewn, lewd, mildew, new, pews, screws, sews, slews, stews, threw

cruise—an ocean trip taken for pleasure: biscuit, bruise, build, circuit, cruise, fruit, guide, guild, guilt, guitar, juice, nuisance, pursuit, suit

cymbal—a percussion instrument consisting of a concave brass disk: medal, metal, principal, pal, gal, fatal, pastoral, corral, tidal, vassal, cyanide, cycle, cyclone, cylinder, cynic, cypress

symbol—something visible that by association or convention represents something else that is invisible: bold, old, told, symphony, sympathy, syllable, syllabus, symbiosis, symmetry, symptom

days—period of time after sunrise and before sunset while it is light outside: ways, says, bays, frays, gays, pays, plays, rays, slays, arrays, betrays, dismays, displays, essays, hoorays

daze—confusion characterized by lack of clarity: blaze, craze, gaze, glaze, raze, amaze, stargaze

dear—a beloved person; used as term of endearment: bear, clear, ear, earl, early, earn, earnest, earth, fear, gear, hear, heard, hearse, heart, hearth, learn, near, pear, pearl, rehearse, search, smear, spear, swear, tear, wear, year, yearn (See -EA- list below)

deer—mammal having two large and two small hooves on each foot and antlers borne predominantly by males: beer, cheer, eerie, engineer, jeer, leer, peer, queer, sheer, sneer, steer

dew—moisture that accumulates on grass blades during dark hours but quickly evaporates once the sun comes out: brew, chew, few, flew, grew, renew, withdrew

do—to act or perform: so, to, non, undo, who, dot, dote, donut, dole

due—amount of money owed on a debt; the last date by which an obligation can be settled, such as the last day a library book can be returned without penalty: avenue, blue, clue, construe, cue, due, flue, fondue, glue, hue, pursue, rescue, revue, subdue, sue, true, value

Doc—nickname for a licensed medical practitioner: doctor, docile, doctrine, document

dock—to land in a harbor next to a pier where ships are loaded and unloaded or repaired; may have gates to let water in or out: block, clock, cock, crock, flock, knock, lock, mock, pock, rock, shock, smock, sock, stock

dough—a flour mixture stiff enough to knead or roll: although, bough, bought, brought, cough, dough, drought, enough, fought, ought, plough, rough, sought, though, thorough, thought, tough, through, wrought

doe—mature female deer; the female of mammals of which the male is called a "buck": canoe, foe, hoe, roe, shoe, toe, woe

die—to suffer or face the pain of death: believe, brief, chief, field, fiend fierce, friend, grief, grieve, lie, niece, pie, piece, pier, pierce, priest, relieve, relieve, retrieve, shield, shriek, siege, thief, tie, yield,

dye—a usually soluble substance for staining or coloring fabrics, hair, etc.: aye bye, lye, rye

earn—to acquire or deserve by one's efforts or actions: ear, earl, early, earn, earnest, earth, fear, gear, hear, heard, hearse, heart, hearth, learn, near, pear, pearl, rehearse, search, smear, spear, swear, tear, wear, year, yearn

urn—a large vase that usually has a pedestal or feet: burn, churn, spurn, turn, return, sunburn, overturn, taciturn

faint—a spontaneous loss of consciousness caused by insufficient blood to the brain: main, abstain, again, bargain, brain, certain, chain, cocaine, contain, curtain, detain, drain, entertain, explain, gain, grain, maintain, mountain, obtain, pain, plain, porcelain, rain, remain, refrain, slain, sprain, stain, strain, taint, train, vain, villain

feint—any distracting or deceptive maneuver as a mock attack: beige, caffeine, ceiling, conceit, conceive, deceit, deceive, either, foreign, heir, leisure, neither, perceive, protein, receipt, rein, seize, their, veil, vein, weird

fair—a competitive exhibition of farm products: air, chair, fair, éclair, hair, stair, air, chair, fair, hair, pair, stair

fare—the food and drink regularly consumed; the sum charged for riding in a public conveyance: are, blare, dare, fare, hare, mare, pare, rare, scare, share, snare, spare, square, stare, ware, aware, compare

fairy—a small, playful human form having magical powers: air, chair, fair, éclair, hair, stair, air, chair, fair, hair, pair, stair

ferry—to transport by boat or aircraft; a boat that transports people or vehicles across a body of water and operates on a regular schedule: blackberry, cherry, error, ferry, merry, mulberry, strawberry

feat—a notable achievement: beat, breath, earth, eat, feat, great, heat, heathen, leather, meat, peat, pleat, seat, sneak, speak, steak, streak, sweat, threat, treat, weak, wheat

feet—the lower part of anything; the lowest extremities of a human: beet, fleet, meet, sheet, skeet, sleet, street, sweet, tweet

find—the act of discovering something; to perceive oneself to be in a certain condition or place: blind, bind, grind, hind, kind, mind, rind, wind, behind

fined—punished by the imposition of a penalty: confined, refined, streamlined, defined, lined, twined, whined, reclined, relined

fir—any of various evergreen trees, chiefly in upland areas: bird, third, sir, stir

fur—dense coat of fine silky hairs on mammals (e.g., cat or seal or weasel): blur, cur, spur, incur, occur, slur, incur, recur

flair—a natural talent; distinctive and stylish elegance: air, chair, fair, éclair, hair, stair, air, chair, fair, hair, pair, stair

flare—a device that produces a bright light for warning, illumination, or identification: are, blare, dare, fare, hare, mare, pare, rare, scare, share, snare, spare, square, stare, ware, aware, compare

flea—any wingless, blood-sucking parasitic insect, noted for its ability to leap: bleak, bleak, clear, gleam, glean, lead, leaf, leak, lean, leap, learn, lease, least, leather, leave, plea, plead, please, pleat

flee—to run away quickly: bleed, fleet, glee, leer, sleep, sleet, sleeve, spleen

flew—having traveled through the air: blew, brew, chew, curfew, dew, drew, few, flew, grew, hewn, lewd, mildew, new, pew, screw, sew, slew, stew, threw

flu—an acute, febrile, highly contagious viral disease: fluent, fluid, fluke, flunk, flush, flute

flue—an enclosed passageway for directing a current; a channel in a chimney for conveying flame and smoke to the outer air: avenue, blue, clue, cue, due, flue, glue, hue, pursue, rescue, subdue, sue, true, value

flower—reproductive organ of angiosperm plants, especially those having showy or colorful parts: owe, flow, glow, low, slow, allow, below, blow

flour—fine, powdery foodstuff obtained by grinding and sifting the meal of a cereal grain: amour, course, court, devour, dour, flourish, four, gourmet, hour, mourn, nourish, our, pour, scour, sour, tour, your (See -OU- list)

for—word that can indicate a goal or purpose, e.g., *for* good grades; can indicate the receiver of a gift, e.g., present *for* Mother: or, nor, furor, pastor, sector, sensor, corridor, cursor

four—the number that comes after three and before five: amour, course, court, devour, dour, flourish, flour, gourmet, hour, mourn, nourish, our, pour, scour, sour, tour, your (See -OU- list)

fore—front part; in the beginning: ore, bore, chore, more, core, tore, shore, folklore, ignore, explore, evermore: bore, chore, fore, gore, lore, more, ore, pore, score, shore, snore, sore, spore, swore, tore, store, swore, wore, yore, adore, ashore, bedsore, before, galore

forth—forward in time, order, or degree: worth, north

fourth—following the third position; number four in a countable series: amour, course, court, devour, dour, flour, flourish, four, gourmet, hour, mourn, nourish, our, pour, scour, sour, tour, your (See -OU- list at end)

foreword—short introductory essay preceding the text of a book: fore, word, bore, chore, gore, lore, more, ore, pore, score, shore, snore, sore, spore, swore, tore, store, swore, wore, yore, adore, afore, ashore, bedsore, before, galore, cord, ford, lord, sword, accord

forward—moving toward a position ahead: nor, or, for, forget, forgive, forlorn, form, formed, former, formal, format, formation, formula, fort, fortune, forum, toward, card, guard, hard, lard, ward, yard, regard

gnu—large African antelope having a head with horns like an ox and a long, tufted tail: gnash, gnat, gnaw, gnome

knew—having become familiarized or acquainted with a person or an object: blew, brew, chew, curfew, dew, drew, few, flew, grew, hewn, lewd, mildew, pew, screw, sew, slew, stew, threw, knack, knave, knee, kneel, knife, knit, knob, knock, knot, know

groan—an utterance expressing pain or disapproval: loan, moan

grown—(of animals) fully developed: arrow, borrow, brow, brown, crow, crown, drown, elbow, frown, grow, growl, row, sorrow, sparrow, tomorrow

great—of major significance or importance: beat, breath, earth, eat, feat, flea, heat, heathen, leather, meat, peat, pleat, seat, steak, wheat

grate—a frame of iron bars to hold a fire: crate, date, grate, hate, state, create, cremate, rate, locate, grateful, gratify

guest—a visitor to whom hospitality is extended: avenue, blue, clue, construe, cue, due, flue, fondue, glue, hue, pursue, rescue, revue, subdue, sue, true, value

guessed—estimated based on little or no information: quest, Guernsey, blessed, chess, dressed, less, mess, pressed, stressed, addressed, compressed, confessed, depressed, distressed, expressed, impressed, possessed, progressed, professed

hail—enthusiastic greeting: ail, avail, bail, detail, fail, flail, frail, grail, jail, mail, nail, rail, sail, snail, tail, trail, wail (See -AI-list)

hale—exhibiting vigorous good health: bale, dale, gale, hale, pale, sale, scale, shale, stale, swale, tale, vale, female, folktale, percale

hair—dense growth of cylindrical filaments covering the body or parts of it (as on the human head) that help prevent heat loss: air, chair, fair, flail pair, stair

hare—swift, timid, long-eared mammal larger than a rabbit, having a divided upper lip and long hind legs: are, blare, dare, fare, hare, mare, pare, rare, scare, share, snare, spare, square, stare, ware, aware, compare

handsome—pleasing in appearance, especially by reason of conformity to ideals of form and proportion: gnome, dome, home, come, become, home, come, income, somebody, someday, sometimes, somewhere

hansom—a two-wheeled, horse-drawn covered carriage with the driver's seat above and behind the passengers: tom-tom, Tom, tomato, from, mom, prom, pom-pom, intercom, sombrero

heal—to provide a cure for and make healthy again: cereal deal, dealt, health, jealous, meal, peal, seal, steal, veal, wealth

heel—the bottom of a shoe or boot; the back part of a shoe or boot that touches the ground: eel, feel, peel, reel, steel, steer, wheel

hear—to perceive (sound) via the auditory sense of the ear: bear, clear, dear, ear, earl, early, earn, earnest, earth, fear, gear, heard, hearse, heart, hearth, learn, near, pear, pearl, rehearse, search, smear, spear, swear, tear, wear, year, yearn

here—the present location; this place: where, mere, were, austere, cashmere, revere, severe, sincere, persevere

heard—having perceived (sound) via the auditory sense of the ear: bear, clear, dear, ear, earl, early, earn, earnest, earth, fear, gear, hear, hearse, heart, hearth, learn, near, pear, pearl, rehearse, search, smear, spear, swear, tear, wear, year, yearn

herd—a group of cattle or sheep or other domestic mammals all of the same kind that are herded by humans; a group of wild animals of one species that remain together: nerd, shepherd, herdsman, perdition, Perdue, verdant, verdict

hi—an expression of greeting: I, pi, xi, Eli, hi-fi, sci-fi, alibi

high—a lofty level, position, or degree: blight, bright, delight, fight, flight, fright, knight, high, light, might, night, plight, right, sigh, sight, slight, thigh, tight

hire—to engage for service under terms of a contract; engage or hire for work: dire, fire, ire, sire, tire, wire, admire, attire, bemire, desire, empire, entire, expire, inspire, perspire, retire, satire

him—a pronoun in the objective case that refers to a male: brim, dim, prim, shim, skim slim, swim, trim, whim

hymn—a song of praise (to God, a saint, or a nation): autumn, column, condemn

hoard—a secret store of valuables or money; to save up as for future use: board coarse, hoarse, oar, roar, roast, soar (See -OA- list)

horde—a vast multitude; a moving crowd: order, chorded, lorded, sword, recorded, worded, accorded

hoarse—deep and harsh sounding from shouting, illness, or emotion: hoard board coarse, hoarse, oar, roar, roast, soar

horse—solid-hoofed mammal domesticated since prehistoric times and used usually for riding: endorse, remorse, worse

hole—an opening deliberately made in or through something: olé, bole, dole, mole, pole, role, sole, stole, cajole

whole—an assemblage of parts that is regarded as a single entity: who, whom, whoop, whoopla, whoosh, whop, whose

holy—belonging to or derived from or associated with a divine power: ho, hold, hole, holiday, holistic, roly-poly

wholly—to a complete degree or to the full or entire extent: whole, who, whom, dolly, folly, golly, holly, jolly, Molly, Polly

hour—a period of time equal to 1/24th of a day: amour, course, devour, dour, flour, flourish, four, gourmet, mourn, mourning, nourish, our, pour, scour, scout, sour, tour, your

our—of or pertaining to us; belonging to us; as our country, our rights, our troops, our endeavors: amour, course, devour, dour, flour, flourish, four, gourmet, hour, mourn, mourning, nourish, pour, scour, scout, sour, tour, your

in—inside an enclosed space, to or toward the inside of: bin, chin, din, fin, pin, thin, tin, twin

inn—a hotel providing overnight lodging for travelers: finny, ninny, shinny, skinny, spinney, tinny, whinny

its—belonging to it: bits, fits, grits, hits, kits, knits, pits, misfits, transmits

it's—contraction for "it is": he's, she's, who's, here's

knead—to make uniform (e.g., "knead dough"); manually manipulate (someone's body), usually for medicinal or relaxation purposes: already, bead, bread, dead, dread, head, lead, plead, spread, steady, thread

need—a condition requiring relief; a state of extreme poverty or destitution: bleed, breed, creed, deed, exceed, feed, greed, heed, need, reed, seed, speed, steed, succeed, tweed

knight—originally a person of noble birth trained to arms and chivalry; today in Great Britain a person honored by the sovereign for personal merit: high blight, bright, delight, fight, flight, fright, knight, high, light, might, night, plight, right, sigh, sight, slight, thigh, tight

night—the period of time after sunset and before sunrise while it is dark outside: high blight, bright, delight, fight, flight, fright, knight, high, light, might, night, plight, right, sigh, sight, slight, thigh, tight

knit—needlework created by interlacing yarn in a series of connected loops using straight, eyeless needles or by machine: knack, knave, knee, kneel, knew, knife, knight, knickers, knife, knob, knock, knot, know, knuckle

nit—egg or young of an insect parasitic on mammals, especially a sucking louse; often attached to a hair or item of clothing: nitpick, nitrate, nitrogen, nitwit, it, bit, chit, fit, flit, pit, sit, skit, wit, writ, admit, benefit, emit, misfit, omit, remit, submit

knot—any of various fastenings formed by looping and tying a rope (or cord) upon itself, to another rope, or to another object: knack, knave, knee, kneel, knew, knife, knight, knickers, knife, knob, knit, knock, know, knuckle

not—negation of a word or group of words: clot, cot, dot, got, hot, jot, lot, not, plot, pot, rot, shot, slot, spot, tot, trot, allot, cannot, apricot, ocelot

know—to be familiar or acquainted with a person or an object: blow, bow, brow, chow, cow, crow, elbow, flow, glow, how know, low, mow, now, plow, row, slow, snow, sow, stow, throw, tow, vow, wow

no—a negative used to express refusal or denial or disagreement, etc., or especially to emphasize a negative statement: go, to, do, fro, ho, so, ago, forgo, gung-ho, hello, oregano

knows—is familiar or acquainted with a person or an object: blows, bows, flows, mows, rows, shows, snows, stows, tows, knack, knave, knee, kneel, knew, knife, knit, knob, knock, knot

nose—the organ of smell and entrance to the respiratory tract; the prominent part of the face of humans or other mammals: rose, chose, hose, nose, pose, depose, expose, suppose, decompose

lead—a mixture of graphite with clay in different degrees of hardness; the marking substance in a pencil: already, bead, bread, dead, dread, head, knead, plead, spread, steady, thread

led—having taken a position of leadership: bed, bled, bred, fed, pled, red, shed, sled, sped, abed, biped

leak—an accidental hole that allows something (fluid or light, etc.) to enter or escape: break beak, bleak, break, creak, feat, peak, sneak, speak, steak, streak, teak, weak

leek—related to onions; white, cylindrical bulb with flat, dark-green leaves: creek cheek, meek, peek, reek, seek, week

lean—to rely on for support: bean, clean, glean, lean, mean, meant, wean

lien—the right to take another's property if an obligation is not discharged: believe, brief, chief, die, field, fiend fierce, friend, grief, grieve, lie, niece, pie, piece, pier, pierce, priest, relieve, relieve, retrieve, shield, shriek, siege, thief, tie, yield

lie—a statement that deviates from or perverts the truth; the position or manner in which something is situated: believe, brief, chief, die, field, fiend fierce, friend, grief, grieve, lien, niece, pie, piece, pier, pierce, priest, relieve, relieve, retrieve, shield, shriek, siege, thief, tie, yield

lye—a strong solution of sodium or potassium hydroxide: aye bye, dye, lye, rye

load—a weight to be borne or conveyed: broad, road, roar, toad

lode—a deposit of valuable ore occurring within definite boundaries separating it from surrounding rocks: bode, code, mode, ode, rode, abode, decode, erode

loan—the temporary provision of money (usually at interest): groan, loan, moan

lone—without anybody else; without any others being included or involved: bone, clone, cone, crone, drone, hone, none, phone, prone, shone, stone, throne, tone, alone, atone, colonel

made—produced by a manufacturing process: bade, comrade, forbade, adenoid, adept, adequate

maid—an unmarried girl (especially a virgin); a female domestic servant: afraid, aid, braid, laid, paid, raid, said, staid

mail—the system whereby messages are transmitted, usually by the postal service: avail, bail, detail, fail, flail, frail, grail, jail, hail, nail, rail, sail, snail, tail, trail, wail

male—a person who belongs to the sex that cannot have babies; opposite of female: ale, dale, pale, sale, swale, shale, female, folktale, percale

main—of or relating to a broad expanse; a principal part: abstain, again, bargain, brain, certain, chain, cocaine, contain, curtain, detain, drain, entertain, explain, faint, gain, grain, maintain, mountain, obtain, pain, plain, porcelain, rain, remain, refrain, slain, sprain, stain, strain, taint, train, vain, villain

Maine—a state in New England: abstain, again, bargain, brain, certain, chain, cocaine, contain, curtain, detain, drain, entertain, explain, faint, gain, grain, maintain, mountain, obtain, pain, plain, porcelain, rain, remain, refrain, slain, sprain, stain, strain, taint, train, vain, villain

mane—long, coarse hair growing from the crest of an animal's neck: bane, lane, pane, plane, sane, wane, arcane, germane, humane, insane, mundane, profane, sugarcane

mantel—a shelf that projects from the wall above a fireplace: antelope, telephone, angel, gel, boatel, hotel, compel, dispel expel, excel, impel, lapel, motel, noel, pixel, rebel, repel, scalpel, caramel, carousel, citadel, parallel

mantle—a cloak that is a symbol of authority; the layer of the earth between the crust and the core: antler, rule, crumple, disciple, example, maple, multiple, participle, principle, apple, scruple, simple

marry—to take in marriage: starry carry, parry, tarry, miscarry, Harry, quarry

merry—offering fun and gaiety; full of or showing high-spirited merriment: blackberry, cherry, error, ferry, merry, mulberry, strawberry

meat—the flesh of animals (including fish, birds, and snails) used as food: beat breath, eat, feat, great, heat, heathen, leather, meat, neat, peat, pleat, seat, teak, threat, treat, wheat

meet—to get together socially or for a specific purpose: beet, feet, fleet, greet, sleet, street, sweet, teeth (See –EE- list)

medal—an award for winning a championship or commemorating some other event: bridal, cymbal, metal, principal, pal, gal, fatal, pastoral, corral, tidal, vassal, dalliance, Dalmatian

meddle—to intrude in other people's affairs or business; interfere in an unwanted manner: peddle, heddle, piddle, diddle, fiddle, middle, riddle, twiddle

metal—a mixture containing two or more metallic elements or metallic and nonmetallic elements, usually fused together or dissolving into each other when molten: fetal, petal, talc, take, talent, talk

mettle—the courage to carry on: fettle, kettle, nettle, settle, teakettle

miner—a laborer who works in a mine: nerve, nervous, diner, finer, liner, shiner, designer, refiner

minor—a young person of either sex; lesser in scope or effect: nor, Nordic, Norma, norm, normal, Norse, north, Norway

might—physical strength: blight, bright, delight, fight, flight, fright, high, knight, light, night, plight, right, sigh, sight, slight, thigh, tight

mite—any of numerous very small to minute arachnids, often infesting animals, plants, or stored foods: bite, malachite, socialite, stalactite, write, miswrite

mist—a thin fog with condensation near the ground: fist, gist, list, twist, wrist, assist, consist, cyclist, insist, coexist, artist, sadist, linguist, egotist, exorcist

missed—failed to perceive or to catch with the senses or the mind: blessed, kissed, dismissed, missed, pressed, oppressed, compressed, dressed, stressed, addressed, confessed, possessed, professed

morning—the period of time between dawn and noon: born, corn, horn, scorn, sworn, thorn, torn, worn, acorn, adorn, forlorn

mourning—a state of sorrow over the death or departure of a loved one: amour, course, devour, dour, flour, flourish, four, gourmet, hour, mourn, nourish, our, pour, scour, scout, sour, tour, your

muscle—animal tissue consisting predominantly of contractile cells: sclerosis, corpuscle, clef, clematis, clemency, clench, clergy, clerk clever

mussel—a marine or freshwater bivalve mollusk that lives attached to rocks, etc.: seldom, select, selenium, self, gel, boatel, hotel, compel, dispel expel, excel, impel, lapel, motel, noel, pixel, rebel, repel, scalpel, caramel, carousel, citadel, parallel

naval—connected with or belonging to or used in a navy: Avalon, Valerie, valor, avalanche

navel—a scar where the umbilical cord was attached: avenge, avenue, averse, avert, velvet, velocity velour, velveteen, brave, cave, crave, gave, grave, knave, rave, save, shave, slave, behave, deprave, forgave, octave, angel, boatel, hotel, compel, dispel expel, excel, impel, lapel, motel, noel, pixel, rebel, repel, scalpel, caramel, carousel, citadel, parallel

none—not any; not at all; in no way: bone, clone, cone, crone, drone, lone, phone, prone, shone, stone, throne, tone, alone, atone, done, one
nun—a woman in a religious order: bun, fun, gun, Hun, pun, run, shun, spun, stun, sun

oh—an exclaim of surprise or puzzlement: Ohio, ohm, alcohol
owe—to be in debt; to be obliged to pay or repay: bowed, browed, cowed, crowed, flowed, flower, mowed, plowed, rowed, showed, snowed, sowed, stowed, towed, vowed

one—a single person or thing; the smallest whole number or a numeral representing this number: bone, clone, cone, crone, drone, lone, none, phone, prone, shone, stone, throne, tone, alone, atone, done
won—having gained victory: on, son ton, crayon, baton, con, yon, bonbon, capon, coupon, icon, neon, peon, salon, moron, octagon, upon

oar—an implement used to propel or steer a boat: boar, board, toward, aboard
or—either: or, oral, choral, coral, floral, orchestra, orchid, order, border, record, furor, fork, stork, cork, world, worm, dorm, form, storm, work
ore—a metal-bearing mineral valuable enough to be mined: bore, chore, fore, gore, lore, more, ore, pore, score, shore, snore, sore, spore, swore, tore, store, swore, wore, yore, adore, ashore, bedsore, before, galore

pail—a container for holding liquid, paste, powder, etc.: avail, bail, detail, fail, flail, frail, grail, hail, jail, mail, nail, rail, sail, snail, tail, trail, wail
pale—(of light) lacking in intensity or brightness; dim or feeble; abnormally deficient in color, as suggesting physical or emotional distress: ale, dale, male, sale, swale, shale, vale, female, folktale, percale

pain—acute discomfort; a symptom of some physical hurt or disorder: abstain, again, bargain, brain, certain, chain, cocaine, contain, curtain, detain, drain, entertain, explain, faint, gain, grain, main, maintain, mountain, obtain, plain, porcelain, rain, remain, refrain, slain, sprain, stain, strain, taint, train, vain, villain

pane—sheet glass cut in shapes for windows or doors: bane, lane, mane, plane, sane, vane, wane, arcane, germane, humane, insane, mundane, profane, sugarcane

pair—two of the same kind: air, chair, fair, flair, éclair, hair, stair, air, chair, fair, grail, hair, stair, wheelchair

pare—to peel off the skin of a fruit, potato, cucumber, etc.: care, dare, mare, rare, scare, share, snare, spare, warfare

pear—a pale grey fruit with a rounded bottom that is much larger than its top rounded part: bear, clear, dear, ear, earl, early, earn, earnest, earth, fear, gear, hear, heard, hearse, heart, hearth, learn, near, pearl, rehearse, search, smear, spear, swear, tear, wear, year, yearn

passed—having thrown an article such as a ball to another member of a team: glassed, passed, sassed, amassed, bypassed, outclassed, surpassed

past—an earlier period in someone's life; time that has elapsed: blast, cast, fast, last, mast, vast, aghast, bedfast, broadcast

pause—a time interval during which there is a temporary cessation of something: applaud, auction, audible, audio, audit, aunt, author, auto, autopsy, autumn, because, cauliflower, cause, caution, cautious, clause, exhaust, faucet, fault, fraud, gauge, gaunt, gauze, haul, haunt, jaunt, laugh, launch, laundry, maudlin, maul, nautical, pauper, pause: plausible, saucer, sauce, sausage, taunt, taut, thesaurus, vault

paws—a clawed foot of an animal, especially a quadruped: awful, claw, bawl, brawl, brawn, crawl, dawn, drawl, draw, fawn, gawk, gnaw, hawk, jaw, law, lawn, pawn, raw, saw, scrawl, shawl, straw, thaw, yawn

peace—a calm state in which people live together in harmony: appeal, beach, pea, peat, peal, peach, pearl, peak, pear, pearl, peat

piece—a part of something: pie, niece, brief, chief, believe, pier, pierce, piety, field, shield, yield

peak—the top point of a mountain or hill: break beak, bleak, break, creak, feat, sneak, speak, steak, streak, teak, weak

peek—a secret look: creek cheek, leek, meek, peek, reek, seek, week

peal—a deep, prolonged sound (as of thunder or large bells): cereal deal, dealt, heal, health, jealous, meal, seal, steal, veal, wealth

peel—to strip the skin off: eel, feel, heel, reel, steel, steer, wheel

peer—a person who is of equal standing with another in a group; to look searchingly: beer, cheer, deer, eerie, engineer, jeer, leer, queer, sheer, sneer, steer

pier—a platform built out from the shore into the water and supported by piles; provides access to ships and boats: believe, brief, chief, die, field, fiend fierce, friend, grief, grieve, lie, niece, pie, piece, pierce, priest, relieve, relieve, retrieve, shield, shriek, siege, thief, tie, yield

plain—an extensive tract of level, open land: abstain, again, bargain, brain, certain, chain, cocaine, contain, curtain, detain, drain, entertain, explain, faint, gain, grain, main, maintain, mountain, obtain, pain, porcelain, rain, remain, refrain, slain, sprain, stain, strain, taint, train, vain, villain

plane—a carpenter's hand tool with an adjustable blade for smoothing or shaping wood; an aircraft that has a fixed wing and is powered by propellers or jets: bane, lane, mane, pane, sane, wane, arcane, germane, humane, insane, mundane, profane, sugarcane

pleas—humble requests for help from someone in authority: beast breast, feast, least, plea, plead, pleat, yeast

please—to give pleasure to or be pleasing to; used in a polite request: crease, grease, lease, ease, tease

poor—having little money or few possessions; unsatisfactory: door, floor, poor, spoor

pore—any small opening in the skin or outer surface of an animal; to gaze intently; to meditate steadily: bore, chore, fore, gore, lore, more, ore, score, shore, snore, sore, spore, swore, tore, store, swore, wore, yore, adore, ashore, bedsore, before, galore

pour—to flow in a spurt; to rain heavily; to move in large numbers: amour, course, devour, dour, flour, flourish, four, gourmet, hour, mourn, mourning, nourish, our, scour, scout, sour, tour, your

pray—to address God; to say a prayer to a higher being: always, away, bay, clay, day, dismay, gay, hay, lay, may, pay, play, pray, ray, repay, say, spray, stay, sway, today, tray, way

prey—an animal hunted or caught for food; to hunt for: alley, chimney, convey, donkey, grey, hockey, honey, jockey, journey, key, kidney, money, monkey, obey, osprey, parsley, prey, survey, they, trolley, turkey, valley, volley

principal—the head administrator of a school: pal, gal, fatal, pastoral

principle—a rule or guideline: crumple, disciple, example, maple, multiple, participle, apple, scruple, simple

rain—water falling in drops from vapor condensed in the atmosphere: abstain, again, bargain, brain, certain, chain, cocaine, contain, curtain, detain, drain, entertain, explain, faint, gain, grain, main, maintain, mountain, obtain, pain, plain, porcelain, remain, refrain, slain, sprain, stain, strain, taint, train, vain, villain

reign—royal authority; the dominion of a monarch; the period during which a monarch is sovereign; to rule over as a sovereign: beige, caffeine, ceiling, conceit, conceive, deceit, deceive, either, foreign, heir, leisure, neither, perceive, protein, receipt, rein, seize, their, veil, vein, weird

rein—one of a pair of long straps (usually connected to the bit or the headpiece) used to control a horse: beige, caffeine, ceiling, conceit, conceive, deceit, deceive, either, foreign, heir, leisure, neither, perceive, protein, receipt, rein, seize, their, veil, vein, weird

raise—the amount a salary is increased; to invigorate or heighten; to lift an object: aisle, appraise, praise, raise, waist

rays—lines of light that appear to radiate from a bright object: days, ways, says, bays, frays, gays, pays, plays, slays, arrays, betrays, dismays, displays, essays, hoorays

raze—to tear down so as to make flat with the ground: blaze, craze, daze, gaze, glaze, amaze, stargaze

rap—a genre of African American music of the 1980s and 1990s in which rhyming lyrics are chanted to a musical accompaniment: cap, chap, clap, crap, flap, lap, map, nap, sap, scrap, slap, swap, strap, tap, trap, yap, zap

wrap—a cloak that is folded or wrapped around a person; to arrange or fold as a cover or protection: wrack, wrangle, wrasse, wrath, wreck, wren, wretched, wriggle, wring, wrinkle, wrist, writ, write, writhe, wrong, wroth, wry

read—interpreted something that is written or printed: already, bead, bread, dead, dread, head, knead lead, plead, spread, steady, thread
red—the quality or state of the chromatic color resembling the hue of blood: bed, bled, fed, fled, led, pled, shed, shred

read—to interpret something that is written or printed: already, bead, bread, dead, dread, head, knead, lead, plead, spread, steady, thread
reed—a vibrator consisting of a thin strip of stiff material that vibrates to produce a tone when air streams over it; a tall, woody, perennial grass with a hollow, slender stem: bleed, breed, creed, deed, feed, greed, heed, need, seed, speed, tweed, weed

real—being or occurring in fact or actuality; having verified existence; not illusory: cereal deal, dealt, heal, health, jealous, meal, seal, steal, veal, wealth
reel—a winder consisting of a revolving spool with a handle, attached to a fishing rod: eel, feel, heel, peel, reel, steel, steer, wheel

right—anything in accord with principles of justice; a privilege; correct: bright, fight, knight, light, tight
rite—a ceremony often of a religious nature: bite, malachite, mite, white, socialite, stalactite, write
write—to record thoughts with pen, pencil, computer, etc.: wring, writ, wringer, wrinkle, wrist, bite, malachite, mite, white, socialite, stalactite

ring—jewelry consisting of a circlet of precious metal (often set with jewels), worn on the finger: bring, cling, fling, king, sing, sling, spring, sting, string, swing, think, wing, zing
wring—to twist, squeeze, or compress in order to extract liquid; a twisting squeeze: wrack, wrangle, wrasse, wrath, wreck, wren, wretched, wriggle, wrinkle, wrist, writ, write, writhe, wrong, wroth, wry

road—an open way (generally public) for travel or transportation: broad, load, toad

rode—having been a passenger in a vehicle; carried or traveled on an animal or in a vehicle: lode, bode, code, mode, ode, abode, decode, erode

rowed—having propelled a small boat with oars: grown arrow, borrow, brow, brown, crow, crown, drown, elbow, frown, grow, growl, grown, row, sorrow, sparrow, tomorrow

role—an actor's portrayal of a character: hole, mole, pole, sole, stole, whole, cajole, console, condole, Creole, parole

roll—to ball into a cylindrical form; to throw a ball, such as a bowling ball; a small, rounded bread, either plain or sweet: doll, droll, knoll, poll, scroll, stroll, troll, enroll

rose—a dusty pink color; having changed location in an upward direction: chose, close, hose, nose, pose, depose, expose, suppose, decompose

rows—arrangements of objects or people side by side in a line; propels a boat with oars: grown arrows, borrows, brows, brown, crows, crown, drown, elbows, frown, grows, growl, grown, sorrows, sparrows, tomorrows

roomer—a tenant in someone's house: boomer, bloomer, groomer

rumor—gossip (usually a mixture of truth and untruth) passed around by word of mouth: humor, tumor, humorous

sail—a large piece of fabric (as canvas) by means of which wind is used to propel a sailing vessel; to travel in a boat propelled by wind: avail, bail, detail, fail, flail, frail, grail, hail, jail, mail, nail, rail, snail, tail, trail, wail

sale—an occasion (usually brief) for buying items at specially reduced prices: ale, dale, male, pale, sale, swale, shale, female, folktale, percale

scene—art consisting of the graphic or photographic representation of a visual percept; a view of landscape, buildings, people, etc.: convene, gene, serene, Nazarene

seen—having perceived by sight: been, preen, queen, screen, sheen, spleen, teen between, canteen, colleen, fourteen, preteen, velveteen

sea—a division of an ocean or a large body of salt water partially enclosed by land: flea, gear, seal, seam, search, seat, smear, tea, yea

see—to perceive by sight or have the power to perceive by sight: bee, fee, glee, tee

seam—a joint consisting of a line formed by joining two pieces: beam, bean, cream, crease, dream, dreamt, gleam, glean, seam, steam, stream, team

seem—to appear to one's own mind or opinion: deem

scents—odors left in passing by which a person or animal can be traced: scene, scenery, scepter, science, scintillating, scissors, scoff, scold, scope, ascent

sense—one of the faculties through which the external world is apprehended: dense, tense, condense, defense, dispense, expense, innocence, incense, intense, nonsense, pretense, suspense

sew, sewn—to create clothes, drapes, etc., with cloth; to fasten with thread; to do needlework: blew, brew, chew, curfew, dew, drew, few, flew, grew, hewn, lewd, mildew, new, pew, screw, sew, slew, stew, threw

so—in order that: do, to, non, undo, who, sober, social, soda, sodium, sofa, solar, solicit, sonar, sophisticated, soprano

sow, sown—to place (seeds) in or on the ground for future growth: know blow, bow, brow, chow, cow, crow, elbow, flow, glow, how know, low, mow, now, plow, row, slow, snow, sow, stow, throw, tow, vow, wow, blown, brown, clown, cow, crow, crown, down, drown, elbow, fellow, flow, flown, grown, known, own, shown, town

shoe—footwear shaped to fit the foot (below the ankle) with a flexible upper of leather or synthetic material and a sole and heel of heavier material: canoe, doe, foe, hoe, roe, shoe, toe, woe

shoo—to cry at to drive away: shoot, hoot, shook, hood, hoof, hook, hoop, hoot

shone—having emitted light, as of the sun or a light; having thrown or flashed the light of a lamp, flashlight, etc.: bone, clone, cone, crone, drone, lone, one, none, phone, prone, stone, throne, tone, alone, atone, done

shown—having made visible or noticeable; having demonstrated something to an interested audience: blown, brown, clown, crown, down, drown, flown, grown, known, own, town

slay—to kill intentionally and with premeditation: always, away, bay, clay, day, dismay, gay, hay, lay, may, pay, play, pray, ray, repay, say, spray, stay, sway, today, tray, way

sleigh—a vehicle mounted on runners and pulled by horses or dogs, for transportation over snow: beige, caffeine, ceiling, conceit, conceive, deceit, deceive, either, foreign, heir, leisure, neither, perceive, protein, receipt, rein, seize, their, veil, vein, weird

soar—to rise upward into the air: boar, oar, board, toward, aboard, oak, boa, approach, loaf

sore—an open skin infection: bore, chore, core, more, pore, shore, snore, sore, store, swore, tore, wore, before, galore, folklore

sole—the underside of footwear or a golf club: hole, mole, pole, role, stole, whole, cajole, console, condole, Creole, parole

soul—the immaterial part of a person; the actuating cause of an individual life: boulder, could, foul, mould, should, shoulder, would

some—(of quantities) imprecise but fairly close to correct; a few: gnome, dome, home, come, become, home, come, income, somebody, someday, sometimes, somewhere

sum—the whole amount: bum, chum, drum, plum, rum, scum, slum, strum, swum

son—a male human offspring: on, ton, crayon, baton, con, won, yon, bonbon, capon, coupon, icon, neon, peon, salon, moron, octagon, upon

sun—a typical star that is the source of light and heat for the planets in the solar system: bun, fun, gun, Hun, nun, pun, run, shun, spun, stun

stake—an instrument of execution consisting of a vertical post that a victim is tied to for burning; a pole set up to mark something (as the start or end of a race track): brake: bake, cake, flake, lake, make, sake, shake, snake, take, wake, awake

steak—a slice of meat cut from the fleshy part of an animal or large fish: break beak, bleak, break, creak, feat, peak, sneak, speak, streak, teak, weak

stare—a fixed look with eyes open wide; to look at with fixed eyes: are, blare, dare, fare, flare, hare, mare, pare, rare, scare, share, snare, spare, square, ware, aware, compare

stair—a support consisting of a place to rest the foot while ascending or descending a stairway: air, chair, fair, flair, éclair, hair, stair, air, chair, fair, grail, hair, pair

steal—to take without the owner's consent: cereal deal, dealt, heal, health, jealous, meal, seal, veal, wealth

steel—an alloy of iron with small amounts of carbon, widely used in construction; its mechanical properties can be varied over a wide range: eel, feel, heel, peel, reel, steer, wheel

straight—having no deviations; without curves: blight, bright, delight, fight, flight, fright, knight, high, light, might, night, plight, right, sigh, sight, slight, thigh, tight

strait—a narrow channel of the sea joining two larger bodies of water: bait, gait, trait, wait

stationary—in a fixed, unmovable condition: car, far, dictionary, canary, wary, necessary

stationery—paper that is used for writing correspondence: cemetery, query, very, her, confer, infer, litter, letter, transfer

tail—the posterior part of the body of a vertebrate, especially when elongated and extending beyond the trunk or main part of the body: avail, bail, detail, fail, flail, frail, grail, hail, jail, mail, nail, rail, sail, snail, trail, wail

tale—a message that tells the particulars of an act, occurrence, or course of events, presented in writing or drama or cinema or as a radio or television program: ale, dale, hale, male, pale, sale, swale, shale, female, folktale, percale

tea—dried leaves of the tea shrub, usually used for making a liquid drink: flea, steady, steak, steal, steam, teach, teak, tear, tease

tee—a short peg put into the ground to hold a golf ball off the ground; the starting place for each hole on a golf course: bee, fee, glee, see, steed, steel, steer, street, succeed, teeth

tear—a drop of the clear, saline solution from an eye: bear, clear, dear, ear, earl, early, earn, earnest, earth, fear, gear, hear, heard, hearse, heart, hearth, learn, near, pear, pearl, rehearse, search, smear, spear, swear, wear, year, yearn

tier—one of two or more layers atop one another: believe, brief, chief, die, field, fiend fierce, friend, grief, grieve, lie, niece, pie, piece, pier, pierce, priest, relieve, relieve, retrieve, shield, shriek, siege, thief, tie, yield

tense—a grammatical category of verbs used to express distinctions of time; uneasy, nervous, or anxious: dense, sense, condense, defense, dispense, expense, innocence, incense, intense, nonsense, pretense, suspense

tents—portable shelters (usually of canvas or nylon stretched over supporting poles and fastened to the ground with ropes and pegs): cents, dents, gents, rents, scents, vents, cements, consents, convents, events, ferments, fragments, indents, intents, invents, laments, percents, pigments, presents, prevents, repents, segments, torments, accidents, arguments, circumvents, compartments, compliments, discontents, documents

their—belonging to them; owned by them: heir, weird, ceiling, receive, conceit, either, seize beige, caffeine, ceiling, conceit, conceive, deceit, deceive, either, foreign, heir, leisure, neither, perceive, protein, receipt, rein, seize, their, veil, vein, weird

there—pointing out; place: here, where, anywhere

they're—contraction for "they are": we're, you're

threw—propelled forward, usually with one's hands and arms: crew, drew, grew, brew, screw

through—a word that indicates in at one side or point and out at another one: dough, thorough, rough, tough, bought, brought, ought, fought, sought

throne—the position and power of one who occupies a throne; the chair of state of a monarch, bishop, etc.: none: bone, clone, cone, crone, drone, lone, none, phone, prone, shone, stone, tone, alone, atone, done, one

thrown—caused to fall to the ground; having propelled something through the air with a rapid movement of the arm and wrist: grown arrow, borrow, brow, brown, crow, crown, drown, elbow, frown, grow, growl, grown, row, sorrow, sparrow, tomorrow

tic—a local and habitual twitching, especially in the face: rubric, heretic, lunatic

tick—any of two families of small parasitic arachnids with barbed proboscis, which feeds on the blood of warm-blooded animals: brick, chick, click, crick, flick, hick, kick, lick, nick, pick, prick, sick, slick, stick, thick, tick, trick, wick

to—toward: do, go, no, so

too—besides, also; excessively, very: took, tool, toot, tooth, toothpick, boo, coo, moo, shoo, soon, zoo, cartoon, kazoo, kangaroo, shampoo, taboo, tattoo, , bugaboo, buckaroo, cockatoo

two—the number between one and three; one doubled: twice, twain, twang, tweed, tweezers, twenty, twice, twin, woman

toe—one of the digits of the foot: canoe, doe, foe, hoe, roe, shoe, toe, woe

tow—the act of hauling something (as a vehicle) by means of a hitch or rope; to drag behind: blow, bow, brow, chow, cow, crow, flow, glow, grow, how, know, low mow, now, plow, row, show, slow, snow, sow, stow, throw, tow, vow, wow

vain—a characteristic of false pride; having an exaggerated sense of self-importance; unproductive of success: abstain, again, bargain, brain, certain, chain, cocaine, contain, curtain, detain, drain, entertain, explain, faint, gain, grain, main, maintain, mountain, obtain, pain, plain, porcelain, rain, remain, refrain, slain, sprain, stain, strain, taint, train, villain

vane—a movable device attached to an elevated object (as a spire) for showing the direction of the wind: bane, lane, mane, pane, plane, sane, wane, arcane, germane, humane, insane, mundane, profane, sugarcane

vein—a blood vessel that carries blood from the capillaries toward the heart; all veins except the pulmonary carry unaerated blood: beige, caffeine, ceiling, conceit, conceive, deceit, deceive, either, foreign, heir, leisure, neither, perceive, protein, receipt, rein, seize, their, veil, vein, weird

vale—a long depression in the surface of the land that usually contains a river: ale, dale, male, pale, sale, swale, shale, female, folktale, percale

veil—a garment that covers the head and face: beige, caffeine, ceiling, conceit, conceive, deceit, deceive, either, foreign, heir, leisure, neither, perceive, protein, receipt, rein, seize, their, veil, vein, weird

vary—to make or become different in some particular way, without permanently losing one's or its former characteristics or essence; to make something more diverse: glary, wary, actuary, coronary, honorary, literary, military, monetary, ordinary

very—really; precisely so: cemetery, query, her, confer, infer, litter, letter, transfer

wail—a cry of sorrow and grief; to cry weakly or softly: avail, bail, detail, fail, flail, frail, grail, hail, jail, mail, nail, rail, sail, snail, tail, trail

whale—any of the larger ocean mammals having a streamlined body and breathing through a blowhole on the head: hale: ale, dale, male, pale, sale, swale, shale, tale, female, folktale, percale

waist—the narrowing of the body between the ribs and hips: aisle, appraise, praise, raise

waste—useless or profitless activity; using or expending or consuming; to spend or use thoughtlessly: baste, chaste, haste, paste, haste, posthaste, taste

wait—time during which some action is awaited; to stay in one place and anticipate or expect something: bait, faith, gait, strait, trait, waitress

weight—a system of units used to express the weight of something; sports equipment used in callisthenic exercises and weightlifting; a weight that is not attached to anything and is raised and lowered by use of the hands and arms: eight, freight, sleigh, neighbor, height, beige, caffeine, ceiling, conceit, conceive, deceit, deceive, either, foreign, heir, leisure, neither, perceive, protein, receipt, rein, seize, their, veil, vein, weird

waive—to do without or cease to hold or adhere to; to lose or lose the right to by some error, offense, or crime

wave—a movement of water on an ocean, sea, lake, etc.; a hairdo that creates undulations in the hair: brave, cave, crave, gave, grave, knave, rave, save, shave, slave, behave, deprave, forgave, octave, navel, avenge, avenue, averse, avert

ware—articles of the same kind or material, usually used in combination: silverware; software: bare, blare, dare, fare, hare, mare, pare, rare, spare, square, stare, aware, compare

wear—the act of having on one's person, as a covering or adornment; to put clothing on one's body: bear, clear, dear, ear, earl, early, earn, earnest, earth, fear, gear, hear, heard, hearse, heart, hearth, learn, near, pear, pearl, rehearse, search, smear, spear, swear, tear, year, yearn

where—in or at or to what place: here, mere, were, austere, cashmere, revere, severe, sincere, persevere

way—a journey or passage; the property of distance in general: always, away, bay, clay, day, dismay, gay, hay, lay, may, pay, play, pray, ray, repay, say, spray, stay, sway, today, tray, way

weigh—to determine the weight of; to show consideration for; to take into account: beige, caffeine, ceiling, conceit, conceive, deceit, deceive, either, foreign, heir, leisure, neither, perceive, protein, receipt, rein, seize, their, veil, vein, weird

weak—physical strength or vigor: break beak, bleak, break, creak, feat, peak, sneak, speak, steak, streak, teak, weak

week—a period of seven consecutive days starting on Sunday: creek cheek, leek, meek, peek, reek, seek, week (See -EE- list)

weather—the state of the earth's atmosphere as to heat or cold, wetness or dryness, calm or storm, clearness or cloudiness: beat breath, eat, feat, great, heat, heathen, leather, meat, neat, peat, pleat, seat, teak, threat, treat, wheat

whether—which one of two: when, whelp, where, whet, whew, whey

wet—covered or soaked with a liquid such as water: bet, fret, get, jet, let, met, net, pet, set, vet, yet

whet—to make keen or more acute; to sharpen by rubbing, as on a whetstone: when, whelp, where, whet, whew, whey

which—what one (of a certain number mentioned or implied): hiccup, enrich, rich, niche, white, whisper

witch—a person, especially a woman, who practices magic, especially black magic or sorcery: ditch, hitch, itch, pitch, twitch

who's—contraction for "who is"

whose—the possessive case of who or which: rose: chose, close, hose, nose, pose, depose, expose, suppose, decompose

wood—the hard, fibrous, lignified substance under the bark of trees; the trees and other plants in a large, densely wooded area: good, hood, stood, mood, blood, noodle, poodle, brood, food

would—strongly desired; used in auxiliary function to a verb to express a wish, desire, or intent: boulder, could, foul, mould, should, shoulder

yolk—the nutritive material of an egg stored for the nutrition of an embryo, especially the yellow mass of a bird egg: folk, talk, walk, balk

yoke—stable gear that joins two draft animals at the neck so they can work together as a team: choke, broke, coke, joke, poke, smoke, spoke, stoke, stroke, woke

yore—of old; years ago; long ago: ore, chore, lore, more, score, store, tore, adore, deplore, explore, galore

you're—contraction for "you are": they're, we're

your—belonging to you: amour, course, devour, dour, flour, flourish, four, gourmet, hour, mourn, mourning, nourish, our, pour, scour, scout, sour, tour, your

O

Student Worksheet for Correctly Spelling "Their," "There," "They're," "To," "Too," and "Two"

See page(s) 134–135

THERE, THEIR, AND THEY'RE

1. **There** is a room in school where students may go to look for **their** lost items, and **they're** always finding lots **there**.
2. The student took **their** books to school, and when they arrived **there**, they put them in **their** lockers.
3. When **they're** ready to start the game outside, all students should have on **their** PE uniforms before going **there**.
4. **There** were a number of students who submitted **their** writings to the "Write Now" contest, and **they're** waiting for the announcement of winners.
5. When the fire alarm rings, students need to leave **their** books in class and walk to **their** assigned stations and stay **there** until **they're** told to return to **their** classrooms.
6. **There** was going to be a fire drill today, but **there** will not be one because the fire officers made up **their** minds that another date would be to **their** advantage.
7. When students go to the library, **they're** to walk quietly in the halls. When they arrive **there**, **they're** to wait in silence for **their** instructions from the librarians.

8. All the students were talking about **their** acting lessons in English, and **they're** telling everyone how everyone laughed **there**.
9. When students view all the student-made movies, **they're** to write a "Rave Review" on each except **their** own.
10. Please stand **there** to take pictures of students while **they're** reading **their** writings to the class.

TO, TOO, TWO

1. I wanted **to** buy **two** books in the Scholastic catalogue, but they cost **too** much.
2. Please don't send me **to** the office **too** with those **two** students who really misbehaved!
3. Janet went with me **to** the restroom **too**, so we could eat **two** candy bars.
4. "It is **too** soon **to** pack up your book bags. There are still **two** minutes left in the period that we are going **to** use!" admonished Mrs. Burkhardt.
5. When students go **to** the library, they may check out only **two** books; three books would be **too** many.
6. **Two** red pencils **to** use when self-correcting papers are not **too** many for students **to** bring **to** English each day.
7. He, **too**, knows **two** ways **to** go school.
8. Michelle was **too** tired **to** listen **to** the **two** oral readings students gave in class.
9. The **two** books I borrowed from the library are **too** hard **to** read.
10. When John went **to** the cafeteria for lunch, he ordered **two** pizzas, but they were **too** much **to** eat.

P

Source List for Writing Memory Tricks for Spellings of Words Commonly Confused

See page 135.

access—the act of approaching or entering; to obtain or retrieve from a storage device, as of information on a computer: accent, accept, accessory, accident, acclaim, accolade, accommodate, accompany, accord, account, accrue, accurate, accuse

excess—immoderation as a consequence of going beyond sufficient or permitted limits; the state of being more than full: excavate, exceed, excel, except, excerpt, exchange, excite, exclaim, exclude, excrete, excuse

affect—the conscious, subjective aspect of feeling or emotion; to have an emotional or cognitive impact upon: affable, affair, affidavit, affiliate, affirm, affix, afflict, afford, affront

effect—a symptom caused by an illness or a drug; a phenomenon that follows and is caused by some previous phenomenon: efface, effeminate, efficiency, effigy, effort

alley, alleys—a narrow street with walls on both sides: alley, barley, convey, galley, grey, honey, key, money, monkey, parley, prey, survey, valley, whey

ally, allies—a friendly nation; an associate who provides assistance; to become an ally or associate, as by a treaty or marriage: dally, rally, Sally, tally

angel—a heavenly being: gel, boatel, hotel, compel, dispel expel, excel, impel, lapel, motel, noel, pixel, rebel, repel, scalpel, caramel, carousel, citadel, parallel

angle—two straight lines that meet at a point: bangle, dangle, eagle, goggle, jungle, mangle, rectangle, spangle, strangle, tangle, triangle, wiggle, wrangle

breath—the process of taking in and expelling air during breathing: beneath, bequeath, death, sheath, underneath, wreath

breathe—to draw air into, and expel out of, the lungs: the, theft, them, theme, thence, theology, theorem, theory, therapist, there, thermal, thermometer

clothes—garments worn on the body: the, these, he, thesis, lot, lotion, other

cloths—pieces of material often used in cleaning: broths, moths

dairy—a farm that raises cows for the production of milk: air, airy, hairy, fairy, hair, stair, chair, chair, pair, stair

diary—a book or journal that records, usually daily, the events that have happened as well as the writer's thoughts and feelings about these happenings: Virginia, Pennsylvania, dahlia, California, via, diamond, diatribe

desert—an arid region with little or no vegetation: describe, deserve, desensitize, deserve, design, designate, desire, desk, desolate, despair, desperate, despondent

desert—to leave someone who needs or counts on you; to leave in the lurch; to describe: deserve, desensitize, deserve, design, designate, desire, desk, desolate, despair, desperate, despondent

dessert—a dish served as the last course of a meal: bless, chess, dress, less, mess, press, stress, caress, confess, excess, express, impress, obsess, princess, process, recess

farther—more distant in space or time; more distant in degree; to or at a greater distance in time or space: fare, farm, farce, bar, car, jar, scar, star, tar, ajar

further—more distant in degree; to or at a greater extent or degree or a more advanced stage: fur, furbish, fury, furious, furlough, furnace, furnish, furor, furtive

formerly—at a previous time: former, burly, curly, early, pearly, surly, whirly

formally—in an established manner; with official authorization: formal, dally, rally, Sally, tally

later—the comparative of the adverb "late"; happening at a time subsequent to a referenced time; at some eventual time in the future: ate, crate, date, fate, gate, hate, late, mate, plate, rate, skate, slate, state

latter—the second of two or the second mentioned of two: batter, chatter, clatter, fatter, flatter, matter, patter, platter, scatter, shatter, splatter

lie—a statement that deviates from truth; to be prostrate in a horizontal position; to assume a reclining position: believe, brief, chief, field, fiend fierce, friend, grief, grieve, lie, niece, pie, piece, pier, pierce, priest, relieve, relieve, retrieve, shield, shriek, siege, thief, tie, yield,

lay—to put into a certain place or abstract location: always, away, bay, clay, day, dismay, gay, hay, lay, may, pay, play, pray, ray, say, spray, stay, sway, today, tray, way

loose—free from confinement; not tight; not closely constrained or constricted or constricting: goose, loose, moose, noose, caboose, footloose, mongoose

lose—to allow to go out of sight; to miss from one's possessions; to fail to keep or to maintain; to cease to have, either physically or in an abstract sense: rose, chose, hose, nose, pose, depose, expose, suppose, decompose

loss—the act of missing something from one's possessions; the failure to keep or maintain: boss, cross, floss, gloss, moss, toss, across, gross

personal—particular to a given individual; concerning or affecting a particular person or his or her private life and personality: tonal, zonal, hormonal

personnel—a group of people willing to obey orders; the department responsible for hiring and training and placing employees and for setting policies for personnel management: bonnet, sonnet, sonny, colonel, boatel, hotel, compel, dispel, expel, excel, impel, lapel, motel, noel, pixel, rebel, repel

sit—to be seated; to travel on the back of animal, usually while controlling its motions; to place one's posterior end on a chair: bit, chit, fit, flit, nit, pit, skit, wit, writ, admit, benefit, emit, misfit, omit, remit, submit

set—to put or place something in position; a number of things of the same kind: bet, fret, get, jet, let, met, net, pet, vet, wet, yet

than—a function word to indicate difference of kind, manner, or identity; used especially with some adjectives and adverbs that express diversity—e.g., anywhere else *than* at home: ban, bran, can, clan, fan, man, pan, ran, scan, span, tan, van, began

then—subsequently or soon afterward (often used as sentence connector): den, glen, pen, ten, when, wren, amen

quiet—not showy or obtrusive; free of noise or uproar; making little if any sound: diet, piety, anxiety, propriety, sobriety, society, variety, notoriety

quit—to give up or retire from a position; to turn away from; to go away or leave; to put an end to a state or an activity: it, bit, chit, fit, flit, pit, sit, skit, wit, writ, admit, befit, emit, misfit, omit, remit, submit

quite—to the greatest extent; completely to a degree (not used with a negative); of an unusually noticeable or exceptional or remarkable kind (not used with a negative); actually or truly or to an extreme: bite, malachite, mite, miswrite, socialite, stalactite, write

Q

List of Words That Have Interesting Etymologies

See page(s) 143–144.

academy	barbarian	cab	daisy
aftermath	barbecue	calculate	damask
aggravate	barber	calico	days of the week
agony	bayonet	cancel	deliberate
alimony	bedlam	candidate	democracy
almanac	bib	cantaloupe	derrick
alphabet	biography	capricious	dilapidated
ambition	biology	choleric	doctor
America	blank	chortle	dunce
aristocracy	blurb	companion	enthrall
astonish	bonfire	congregation	enthusiasm
avocation	boycott	conspiracy	extravagant
ballot	bravo	curfew	filibuster
ballyhoo	bus	cute	fiscal
Florida	maverick	picnic	sincere
frankfurter	mayor	plutocracy	slush fund
funeral	melancholy	pocket	sophomore
galvanize	mercurial	poll	soprano
gerrymander	metropolis	precocious	sousaphone
gingham	milliner	preposterous	stilettto
gobbledygook	mob	prevaricate	supercilious

good-bye	model	propaganda	syrup
governor	Montana	pseudonym	tantalize
guppy	months of the year	psychology	telegraph
gypsy	nickname	radical	telephone
humble pie	nicotine	radio	television
hurricane	noodle	record	terrier
ignoramus	panic	regal	tomato
inauguration	paraffin	remorse	tuxedo
journey	parliament	rival	vandal
khaki	pedigree	sadism	veranda
lunacy	peninsula	salary	veto
macadam	pert	salve	villain
mammoth	phlegmatic	satin	volume

R

Student Worksheet for Guessing Meanings of Vocabulary Words Used in Context

See page(s) 148–150.

Directions: For each of the following sentences, list the **word** in **boldface type** along with the word's number. Then follow each word with your guess: Use your good thinking skills! DO NOT LOOK UP THE MEANING IN A DICTIONARY!

1. Mrs. Jones is so **altruistic** that she has made a will that will give all she owns to the homeless.
2. Students who **procrastinate** working on a major project will most certainly fail if they start working on it the night before the due date.
3. The **proponents** for the additional tax proposal could easily afford the increases, whereas the opponents objected, stating they could not afford to pay more.
4. Pens and pencils are **indispensable** tools in our English class.
5. Understanding basic phonetic concepts is a **prerequisite** to learning logical spelling rules.
6. Some real estate agents find they cannot make enough money selling property, so they decide to change to another, more **lucrative** profession.
7. Others describe John as **astute**, shrewd, wise, crafty, and cunning.
8. The teacher explained that students would be giving **extemporaneous** speeches, ones they would give without preparation.

9. The dwarf cringed in fear when the witch pronounced a **malediction** to turn him into a frog.

10. An **orthographic** description of a word is giving the word's correct spelling.

11. The police describe the thief as a **kleptomaniac** since they had caught him twenty times stealing from the toy store.

12. Since the lady was amazed that the special makeup completely **obliterated** the severe scar on her cheek, she felt confident that no one would notice this imperfection at her wedding.

13. Normally cats and dogs are **incompatible**, but my cat and dog love each other so much they often curl up together to sleep.

14. My sister Dianne is **ambidextrous** and can write legibly and easily with both her left and right hands.

15. The DNA analysis presented **inconvertible** evidence that the accused murderer had killed all three victims.

16. An **antihistamine** is a drug used against certain allergies and cold symptoms.

17. Jim ran so long and rapidly on the treadmill, he had such an **unquenchable** thirst for water he had to stop to get a drink from a nearby fountain.

18. To say that Benjamin Franklin used a computer for writing would an example of an **anachronism**.

19. Students must learn to **collaborate** with all members of their group to be able to complete the assigned task successfully.

20. Becoming a **proficient** writer will help to guarantee success throughout all school years.

S

Noun, Verb, Adjective, and Adverb Suffixes

See page(s) 150–158 in Chapter 8.

NOUN SUFFIXES

-an, -ian: native of; relating to (Canadian, African)

-ance, -ence: act, quality, or state of being (resistance, persistence)

-ant, -ent: one who (servant, agent)

-ary, -ery, -ory: condition of; quality; place where (dictionary, bravery, dormitory)

-dom: position of; realm of; state of being (kingdom)

-ee: one who receives the action (employee, refugee)

-er, -or: one who; person who does; that which (debater, author)

-ess: female (actress, authoress)

-hood: order; condition; quality (statehood, manhood)

-ion, -sion, -tion: act; process; or condition of being (union, division, action)

-ism: act or fact of doing; state or condition (alcoholism, heroism)

-ist: one who; that which (artist, perfectionist)

-ity, -ty: condition or quality of being (captivity, clarity)

-ment: act of; state of; result of (contentment, achievement)

-ness: condition or quality of being; state of (carelessness, restlessness)

-ship: office, statue, rank; state of being; act of; power in; skill in (authorship, dictatorship)

-tude: condition or quality of being (gratitude, multitude)

-ture: act of; state of; process; rank (literature, rupture)

-ty: something or someone that exemplifies an act, quality, or state of being (beauty, unity)

VERB SUFFIXES

-ate: to cause or make (liquidate, segregate)

-en: to make or become (soften, lighten)

-ify: to make (fortify, falsify)

-ize: to make (idolize, penalize)

ADJECTIVE SUFFIXES

-able, -ible: able (suitable, edible)

-al: relating to (manual, natural)

-ant, -ent: being like; acting with (resultant, persistent)

-en: made of (silken, wooden)

-ern: belonging to; characterized by (southern, modern)

-ful: full of; characterized by (beautiful, bountiful)

-ic, -ical: pertaining to; of the nature of, or like (ironic, comical)

-ish: resembling; relating to; characteristic of (foolish, boorish)

-ive: having the nature of; like; tending to (abusive, exhaustive)

-less: free from; without (fearless, helpless)

-ly: like; characteristic of; suitable to (lonely, comely)

-some: characterized by; tending to be (lonesome, gruesome)

-ous: having; full of; abounding in (glorious, generous, vivacious)

-y: full of; characterized by (soapy, cheery)

ADVERB SUFFIXES

-ly: in the manner of; in or at the time or place of; in order of sequence
(fearlessly, timely, secondly)

-wise: in the direction of; in the position or manner of; with regard to
(lengthwise, clockwise, dollar-wise)

T

Words That Have a Minimum of Four Grammatical Forms

See page(s) 158–160.

accept, acceptance, acceptable, acceptability, acceptably
achieve, achiever, achievable, achievement
act, actor, actress, active, activeness, activity, actively
advise, adviser, advisable, advisability, advisably
advise, adviser, advisable, advisably
alphabet, alphabetize, alphabetical, alphabetically
apply, applicant, applicable, applicability
apprehend, apprehender, apprehension, apprehensive, apprehensively
art, artist, artistic, artistically
automate, automation, automatic, automatically
biology, biologist, biological, biologically
blame, blamer, blameless, blamelessly, blamelessness
blur, blurry, blurrily, blurriness
care, careful, carefully, carefulness, careless, carelessness, carelessly
chauvinism, chauvinist, chauvinistic, chauvinistically
collect, collector, collective, collection, collectively
comfort, comfortable, comfortably, comforter
communicate, communicator, communicative, communication, communicable
compete, competition, competitor, competitive
conserve, conservationist, conservation, conservative, conservatively

269

contradict, contradicter, contradiction, contradictory
convene, convention, conventional, conventionally
create, creator, creative, creativeness, creatively
critic, criticize, critique, criticism, critical, critically
decorate, decorator, decoration, decorative, decoratively
defend, defender, defensive, defensiveness, defensively
dictate, dictator, dictatorial, dictatorship, dictatorially
direct, director, direction, directional, directory
divide, divider, divisional, divisible
drama, dramatist, dramatic, dramatically
economy, economist, economical, economically, economize
edit, editor, editorial, edition, editorially
educate, educator, educational, educationally
electric, electrician, electrical, electronics, electrically
employ, employee, employer, employment
energy, energize, energetic, energizer, energetically
environment, environmental, environmentalist, environmentally
equal, equality, equally, equation
finance, financier, financial, financially
glory, glorify, glorification, glorifier
govern, governor, government, governmental, governmentally
grace, gracious, graciously, graciousness
history, historian, historical, historic
hope, hopeful, hopefully, hopefulness, hopeless, hopelessly, hopeless-
ness
indicate, indicator, indication, indicative, indicatively
individual, individualize, individualization, individuality, individually
inspire, inspirer, inspirational, inspiration
introduce, introducer, introduction, introductory, introductive, intro-
ductorily
joy, joyfully, joyfulness, joyless, joylessly, joylessness
love, lover, lovely, loveliness, lovable, lovably
magic, magician, magical, magically
music, musician, musical, musically
observe, observer, observation, observational, observatory
optimism, optimist, optimistic, optimistically
perform, performer, performance

permit, permission, permissible, permissibility, permissibly
person, personalize, personable, personality, personally
physic, physician, physical, physically
please, pleasant, pleasantness, pleasantly
politics, politician, political, politically
prepare, preparer, preparation, preparatory
progress, progressive, progression, progressively
question, questioner, questionable, questionably, questionnaire
real, realism, realistic, realistically
regular, regulate, regularity, regularly, regulator
separate, separator, separatist, , separately, separateness, separation
special, specialist, specialize, specialty, specially
waste, wasteful, wastefully, wastefulness

U

A Word Web Generated from the Roots "-Spec-," "-Spect-," and "-Spic-"

See page(s) 161–163.

aspect, noun. A noticeable characteristic to be considered **aspectual**, adjective.

auspicious, adjective. Of good omen. Favorable. Propitious.

circumspect, adjective. Heedful of potential consequences by looking at all aspects. **circumspection**, noun. **circumspectly**, adverb.

disrespect, noun. A manner that reveals contempt. **disrespectful**, adjective, **disrespectfully**, adverb.

expect, verb. To look forward to something. **expectation**, noun.

inspect, verb. To look over carefully. **inspection**, noun. **inspector**, noun.

irrespective, adjective. In spite of everything already known or seen.

irrespectively, adverb.

introspective, adjective. Examining own sensory and perceptual experiences.

introspection, noun.

perspective, adjective. The appearance of things relative to one another as determined by their distance from the viewer

perspicacity, noun. The capacity to assess situations or circumstances shrewdly and to draw sound conclusions perspicacious, adjective. **perspicuousness**, noun. **perspicaciously**, adverb. **perspicuity**, noun.

prospect, noun. A vision of future success. **prospector,** noun. **prospective,** adjective.

respect, verb. An attitude that shows admiration or esteem. **respectful,** adjective.

respectfully, adverb.

respective, adjective. Noticing with attention; hence, careful; wary; considerate. **respectively,** adverb.

retrospect, noun. Contemplation of things past. **retrospective,** adjective.

specialty, noun. A distinguishing trait or area of expertise. **specialist,** noun.

specialization, noun.

species, noun. A specific kind of something that has distinguished characteristics.

specific, adjective. Relating to a distinguished characteristic. **specification,** noun.

specimen, noun. An example to look at.

speck, noun. A very small spot one notices. **speckle,** noun.

spectacle, noun. Eye glass worn to improve vision. **specs,** noun.

spectacle, noun. An elaborate or remarkable display on the lavish side. **spectacular,** adjective.

spectator, noun. A close observer; someone who looks at something such as an exhibition of some kind. **spectate,** verb.

specter, noun. A ghostly appearing figure. **spectral,** adjective.

spectrophobia, noun. Fear of seeing a ghost.

spectrum, noun. A broad range of related values or qualities or ideas or activities; an ordered array of the components of an emission or wave.

speculate, verb. To talk over conjecturally, or to review in an idle or casual way and with an element of doubt or without sufficient reason to reach a conclusion; to reflect deeply on a subject. **speculation,** noun. **speculative,** adjective. **speculator,** noun.

V

Magniloquence Word List

See page(s) 163–164.

acquiescent	compliant	enterprising	gregarious
affable	conciliatory	pulchritude	hospitable
altruistic	confabulator	equanimity	humanitarian
amicable	congenial	erudite	inimitable abilities
amenable	convivial	extroverted	insatiable curiosity
benevolent	divergent thinker	facetious	jocular
chimerical	effervescent	felicitous	jovial
loquacious	philanthropic	superlative skills	vociferous
meditative	perspicacious	tractable	winsome
mellifluous	writer	punctual	trenchant
meritorious scholar	punctilious	talented	thespian
perseverant	quiescent	veracious	

References

Allred, Ruel A. 1977. *Spelling: The Application of Research Findings.* Washington, DC: National Education Association.

Applebee, Arthur N., et al. 1994. "Senior Consultants." In *Literature and Language.* Red Level: Grade 7. Evanston, IL: McDougal, Littell.

Baring, Evelyn, 1st Earl of Cromer (Lord Cromer). 1902. "Our Strange Lingo." *Spectator,* August 9. http://www.spellingsociety.org/news/media/poems.php.

Bear, Donald R. 2004. *Words Their Way: Word Study for Phonics, Vocabulary, and Spelling Instruction.* Upper Saddle River, NJ: Pearson/Merrill/Prentice Hall.

Boddy-Evans, Marion. 2010. *Right Brain/Left Brain: What Is It All About?* http://painting.about.com/od/rightleftbrain/a/Right_Brain.htm.

Bolton, Faye, and Diane Snowball. 1993a. *Ideas for Spelling.* Portsmouth, NH: Heinemann.

———. 1993b. *Teaching Spelling: A Practical Resource.* Portsmouth, NH: Heinemann.

Belloc, Hillare. *Poet's Corner: Selected Verses from Cautionary Tales.* http://theotherpages.org/poems/belloc01.html.

Bradley, Lynette, PhD, and Peter Bryant, PhD. 1985. *Rhyme and Reason in Reading and Spelling.* Ann Arbor: University of Michigan Press.

Brainerd, Charles J. 1976. *Piaget's Theory of Intelligence.* Englewood Cliffs, NJ: Prentice-Hall.

Brand, Max. 2004. *Word Savvy: Integrated Vocabulary, Spelling, & Word Study, Grades 3–6.* Portland, ME: Stenhouse.

Bruner, Jerome. 1996. *The Culture of Education.* Cambridge, MA: Harvard University Press.

Burkhardt, Sally E. 1987a. "Laughing While Learning." *Arizona English Bulletin* 29, no. 3 (Spring): 25–28.

———. 1987b. "My Ladies." *Doberman World* 9, no. 1 (March/April): 78.

———. 1987c. "A Test for Teachers." *Virginia English Bulletin* 37, no. 1 (Spring): 100, 112.

Carroll, David W. 1986. *Psychology of Language.* Monterey, CA: Brooks/Cole Publishing.

Carroll, Lewis (Charles Lutwidge Dodgson). 1923. "Jabberwocky." In *Through the Looking Glass.* London: Macmillan.

Chandler, Kelly, and Mapleton Teacher Research Group. 1999. *Spelling Inquiry: How One Elementary School Caught the Mnemonic Plague.* York, ME: Stenhouse.

———. 2000. "What I Wish I'd Known about Teaching Spelling." *English Journal* 89, no. 6 (July): 87–95.

Chekhov, Anton. 2003. "To Gorky" (Yalta, December 3, 1899). *Letters of Anton Chekhov.* Rendered into HTML by Steve Thomas for The University of Adelaide Library Electronic Texts Collection, January 17 (accessed on February 8, 2010).

Coleman, Lawrence, and Tracy L. Cross. 2001. *Being Gifted in School.* Waco, TX: Prufrock Press.

Cootes, Claire, and Juliet Jamieson. 1985. *Spotlight on Spelling: A Structured Guide to the Assessment and Teaching of Spelling.* Colchester, UK: Alphabet Books.

Cramer, Ronald L. 1998. *The Spelling Connection: Integrating Reading, Writing, and Spelling Instruction.* New York: Guilford Press.

Dahl, Roald. 1982. *Revolting Rhymes.* Illustrations by Quentin Blake. London: J. Cape.

———. 1983. *Dirty Beasts.* Pictures by Rosemary Fawcett. London: J. Cape.

———. 1989. *Rhyme Stew.* Illustrations by Quentin Blake. London: J. Cape.

Dean, John F. 1977. *Games Make Spelling Fun: Activities for Better Spelling.* Belmont, CA: Pitman.

DeVault, Lillian. 1973. *Word Lists for the American English Language.* Cleveland, OH: Montessori Development Foundation.

Ehrlich, Ida. 1968. *Instant Vocabulary.* New York: Pocket Books.

Fisher, Carol J., and Catherine E. Studier. 1977. *Misspellings of Children in the Middle Grades.* Report No. 29 RIE. Athens: University of Georgia, . ED 143030.

Forte, Imogene, and Mary Ann Pangle. 1976. *Spelling Magic: Activities, Gimmicks, Games galore for Making Learning Mean Lots More!* Nashville: Incentive Publications.

Fountas, Irene C., and Gay Su Pinnell, eds. 1999. *Voices on Word Matters: Learning about Phonics and Spelling in the Literacy Classroom.* Portsmouth, NH: Heinemann.

Fresch, Mary Jo, and Aileen Wheaton. 2002. *Teaching and Assessing Spelling.* New York: Scholastic Professional Books.

Furness, Edna L. 1977. *Spelling for the Millions*. Nashville, TN: Rhomas Nelson.

Gentry, J. Richard. 1993. *Teaching Kids to Spell*. Portsmouth, NH: Heinemann.

——. 2004. *The Science of Spelling: The Explicit Specifics That Make Great Readers and Writers (and Spellers!)*. Portsmouth, NH: Heinemann.

Glasser, William. 2006. *William Glasser Quotes*. http://thinkexist.com/quotations.

Hanna, Paul R., Richard E. Hodges, and Jean S. Hanna. 1971. *Spelling: Structure and Strategies*. Boston: Houghton Mifflin.

Hanna, Paul R., Richard E. Hodges, Jean S. Hanna, and Edwin H. Rudorf Jr. 1966. *Phoneme-Grapheme Correspondences as Cues to Spelling Improvement*. Washington, DC: Government Printing Office, U.S. Office of Education. ED 003 321.

Henderson, Edmund. 1981. *Learning to Read and Spell: the Child's Knowledge of Words*. Dekalb: Northern Illinois Press.

——. 1985. *Teaching Spelling*. Boston: Houghton Mifflin.

Henderson, Edmund H., and James W. Beers. 1980. *Developmental and Cognitive Aspects of Learning to Spell*. Newark, DE: International Reading Association.

Henry, Marcis. 2003. *Unlocking Literacy: Effective Decoding & Spelling Instruction*. Baltimore, MD: P.H. Brooks.

Hill, Ada, and Beth Boone-Bradford. 1982. *If Maslow Taught Writing: A Way to Look at Motivation in the Composition Classroom*. Berkeley: University of California, National Writing Project.

Hiskes, Dolores G. 2005. *Phonics Pathways: Clear Steps to Easy Reading and Perfect Spelling*. San Francisco: Jossey-Bass.

Hodges, Richard E. 1981. *Learning to Spell*. Urbana, IL: ERIC Clearinghouse on Reading and Communication Skills and the NCTE.

——. 1982. *Improving Spelling and Vocabulary in the Secondary School*. Urbana, Illinois: ERIC Clearinghouse on Reading and Communication Skills and the NCTE.

Hunter, Madeline. 1990. *Mastery Teaching*. El Segundo, CA: TIP Publications.

Kavanaugh, James F., and Richard Venezky. 1980. *Orthography, Reading and Dyslexia*. Baltimore, MD: University Park Press.

Keyes, Daniel. 1988. *Flowers for Algernon*. New York: Bantam Books.

Kimble, Cornell. 2006. *A Study of Some of the Most Commonly Misspelled Words*. http://www.Barnsdle.demon.co.uk.

Laminack, Lester L., and Katie Wood. 1996. *Spelling in Use: Looking Closely at Spelling in Whole Language Classrooms*. Urbana, IL: NCTE.

Landin, Leslie. 1956. *100 Blackboard Games*. Belmont, CA: Pitman.

Levine, Harold, Norman Levine, and Robert T. Levine. 1989. *Vocabulary for the High School Student, Book A*. New York: Amsco School Publications.

——. 1994. *Vocabulary for the High School Student*. 3rd ed. New York: Amsco School Publications.

Mallett, Jerry J. 1976. *101 Make-and-Play Reading Games for the Intermediate Grades*. New York: Center for Applied Research in Education.

Manning, Maryann Murphy, and Gary L. Manning. 1981. *Improving Spelling in the Middle Grades*. Washington, DC: National Education Association.

Mapes, Lola. 1983. *Name Games: Personalized Language Games and Activities*. Nashville, TN: Incentive Publications.

Marland, Ken. 2002. *High Frequency Words: Strategies That Build Skills in Spelling, Vocabulary and Word Play*. Markham, ONT: Pembroke.

Marten, Cindy. 2003. *Word Crafting: Teaching Spelling, Grades K–6*. Portsmouth, NH: Heinemann.

Maslow, A. H. 1970. *Motivation and Personality*. 2nd ed. New York: Harper & Bros.

McAlexander, Patricia J, Ann B. Dobie, and Noel Gregg. 1992. *Beyond the "SP" Label: Improving the Spelling of Learning Disabled and Basic Writers*. Urbana, IL: NCTE.

Meyers, Judith N. 1998. *Vocabulary & Spelling in 20 Minutes a Day*. New York: Learning Express.

Miller, Robert D. 1976. *Spelling Games and Puzzles for Junior High*. Belmont, CA: Fearon.

Milton, Roger. 1996. *English Spelling and the Computer*. New York: Longman.

Montgomery, Diane. 2007. *Spelling, Handwriting, and Dyslexia: Overcoming Barriers to Learning*. New York: Routledge.

Nurnberg, Maxwell. 1970. Fun with Words. Englewood Cliffs, NJ: Prentice Hall.

O'Donnell, Laurence. 2010. *Music and the Brain*. http://www.cerebromente.org .br/n/15/mente/musica.html.

Oglan, Gerald. 2001. "Grocery Lists, Shopping, and a Child's Writing and Spelling Development." *Talking Points* 12, no. 2 (April/May): 2–6.

O'Sullivan, Olivia. 2007. *Understanding Spelling*. New York: Routledge.

Peters, Margaret L. 1985. *Spelling: Caught or Taught? A New Look*. Rev. ed. London: Routledge & Kegan Paul.

Pflug, Barbara S. 1981. *Do Fifth Grade Students Learn to Spell Better Using an Individualized Approach or a Traditional Workbook Approach?* Kean College of New Jersey: RIE. ED 200992.

Phenix, Jo. 2001. *The Spelling Teacher's Handbook*. Markham, ONT: Pembroke.

———. 2003. *The Spelling Teacher's Book of Lists: Words to Illustrate Spelling Patterns and Tips for Teaching Them*. Portland, ME: Stenhouse, 2003.

Pinnell, Gay Su. 1998. *Word Matters: Teaching Phonics and Spelling in the Reading/Writing Classroom*. Portsmouth, NH: Heinemann.

Podhaizer, Mary Elizabeth. 1998. *Painless Spelling*. Hauppauge, NY: Barron's Educational Series.

Potter, Charles Francis. 1964. *More Tongue Tanglers and a Rigmarole*. Cleveland, OH: World Publishing.

Read, Charles. 1975. *Children's Categorization of Speech Sounds in English.* Urbana, IL: NCTE.

Rosencrans, Gladys. 1998. *The Spelling Book: Teaching Children How to Spell, Not What to Spell.* Newark, DE: International Reading Association.

Rycik, Mary Taylor. 2007. *Phonics and Word Identification: Instruction and Intervention, K–8.* New York: Pearson Merrill Prentice Hall.

Sears, Nedra C., and Dale M. Johnson. 1986. "The Effect of Visual Imagery on Spelling Performance and Retention among Elementary Students." *Journal of Educational Research* 79 (March–April): 230–33.

Sebranek, Patrick, Verne Meyer, and Dave Kemper. 1995. *Write Source 2000.* 3rd ed. Burlington, WI: Write Source Educational Publishing House.

Shackle, Eric. 2010. "Double English: Worse Than Double Dutch." http://www.fun-with-words.com/double_english.html.

Shaughnessy, Mina P. 1977. *Errors and Expectations.* New York: Oxford.

Shefter, Harry. 1976. *6 Minutes a Day to Perfect Spelling.* Rev. ed. New York: Pocket Books.

Simon, Liz. 2004. *Strategic Spelling: Every Writer's Tool.* Portsmouth, NH: Heinemann.

Sipe, Rebecca Bowers, et al. 2002. "Supporting Challenged Spellers." *Voices from the Middle* 9, no. 1 (March): 23–32.

———. 2003. *They Still Can't Spell: Understanding and Supporting Challenged Spellers in Middle and High School.* Portsmouth, NH: Heinemann.

Smith, Carl Bernard. 2001. *Spelling for Writing Instructional Strategies.* Bloomington, IN: Family Learning Association. ED 448460.

Snowball, Diane, and Faye Bolton. 1999. *Spelling K–8: Planning and Teaching.* York, ME: Stenhouse.

Stotsky, Sandra. 1984. "The Role of Writing in Developmental Reading." *Journal of Reading* 25, no. 4 (January): 330–39.

Templeton, Shane. 1998. *Houghton Mifflin Spelling and Vocabulary. Teacher's Book: A Resource for Planning and Teaching.* Boston: Houghton Mifflin.

———. 2004. "Spell-Check This! The Limitations and Potential of Technology for Spelling." *Voices from the Middle* 11, no. 3 (March): 58–59.

Tennyson, Alfred Lord. "Flower in the Crannied Wall." In *Alfred Lord Tennyson's Poetry.* http://home.att.net/%7ETennysonPoetry/flow.htm.

Terban, Marvin. 1982. *Eight Ate: A Feast of Homonym Riddles.* New York: Ticknor & Fields.

———. 1985. *Too Hot to Hoot: Funny Palindrome Riddles.* New York: Ticknor & Fields.

Terrell, Catherine. 1983. "The Effect of a Systematic Study Interval Peer Tutoring, and Mutual Behavioral Contracting on Unit Spelling Accuracy of Adolescent Learning Disabled Students." Paper Presented at the International Conference of the Association for Children and Adults with Learning Disabilities. ED 232374.

Thibodeau, Gail. 2002. "Spellbound: Commitment to Correctness." *Voices from the Middle* 9, no. 3 (March): 19–22.

Topping, Keith J. 1995. *Paired Reading, Spelling, and Writing: The Handbook for Teachers and Parents.* New York: Cassell.

Untermeyer, Louis, ed. [1935], 1963. *Rainbow in the Sky.* New York: Harcourt Brace.

Wagner, Guy, Max Hosier, Dorlan Mork, and Joan Cesinger. 1972. *Learning Games for Intermediate Grades.* New York: Teachers Publishing Division, Macmillan.

Weaver, Constance, comp. 1996. "On the Teaching of Spelling." *NCTE SLATE Starter Sheet* no. 2: 1–2. Prepared for the Michigan English Language Arts Framework and copyrighted 1995 by Constance Weaver. In *Creating Support for Effective Literacy Education,* ed. C. Weaver, L. Gillmeister-Krause, and G. Vento-Zoaby. Portsmouth, NH: Heinemann.

Webster's Compact Rhyming Dictionary. 1987. Springfield, MA: Merriam-Webster.

Webster's Ninth New Collegiate Dictionary. 1983. Springfield, MA: Merriam-Webster.

Westwood, Peter S. 2005. *Spelling Approaches to Teaching and Assessment.* Camberwell, Victoria: ACER Press.

Wilde, Sandra. 1992. *You Can Read This!—Spelling and Punctuation for Whole Language Classrooms, K–6.* Portsmouth, NH: Heinemann.

———. 1996. "A Speller's Bill of Rights." *Primary Voices K–6* 4, no. 4 (November): 7–10.

———. 1997. *What's a Schwa Sound Anyway?—A Holistic Guide to Phonetics, Phonics, and Spelling.* Portsmouth, NH: Heinemann.

———. 2004. "Spelling: What We Still Worry About." *NCTE School Talk* 9, no. 2 (January): 1–6.

Wordsworth, William. "She Dwelt Among the Untrodden Ways." http://www.rainsnow.org/csh_sampler_of_english_poetry.htm#She Dwelt Among The Untrodden Ways: By William Wordsworth.

Zar, Jerrold. 1994. "Candidate for a Pullet Surprise." *Journal of Irreproducible Results* (January/February): 13. Reprinted in *Journal of Irreproducible Results* 45, nos. 5/6 (2000): 20.

Index

Allred, Ruel A., 142
Applebee, Arthur N., et al., *See
Literature and Language*
assessment of student misspellings
or writing errors: beginning
research studies: Charles Read's,
6–7; Edmund Henderson's, 7; by
patterns of errors, 34, 40–42. *See
also* Mina Shaughnessy; current
complex systems, 41; state writing
tests, 26; student accountability for
spelling, 26, 41–42.
auditory strategies, xiv, 41, 42,
77, 101; phoneme-grapheme
correspondences, 79, 88, 90, 94;
sounds of syllable parts and words,
7, 11, 14; versus visualization
strategies, 77. *See also* logical
spelling, phonetics

Bear, Donald R., 5, 41
Beers, James W., 5, 7
Belloc, Hillare, 109
Boddy-Evans, Marion, 25
Bolton, Faye, 5, 39, 89

Boone-Bradford, Beth, 17, 18
Bradley, Lynette, 101
brain connections: assimilating new
information, 14; building memory
banks of deviant letter patterns,
79, 81, 82, 84, 85, 87, 89–90,
93–96, 97, 110, 136; building
memory bases of knowledge, 6,
12, 14, 88, 91, 133, 139, 165;
cursive handwriting to spelling
and legibility, 16, 37–39;
information that connects to
learners, 2, 9, 13, 14, 27, 37, 38,
83, 88, 97, 110, 136, 164; learning
difficulty when few connections,
14, 88; to knowledge already
known, 14–15; to learn spellings,
83, 85, 88, 91, 97, 100, 110,
129, 161. *See also* language and
spelling acquisition, mnemonic
strategies, psycholinguistics
communication skills. *See*
listening skills, reading skills,
speaking skills, whole-language
curriculum, writing skills

correction, 30, 34; misspellings of given words, 34, 36; parent/peer correcting help, 32; using different colors, 18, 29–30, 116.

grammar instruction: avoid explicit terminology, 10, 11, 31; basic parts of speech, 150–51, 153, 154–55; suffix sense, 6, 150–58, 263–65; tacit understanding, 10, 33, 35, 36; transformational grammar, 31.

Gregg, Noel, 5, 41, 75, 128, 133

group work: accountability of each member, 49; enjoyable way to learn 115, 119; fulfills psychological needs, 49; 4–5 members, 49; paired learning, 49–50; peer pressure, 22–23; ways to select members, 49.

Hanna, Jean S., 53, 79, 88, 90, 142

Hanna, Paul R., 53, 79, 88, 90, 142

Harper, Pennye, 127

Henderson, Edmund, 7, 14, 21, 142

Henry, Marcis, 5

high-frequency words, 6, 39–40

Hill, Ada, 17

Hiskes, Dolores G., 5

Hodges, Richard E., 53, 79, 88, 90, 101, 137, 142, 143

Holmes, Oliver Wendell, 104

homonym & words often confused instruction, 127–136; homonym riddles, 134; memory trick writing, 129–133, 135, 221–53, 257–60; "Spellbound," 127–28. *See also* Eric Shackle, Jerrold Zar

Hosier, Max, 134

Houghton Mifflin, 5

Hunter, Madeline, 30, 114

Hunter, Meredith, 34

"Jabberwocky," 153–54

Jackson, Shirley, 31

Jamieson, Juliet, 78, 85, 86, 88, 95

Johnson, Dale M., 77, 78

Kavanaugh, James F., 38

Kemper, Dave. *See Write Source 2000*

Keyes, Daniel, 15–16

Kimble, Cornell, 137–38, 140

Laminack, Lester L., 5, 8, 41, 76

Landin, Leslie, 63, 64

language and spelling acquisition: comparison to a tree's growth, 8–9; developmental spelling stages: initial, 7, 8–9, 10; intermediate, 7; highest levels, 7, 9, 10; first word, 1, 4, 8, 9, 12, 18, 164, 166, 167;

language innate, 10; recursive, xiv, 7–8; slow process, xiv, 11, 14–15, 139.

lesson planning: focus on whole language skills, 2, 3, 5; middle school vs. high school, 48–49; lessons in short time segments, 35, 48, 59, 61, 62, 65, 76, 125; closure activities, 34, 48, 59, 62, 65, 76, 98, 99, 152. *See also* Madeline Hunter, teaching strategies

levels of learners: adults, 17, 20, 106, 126, 132, 133; advanced/gifted, 16, 19, 68, 124, 143, 166, 167; drop-out prone: gifted, 15–16, 19; reluctant/unmotivated, 19, 20, 21; low-level, 19, 21, 22, 30, 34, 87–88; preschoolers, 8.

levels of spellers: competent/tacit spellers (self-taught learners), xiv, 2, 4, 14, 26–27, 69, 78, 87, 92,

About the Author

Sally E. Burkhardt is a retired English teacher who attended and graduated from Ohio State University in December 1962 attaining a Bachelor of Science in Education degree with a major in English and a minor in Biological Sciences. When attending OSU, she became a proud member of Ohio Beta Chapter of Pi Beta Phi Sorority.

Dr. Frank Zidonis, known for developing Transformational Grammar, was her undergraduate and graduate advisor at OSU. His superior evaluations and recommendations enabled her to obtain her first English teaching position starting in January 1963, at Worthington High School located in a suburb of Columbus, Ohio, where she taught all grades for 6 years.

Under Dr. Zidonis's instruction, she wrote "A Compromise Unit," which proposed sentence-generating strategies known today as sentence combining. She completed this document on November 30, 1964, five years before John Mellon, commonly called the "father of sentence combining" published his first work on this subject.

In a graduate-level independent study under Dr. Zidonis's direction, she produced "The Versatility of Verbs," a writing on her teaching the AUX Rule to her high school English students to help learn how to write in present tense. The AUX Rule, developed by Dr. Zidonis and Donald Bates, is one that generates every possible form for any verb in the English language. Application of the AUX Rule uses the 23 helping verbs to produce all forms of English verbs: A transitive verb has over 200 forms.

In 1981, she and her family moved to Midlothian, Virginia. Even though she was not an employed teacher, she resumed graduate work at Virginia Commonwealth University in January 1985, with the goal of obtaining a teaching position. She was thrilled to be accepted as a Fellow in VCU's 1985 Capital Writing Project, an experience that helped her to obtain an English position at Swift Creek Middle School in the Chesterfield County School System, a district always inundated with thousands of applicants. Originally, she was a reading teacher in 6th grade. For the following years, she then obtained an English assignment teaching all levels of seventh graders, a grade she found by far the hardest but most rewarding to teach.

Three of the writings she produced as a Fellow were published: "A Test for Teachers," *Virginia English Bulletin*, Spring 1987; "Laughing While Learning," *Arizona English Bulletin*, Spring 1987; and "My Ladies," *Doberman World*, March/April 1987.

As part of CWP, she also prepared a presentation titled "The Reading/ Writing Connection" that she delivered at two state level conferences— Virginia Association of Teachers of English's "Promote Critical Thinking" in 1987 and Virginia State Reading Association's "Literacy: Objective of Virginia Educators" in 1988.

While teaching, she continued pursuing a Master's Degree at VCU in English-Education, focusing on the teaching of writing, and finished the program in August 1989 with a 4.0 GPA.

Upon retirement in June 2000, she started working on writing her book on spelling but only dabbled in composing it because she did an abundance of substitute teaching along with other pleasurable pursuits. Finally in the late fall of 2004, she became serious about completing her book and finished the first manuscript in the spring of 2006.

From that point on, she has made many revisions and corrections especially after obtaining a contract from Rowman & Littlefield Publishing House in September 2009.

While she has always enjoyed reading more than writing, she has developed writing skills from learning to be a writing teacher. She probably revises more than she writes and always struggles to produce quality written work.